THE POWER OF

POINT OF VIEW

THE POWER OF
POINT OF VIEW

Make Your Story Come to Life

Alicia Rasley

WRITER'S DIGEST BOOKS
Cincinnati, Ohio
www.writersdigest.com

Distributed in Canada by Fraser Direct, 100 Armstrong Avenue, Georgetown, Ontario, Canada L7G 5S4; Distributed in the U.K. and Europe by David & Charles, Brunel House, Newton Abbot, Devon, TQ12 4PU, England, E-mail: postmaster@davidandcharles.co.uk; Distributed in Australia by Capricorn Link, P.O. Box 704, Windsor, NSW 2756 Australia.

12 11 10 09 08   5 4 3 2 1

Library of Congress Cataloging-in-Publication Data

Rasley, Alicia.
  The power of point of view : make your story come to life / by Alicia Rasley.
      p. cm.
  "Writer's Digest Books."
  Includes index.
  ISBN 978-1-58297-523-8 (alk. paper) -- ISBN 978-1-58297-524-5 (pbk. : alk. paper)
  1. Fiction--Authorship. 2. Point of view (Literature) I. Title.
  PN3383.P64R37 2008
  808.3--dc22

                                                    2007043570

Edited by Lauren Mosko
Designed by Terri Woesner
Production coordinated by Mark Griffin

dedication

This is dedicated to my parents, Jeanne and Robert Todd, who guided all of their eight children to be avid readers.

acknowledgments

Too many fellow writers have helped me to name them all individually. But special thanks go out to the members of Indiana RWA, WITTS, Romex, and the Demo Dames, who patiently suggested examples for my most arcane points. I truly don't know how any writer gets by without a little help from friends! Also many thanks to my editor, Lauren Mosko, for her unending patience and savvy in revamping the book. And I also owe my husband, Jeff, and my sons, JJ and Andrew, for the many passages they suggested and all the hours they listened patiently to my obsessive lectures on point of view.

table of contents

INTRODUCTION

Readers are different these days.

But not in the way so many social critics assert. Today's readers aren't worse readers than their predecessors or more shallow or less discriminating—far from it. Anyone who reads fiction for pleasure instead of watching television, playing video games, or surfing the Web is probably a very experienced, very educated reader—not necessarily someone with a PhD in literature, but someone educated in how stories work. In fact, they often know more, consciously or subconsciously, about story structure than we writers do.

Think about it: A reader who has read three hundred mystery stories is hard to fool. She notes that casual mention of Deborah's grandmother's brooch, immediately labels it a "clue," and puts Deborah in the suspect column. A thriller reader has had his fill of stalkers—another isn't going to chill him much. A reader of romances has seen a hundred couples paired off happily, and when she's three chapters into a new novel, she might already know how this couple is going to overcome the barriers to love.

This doesn't mean the books are bad—only that readers of popular fiction are often hard to impress in this new millennium. Readers like to read and they like to buy books, so they are definitely the writer's friend. But the more they read, the more it takes to impress them because they are so familiar with the traditional storytelling forms.

UNIVERSAL THEMES, FAMILIAR FORMS

Familiarity of form is not, as some critics might aver, a sign of lack of creative imagination. That's like saying a pitcher throwing three fast balls in a row to strike out a batter also lacks imagination. In fact, these storytelling traditions are one of the reasons genres have survived for so long—because they lead writers to explore themes of universal interest (for example, justice, love, or survival). Genre readers like to see old stories done in new ways. This doesn't mean they're afraid of experiments, only that they get more pleasure when a writer's experimentation is performed within the boundaries of the genre's expectations. These readers are sophisticated enough in "story grammar" to tie us poor writers into knots trying to keep them intrigued, when they have pretty much seen it all before.

I remember the astonishment of a friend after reading his first mystery. He was blown away by the ending—you know, when the sleuth figures out who the murderer is? My friend went on and on about how smart this sleuth was, how he never guessed the bad guy was so-and-so, and how, wow, it was a great book. To get that sort of reaction from an experienced fiction reader, you have to do a lot more than out a murderer. But this is good news, because trying to impress those experienced readers makes us become more innovative in our writing techniques.

One way to make fresh the familiar story structure is through point of view (POV)—the narrative perspective through which the reader experiences the story. From the earliest times, storytellers realized that a story changes depending on the narrator: Victorious Achilles's version of what happened during the Trojan War will differ in experience, detail, interpretation, and attitude from the defeated Hector's. (Homer, trickster that he was, started the trend toward multiple viewpoints by giving us both versions in *The Iliad* and *The Odyssey*.) Unique characters can offer unique experiences even of common, familiar events—and this truth lies at the center of the POV-construction process.

The Amazing Doubling Trick

To better understand the power of POV, add to this uniqueness of perspective the educated readers' amazing cognitive "doubling" trick: They can descend entirely into the experience of a compelling character, while maintaining the distance of the outside observer. In this way, they simultaneously participate vicariously in a fictional event *and* analyze their participation rationally. This is how law-abiding readers can understand very well why Hannibal the Cannibal bites off a guard's nose and still remain amazed at themselves for being so taken in by this serial murderer, all the while rooting for Clarice to get him in the end.

This cognitive doubling trick isn't understood by the puritanical social critics who assume that those who read Stephen King have a death wish, those who read Thomas Harris are latent murderers, and those who read Nora Roberts must be unhappy in love. The truth is, experienced readers are much more capable than nonreaders of distinguishing between fiction and reality, because they do it constantly as they read. Unfortunately for us fiction writers, this makes sustaining our readers' interest and belief doubly hard.

In this book, I'll be exploring how varying POV can help writers provide readers with a complex, sophisticated, interactive experience and make every book, even one with old themes, seem new. First, writers must create vivid characters with strong motivations who are placed into difficult or interesting situations; next, they must designate and develop POV to make the story come to life within the readers' heads.

Thinking About POV Like a Writer

I first got intrigued with POV while writing my master's thesis on the stories of Edgar Allan Poe. Poe wrote almost exclusively in first-person POV, experimenting with the "unreliable narrator" technique that makes this type of narration so much fun. (That is, you don't quite trust the narrator of Poe's "Berenice" when he says he can't imagine how his fiancée came to be buried alive in that tomb.)

There are one hundred and fifty years worth of literary criticism on this seminal writer, but I found few critics had the same understanding of his POV approach as I did. It isn't that I am smarter than they are, but I am a writer, and I found myself analyzing his POV approach as I'd analyze my own: How did he convey what other characters were thinking and feeling when confined to the narrator's solipsistic POV? How did he make a narrator's voice sound both rational and insane? Why did he pull away from sharp perception and go into abstraction right at the moment when the narrator gets his hands on the poison? When did the narrator start lying to the reader?

In fact, I found only a few critics who truly explore Poe's POV approach, and these were all writers themselves: Baudelaire, Dostoyevsky, and D.H. Lawrence. (You can tell what a significant influence Poe was to attract such critics.) This confirmed my supposition that only writers fully understand the mechanics of POV (consciously or not) and that only writers care how it's done.

Writing that thesis also taught me that mastering POV can add layers of meaning to one's stories: It was Poe's control of POV that led generations of readers to know in their bones that Poe's narrators were lying when they proclaimed that they really didn't mean to bury their wives alive, which, in turn, led generations to assume Poe himself must have buried a wife or two. (One hazard of writing in first person is that your readers tend to think that *I*-the-narrator is actually *I*-the-author.) Poe would have enjoyed knowing that his readers dug beneath the surface of his stories and sought the hidden mysteries underneath, even if it came at the cost of his own reputation. He would have applauded Robert Frost's observation, "I want people to understand me. I just want 'em to understand me *wrong*." Intense reader involvement through the mastering of POV is precisely what we modern writers should be seeking as we craft our own stories.

POV is a writer's closest connection to her readers. It creates meaning beyond that offered by the simple combination of character and plot; it adds subtext and secrets and suspense. POV is a writing element every bit as important as pacing or setting and, for that matter, is an essential part of developing plot and character. In fact, writers actually work with many facets of POV, consciously or not; with every scene, they explore the ways POV affects the reader's experience of the work.

This book is meant both to explain the basics and to explore the complexities of the elusive but essential elements of POV. You'll probably notice I love this subject. The more I study it, the more it fascinates me. I hope you find it even half as interesting as I do.

HOW TO USE THIS BOOK

This book is comprehensive: You'll find both the basic information—the types of POV, its purposes, its history—and more advanced sections, such as POV levels, tricks, subtleties, and maneuvers. I will continually focus on how these affect the reader's experience of the story. More experienced writers may be inclined to just skim or skip the basic information section. However, this might be valuable for even advanced authors because I frame those fundamental concepts in a new way.

Because POV is, above all, an interactive subject, I'll use published examples to explore each topic. I'll finish with some exercises that you can apply immediately to your own book. It's best just to freewrite answers to these questions, without trying to edit or censor yourself. For instance, sometimes I'll ask you to write in the first-person voice of your character, and you'll be amazed—once you let yourself "become" that person—how your subconscious creates that voice and persona to reveal attitudes and events you never imagined before.

I do want to stress that you should try to apply what you've learned to the book you're currently working on. While I'll use well-known examples in discussing these concepts, you'll learn a lot more from trying out the techniques and exercises on your own story and on the characters you know even more intimately.

It will help if you can stay open to the need for revision. Revision is as much a part of writing as the initial drafting. In fact, revision is what turns "writer therapy" into "reader enjoyment" by aiding in the transferal of the story from the writer to the reader. (That's why revision is so scary, because when you start considering what the reader needs to know rather than just what you want to say, you're giving up ownership of your story, in a way.) Don't be surprised if an exercise has you analyzing your own POV choice in an already written scene and concluding ruefully that it wasn't the best choice after all.

You'll notice that I can't avoid talking about plot and character as I discuss POV. That's because POV filters the experience of the plot events through the personalities and perceptions of the characters. *Who* is narrating the event (that is, the POV character) determines in great part how the reader experiences it.

The Book's Structure

I've arranged this book in three parts so you can easily find the information you need.

Part One: The Basics contains an overview of the elements of POV.

Part Two: Building Your Story defines each of the major POV choices and helps you determine which is best suited to shape your story.

Part Three: The Master Class goes beyond mere definition to an exploration of how to use POV to deepen characterization, increase suspense, and enhance your readers' experiences. My overall purpose is to equip you with the tools to experiment with POV, to teach you how to control your readers' experiences of your book, and to help you build stronger, more dynamic and compelling fiction—using POV as the core of your story-building process.

EXERCISE

GETTING ACQUAINTED WITH POV

1. Pick up whatever book you're currently reading and reread the first scene, analyzing your own response to it. Whose experience are you feeling most intensely? If you're not feeling any character's experience, look back and see if you can decipher why. What has the author done, or failed to do, to keep you at a distance?

2. Now go back to the first scene you wrote in your own story. Try to analyze it as if you were a reader. (I know that's hard!) When do you know which character is central to this first scene? What sense do you get of that person? Can you identify the words or phrases that first clue you in?

3. In the first-person voice of your central character, answer this question: "How did you get yourself into this situation?"

   Here is an example from Shakespeare—riffing off Hamlet's first soliloquy:

   > O, that this too too solid flesh would melt
   > Thaw and resolve itself into a dew!
   > Or that the Everlasting had not fix'd
   > His canon 'gainst self-slaughter! O God! God!
   > How weary, stale, flat and unprofitable,
   > Seem to me all the uses of this world!
   > Fie on't! ah fie! 'tis an unweeded garden,

That grows to seed; things rank and gross in nature
Possess it merely. That it should come to this!
But two months dead: nay, not so much, not two:
So excellent a king; that was, to this,
Hyperion to a satyr; so loving to my mother
That he might not beteem the winds of heaven
Visit her face too roughly.

Hamlet: How did I get into this situation? Well, that is the question, isn't it? It is quizzical, how we go through life, growing into our mature selves, gathering knowledge, planning our future, honoring our loving father and our gentle mother, and then, out of nowhere, death comes and deprives us of it all—the purpose, the certainty, the knowledge. That is what happened to me when my father died two months ago. Since then, life has been weary, stale, flat, and unprofitable. There is no future. I have no kingdom; it was taken from me with my father. My mother, too, was taken from me. The same usurper took her. Once I admired her, but now I see her giggling with him, letting him put his hands all over her. Disgusting. What would my father think? What do I think? I don't know. I just know that I feel such disgust that I can't go on like this much longer, but I don't have any idea what else to do but accept.

4. Finally, read over what you've just written, and consider what sort of attitude, value, and POV come through in that passage. In the Hamlet example, we hear from a man whose attitude is depression, but moving now into desperation. It's clear that he values his father above all and that since his father's death, nothing is right—everything is "weary, stale, flat, and unprofitable." We also get a sense that he idealized his parents' marriage. This sets up for the conflict of the mother's remarriage and the realization that her new husband has usurped the throne. As far as POV goes, we see a man given to analysis at length, who worries at his emotions and situation rather than taking action. It will come as no surprise when this character later responds to the "call to adventure" (his father's ghost demanding vengeance) with indecision and a need for proof.

part one

the
BASICS

WHAT IS POV?

1

You might remember from school that there's first person (I), second person (you), and third person (he/she). But "person," in the grammatical sense, is only the beginning of POV. That I/you/he/she is a person in the literal sense, too—a person with values, thoughts, emotions, attitudes, and a unique way of perceiving the world and telling a story. An author can individualize his story and liven up his prose by considering who this POV character is and how that affects the narration of the plot.

So what is *viewpoint* or *point of view*? It is the perspective from which the reader experiences the action of story. *Perspective* means perception, thought, and emotion, and POV determines whose perceptions (sight, hearing, and the rest of the senses), whose thoughts, whose emotions you get as you read a passage. That's the simple definition. As you might expect, it gets more complicated the more you explore the subject.

POV is the vehicle your reader uses to travel through the story. At most junctures, the vehicle is "driven" by one of the characters; we see and hear and feel a particular event from the perspective of one person. We might not consciously think that we are in Johnny's head and body during the battle scene, but we know that Johnny's ears are ringing from the artillery fire, his vision is blurring, and he's seriously considering dropping his weapon and heading for the woods. We get the vicarious experience of exhaustion, despair, and pain without actually having to fight the battle. But at any point, if the author chooses, the viewpoint could shift to another character—maybe the veteran reporter who is doing the stand-up summary for evening news back home. Then our vicarious experience becomes the relief and guilt of a man standing under a shelter with a microphone while other men are dodging bullets.

It's the author's use of narrative that determines whose viewpoint we're in at any given moment. There are several ways to do this well and many ways to do it badly; we'll explore both in this book. But the most important factor to remember is this: *POV is reader-oriented but author-controlled.* You, as the author, are in charge. Your choices will control whether your reader experiences this battle scene through the perspective of the general who is commanding the army or the raw recruit trembling in the trench or the war correspondent who reports but does not fight or the nurse waiting in the hospital tent for broken bodies to mend.

THE ELEMENTS OF POV

Now that you have a general idea of what POV is, I'll go a little deeper and explain its basic elements: narration, perception, introspection, and voice.

Narration is the way the action of the story is told, whether it's from above (omniscient), from within a single person (first-person single or third-person single), or from within more than one person (first-person multiple or third-person multiple). This will determine whether the reader gets a deep, individual, but narrow (single) understanding of what happens, a juxtaposed and perhaps contradictory (multiple) understanding, or a comprehensive but distant (omniscient) understanding.

The term *narration* in the limited sense applies to the telling of action within a scene, as opposed to a description of the setting or a dialogue between the characters. So you'll see guidelines like "Only 40 percent of your lines should be devoted to narration; the rest should be dialogue." (I don't agree with this "rule" either; the proportion of narration and dialogue will vary with the type of book and the requirements of the story.) This expository type of narration is also POV related, in that the very prose you use to describe action will often reflect your choice of POV character. For instance, a stuffy Oxford dean will narrate a student dance with terminology and attitude considerably different than those of a dreadlocked freshman.

Perception is the unique way the narrator perceives an event and its effect on the narration, both in sensory terms (for example, a musician will "hear" in more detail than a painter will) and in position terms (the private in the trenches will perceive the battle differently from the general back at headquarters).

Introspection includes the thoughts and feelings of the narrator and (in omniscient POV) the characters. This deepens the reader's understanding of the human consequences of the plot and individualizes the story because only this character would have this specific internal response.

Voice is the diction, style, and attitude of the narration. Sometimes only the author's voice is displayed in the narrative, but often the narrating character's own voice comes out.

Good scenes, of course, typically reflect all of the above. But for the sake of clarity, I'm going to focus on each individually in passages from Mark Twain's *Extracts from Adam's Diary*, written through the POV of Adam (of Adam and Eve, that is), whose diary is a true *tour de force* of a naive and eloquent perspective.

> FRIDAY—She has taken to beseeching me to stop going over the Falls. What harm does it do? Says it makes her shudder. I wonder why; I have always done it—always liked the plunge, and coolness. I supposed it was what the Falls were for. They have no other use that I can see, and they must have been made for something. She says they were only made for scenery—like the rhinoceros and the mastodon.
>
> I went over the Falls in a barrel—not satisfactory to her. Went over in a tub—still not satisfactory. Swam the Whirlpool and the Rapids in a fig-leaf suit. It got much damaged. Hence, tedious complaints about my extravagance. I am too much hampered here. What I need is a change of scene.

This is the narrative, the necessary description of the action and setting of the scene. Adam's POV shapes the narrative because he is the one who gets pleasure from his plunges over the Falls but then must deal with his wife's disapproval.

> WEDNESDAY—I have had a variegated time. I escaped last night, and rode a horse all night as fast as he could go, hoping to get clear of the Park and hide in some other country before the trouble should begin; but it was not to be. About an hour after sun-up, as I was riding through a flowery plain where thousands of animals were grazing, slumbering, or playing with each other, according to their wont, all of

a sudden they broke into a tempest of frightful noises, and in one moment the plain was a frantic commotion and every beast was destroying its neighbor. I knew what it meant—Eve had eaten that fruit, and death was come into the world.

The sensory descriptions are the signal that this is his perception. He sees the flowers and the animals; hears the noise and commotion; and derives meaning from that: Eve had eaten the forbidden fruit. His POV reveals the fear that drives him to flee from the Park and regard the unprecedented activity around him as proof he has lost his home in Eden.

TEN DAYS LATER—She accuses ME of being the cause of our disaster! She says, with apparent sincerity and truth, that the Serpent assured her that the forbidden fruit was not apples, it was chestnuts. I said I was innocent, then, for I had not eaten any chestnuts. She said the Serpent informed her that "chestnut" was a figurative term meaning an aged and moldy joke. I turned pale at that, for I have made many jokes to pass the weary time, and some of them could have been of that sort, though I had honestly supposed that they were new when I made them. She asked me if I had made one just at the time of the catastrophe. I was obliged to admit that I had made one to myself, though not aloud. It was this. I was thinking about the Falls, and I said to myself, "How wonderful it is to see that vast body of water tumble down there!" Then in an instant a bright thought flashed into my head, and I let it fly, saying, "It would be a deal more wonderful to see it tumble UP there!"—and I was just about to kill myself with laughing at it when all nature broke loose in war and death and I had to flee for my life. "There," she said, with triumph, "that is just it; the Serpent mentioned that very jest, and called it the First Chestnut, and said it was coeval with the creation." Alas, I am indeed to blame. Would that I were not witty; oh, that I had never had that radiant thought!

The above excerpt demonstrates the introspection of Adam's POV; we're inside his head. He's puzzling through what he's learned and coming to a conclusion, albeit the wrong one. His appealing vanity (he thinks his great sense of humor caused The Fall) is a POV filter that helps individualize his thinking, giving a new spin to the old tale of Adam and Eve.

WEDNESDAY—Built me a shelter against the rain, but could not have it to myself in peace. The new creature intruded. When I tried to put it out, it shed water out of the holes it looks with, and wiped it away with the back of its paws, and made a noise such as some of the other animals make when they are in distress. I wish it would not talk; it is always talking. That sounds like a cheap fling at the poor creature, a slur; but I do not mean it so. I have never heard the human voice before, and any new and strange sound intruding itself here upon the solemn hush of these dreaming solitudes offends my ear and seems a false note.

Here's a bit of voice: "Built me a shelter" is something Adam would say if he were saying this out loud. We're so deep in Adam's POV we're hearing his voice—a mix of down-home plainness ("back of its paws"), naiveté ("never heard the human voice before"), and poetry ("solemn hush"). This is an example of using the levels of POV to get closer to the character.

Consider that we are only in Adam's head and body here. We don't get to "hear" any of Eve's defensiveness about her involvement with the serpent, or the serpent's triumph at seducing her. This is Adam's passage, and we get only his view and interpretation of the action. This is the most typical POV approach in modern fiction, a fairly tight focus on one person's perspective to narrate an extended sequence of action. To have switched to Eve's POV would have derailed the descent from Adam's experience (narration and perception) into his thoughts and feelings (introspection). We'll focus more on the use of levels of POV in chapter ten.

WHAT POV CAN DO FOR YOUR STORY

In order to maximize the impact POV has on your readers, an understanding of its potential is essential. The choices you make regarding POV have the power to do the following:

1. *Give readers the vicarious experience* of a certain perspective on an event (such as what the Battle of Waterloo felt like from the trenches with the privates or from headquarters with the generals).

This broadens readers' worldviews by allowing them to explore how someone other than themselves—the POV character—thinks and feels and perceives reality. This insight provides clues as to who a character is and how perspective affects his behavior.

2. *Create an interactive experience* of the story, by inviting readers to participate with the characters and second-guess their decisions and actions.

3. *Increase reader identification,* so the POV character's goals and conflicts become, for the moment, important to the readers (which keeps them turning pages).

4. *Convey (or conceal) information* that is known to a particular character in order to create affiliation (or suspense) with the readers.

5. *Individualize characters* and distinguish them from each other by showing how differently each feels and thinks about the same event.

6. *Provide the contrast between the apparent and the internal* in order to create subtext. POV can create tension between what the character says and what she means; between her vision and reality; between what is said and what is interpreted.

These will be explored in greater depth throughout the book, but one point I'll make now is that not all these purposes will come into play in every scene or book, and there is no one approach that will effortlessly fulfill all of them. In fact, sometimes you will sacrifice one effect (such as conveying information) for another (creating suspense). The choices you make, the purposes you emphasize, will be what really individualizes your narrative, no matter how conventional or radical your plot.

THINKING ABOUT POV LIKE A READER

We're all readers as well as writers, and when we explore POV, we should use both perspectives. As you write your own story, always consider how the eventual reader will experience it. Most readers don't consciously record whose POV they're in at any given moment. In fact, most readers won't even notice POV as a separate element as they read. But then, if the author is doing a good job, the reader also doesn't immediately register plot; all she knows is she can't put the book down. Yet we never tell authors, "Don't worry about plot! The reader doesn't notice it."

Readers *do* notice when something is wrong with POV. While they won't pinpoint it as being a POV problem, they'll feel distanced from the characters or feel that the book was "jumpy" or "hard to follow." Or maybe their response will be, "I never bonded with the hero. In fact, it was chapter four before I figured out *he* was the hero; there were so many other characters." These are all signs of POV problems that could have been fixed with more analysis and revision.

Readers will also notice when POV is done well, even if they don't consciously register what choices an author makes. In fact, if the author does a good job, all the reader should notice is that she really understood the protagonist, was thrilled by the action, or laughed and cried. I think of myself as extremely sensitive to POV in books, but recently when I was having a discussion with a friend about a book we both loved, I found that neither of us could remember if it was a first-person or third-person narrative. All we remembered was that we truly knew the protagonist and identified with her, so even if the author's choice wasn't obvious, it was effective.

Think about why readers read fiction, especially popular fiction: to be entertained, to learn something, to get involved in a story and forget their own troubles. What's intriguing to me, however, is the way fiction makes a reader both an observer of and a participant in someone else's life. That is, while the reader maintains her own life, her own external and internal reality, she experiences what it's like to be someone else.

And that dual status of observer and participant is made possible by the author's use of POV to provide an "insider's view" of the characters' experience of the story's events. What's fun is that the reader gets to contrast this, whether aware of it or not, with what her own experience might be in the same situation and, in this way, interact with the book. There can be a running internal monologue like this: *That was pretty stupid. I wouldn't have let him have the money. But then, I'm not seventeen and in love, like Tillie. She's naive and she's been sheltered by her parents and she's never been exposed to cheats and scoundrels before. She's easy prey for someone like Raphael. Me, well, I would have had him pegged the first time he called me 'darling,' but then, he's a lot like my handsome dog of a dad.*

At the same time, the reader might like to participate in what he'd never want to do in real life, whether it's bungee jumping or serial murder. That type of back-and-forth, me-and-them, reader-character dynamic is essential to the sort of reading experience most authors want to provide—captivating and enjoyable. The most successful and compelling books are the ones in which the reader can simultaneously be the character and the outside observer of the character.

It is possible to write a great book without spending one moment thinking about POV; some authors have done it. And some instinctively great authors also write great books without any revisions. I don't know about you, but I'm not going to try that. I'm going to do everything I can to make the book a great experience for my reader, and this means utilizing POV as a powerful tool.

BASIC TYPES OF POV

Usually in modern fiction, if POV resides at any given moment in a single character, whether first person or third person, that's *personal POV*. But there are a couple of *impersonal POV* types that aren't confined to an actual sentient being. In *omniscient POV*, there's an overall narrative presence that is not any character in the story—more of an authorial stand-in, able to report on the doings and feelings of any character. In *objective POV*, the narrative is limited to what might be recorded by a video camera, such as the movement and sound of the characters. So going from most detached to most intimate POV, here are the basic types (each will be explained in greater depth in Part Two):

- Objective or camera-eye
- Classical omniscient
- Contemporary omniscient
- Second person
- First person
- Third-person multiple (also called multiple third)
- Third-person single (also called single third)
- Deep third person

How to Know Which POV You're In

If we're in a character's personal POV, we feel what the character feels, think what he thinks, see what he sees, and move from one setting to another when he moves. It's easy to know what person we're in when first person is used—we're the "I" character. But in third person, the distinction can be subtler, relying on words that present the internal and perceptual reality of the viewpoint character. For example:

> John's stomach *clenched* as he *absorbed* the bad news.

"Clenched" is a perception and "absorbed" is a process of thought. This line shows John's perspective or POV, because only John can feel his stomach clenching.

But try this:

> John's *face contorted* as he absorbed the bad news.

This could be from John's POV (he can feel his face contorting, presumably) or it could be from someone observing his face. Let me add a bit to clarify the POV:

> John's face *contorted* as he absorbed the bad news. Terry sympathized. She'd also had a hard time accepting that their mother had run off with their high-school principal.

That's more clearly in Terry's POV. She's told her brother the bad news and is watching her brother's face contort. She knows he's *absorbing* the news and that he thinks it's bad news, because, presumably, she knows him well enough to read his expression and body language.

Usually an author starts a new paragraph when she switches to a new POV, as a signal to the reader that there is some shift about to take place. But I've seen cases where the author deliberately chose to juxtapose two POVs even in one sentence. However, some authors like to mix POVs in passages. So you might get:

> John's stomach *clenched* as he absorbed the bad news. [John's POV: Only he can feel his stomach pain.] Terry sympathized. She'd also had a hard time accepting that their mother had run off with their high-school principal. [Terry's POV: Only she can "hear" her thoughts.]

Personally, I would mix POV within passages seldom and only for a specific purpose, as it's confusing to the reader. But it can be done effectively if it's done for a good reason. (More on switching POV in chapter eight.)

Looking From the Inside Out

We get the POV character's actions and perceptions from the *inside* and the other characters' actions and perceptions from the *outside*. So when it comes to motion and vision, be careful about your verbs. You want to convey that inside/outside distinction. Consider this example:

> John *managed to raise* his head off the pillow and open his eyes, and *he saw* the shock on Lainie's face. "Yeah, I'm alive," he said.

This is an *inside* perspective because we feel the effort of him raising his head, and because we "see" through his eyes. We get Lainie's shock not from inside of her, but from John's perception of her facial expression. We're in *John's* POV. However, consider the same incident from Lainie's POV:

> As Lainie watched, John's slack face suddenly *contorted,* and he *raised his head* from the pillow. Then his eyes were open and *staring right at her.* "Yeah, I'm alive," he said.

This is *outside* because we are outside of him, watching him look at her; we're not seeing from within him. We are seeing him through her eyes; we're in *Lainie's* POV.

This is a signal to be careful with your wording of even minor actions and perceptions, because the reader subconsciously uses these to locate himself in the POV of the character. As a reader, not a writer, think about which character you're "in" here:

> The door closed behind the young detective, leaving Inspector Weems alone in his office.

We're Inspector Weems, right? We're seeing through his eyes (the door closed behind), and we're left in the office with the inspector. How about the same mini-event, but with slightly different wording:

> Paula let the door close behind her, and, fists clenched, she strode down the corridor, away from Inspector Weems's office and his condescending smirk.

We're in Paula's head in this instance; she "let" the door close behind her, so we know from the inside what she intended. We also stride with her away from the inspector's office and interpret his look as she would.

Even the use of identifiers can provide subtle information or identification. The inspector thinks of Paula as "the young detective," whereas Paula thinks of herself by her first name. The inspector is stuffy and pompous; we know that because he thinks of himself by his title and last name.

NARROWING IN ON POV

As you start writing your own story, you'll want to experiment because different situations call for different approaches. But let's look at a single situation to see how varied POV approaches create a distinctive feel to the scene.

Here's a paragraph of old-fashioned objective POV from the opening of Ernest Hemingway's story "The Short Happy Life of Francis Macomber":

> Francis Macomber had, half an hour before, been carried to his tent from the edge of the camp in triumph on the arms and shoulders of the cook, the personal boys, the skinner and the porters. The gun-bearers had taken no part in the demonstration. When the native boys put him down at the door of his tent, he had shaken all their hands, received their congratulations, and then gone into the tent and sat on the bed until his wife came in. She did not speak to him when she came in and he left the tent at once to wash his face and hands in the portable wash basin outside and go over to the dining tent to sit in a comfortable canvas chair in the breeze and the shade.

Notice that we're in no one's mind. This is an objective view of the scene, not one filtered through an actual character. The objective viewpoint is generally used in small doses, perhaps to introduce a setting or character, and many writers don't even use it then. It's too distancing to narrate most scenes, and it reveals little about the characters.

Hemingway's choice here is an intriguing one because the objective approach highlights the irony of the situation (far from bravely "getting his lion" earlier that day, Macomber shows himself a coward by running from it) as well as the author's own dispassionate, detached voice. Just to illustrate how the POV approach changes the experience of the passage, I've rewritten that passage with an omniscient narrator to provide some greater context:

> We see what we want to see. The camp servants wanted to see a triumphant return from the hunt by the great white hunter, and that was what they saw. Or that was what they created: the cook, the personal boys, the skinner, and the porters bearing Francis Macomber to his tent on their arms and shoulders. They were all cheering too loudly to notice that the gun-bearers, who had been with Macomber on the hunt, took no part in the celebration. And Macomber did his gracious part when the native boys put him down, shaking their hands and receiving their congratulations and tipping them generously. They went back to their chores happily, the order restored and their pockets full, and left Macomber on his bed—waiting with dread for his wife. Wives, like gun-bearers, are more observant than cook boys, and she did not speak to him when she came in. He quit the tent at once and went to wash his face and hands in the portable wash basin, scrubbing harder than usual as if to scrub off what he knew, what his wife knew, what the gun-bearers knew. Then he went over to the dining tent to sit in a comfortable canvas chair in the breeze and the shade. He raised his hand for a bottle of whiskey to drown the new, dangerous self-knowledge.

The omniscient approach allows for more explanation of the context, more interpretation of attitude and action, and more conclusion about what it all means. Notice that there is a narrator, however removed (it's not any one of the characters), who knows that the servants are misunderstanding the situation and that Macomber's actions result from shame. "Omniscient" means "all-knowing," and

THE POWER OF POINT OF VIEW

the omniscient narrator is most useful when you want to direct the reader toward interpreting a scene.

But usually the story is told through the perspective of one or more characters who narrate the events. Readers are more engaged by stories that put them inside someone's head so they can "experience" the events through a particular character.

Keeping that in mind, here's another version that sounds more modern, using single POV:

> *I should confess*, Francis Macomber told himself as the cook, the personal boys, porters, and skinner lifted him onto their shoulders for a triumphant procession to his tent. They were treating him like a hero, and he wasn't one. He couldn't help but notice that the gun-bearers were turning away from him, refusing to participate in the celebration. They'd been there. They knew. But at least he could count on them not telling what they knew about the not-so-great great white hunter. Too bad he couldn't count on a similar discretion from his own wife. He'd only been in his tent a moment before she came in, and she refused to greet him. He couldn't stand it another minute. He got up and went outside and washed his hands at the portable washbasin. The cook would probably think he was washing off the blood of the lion; in fact, he was just ridding himself of the dust of the path he had run down. He dried off and dropped into a chair and waited for someone to bring him dinner.

We're in Macomber's head here. We're seeing the scene through his eyes, and we're privy to his thoughts about what is happening. But we also feel his shame at his own behavior. Notice that he can speculate about what others might think ("the cook would probably think that ...") but not really know it as an omniscient narrator might. Single POV means we are confined to only one perspective, but we get a deeper, more intimate glimpse of his thoughts and emotions.

Here's how the scene might unfold with two POV characters sharing that opening moment (multiple POV):

> The tent was finally empty, and Francis Macomber no longer had to act like a hero. As his wife entered, he sank onto the narrow bed. She was

lovely there, with the sunlight filtering through the mosquito screen and gilding her hair. He sighed with relief. He didn't have to pretend with her. She had been there this afternoon. She knew the truth, and she wouldn't condemn him. He was sure of that. She loved him.

So why didn't she say anything?

Mrs. Macomber glanced over at her husband and then away. There was no getting around it: She'd married a coward. Now he sat there on the camp bed, head down, his hands hanging between his knees. He was such a coward, he wouldn't even look at her. In fact, now he fled from her just like he'd fled from the lion.

She should go to him, tell him it didn't matter, that he was her hero still. But she stayed where she was, in the hot, airless tent, until the cook rang the gong for dinner.

Here, we get more physical anchoring because there are two people giving their impressions of the situation. We see that they have two different expectations of their marriage: He thinks she will support him no matter what, and she realizes that she can't respect him when she knows his heroics are false. It's the juxtaposition of different perspectives that makes multiple POV interesting.

First person, however, will offer another dimension: The voice of the narrator is an actual character. Usually in modern fiction, the first-person narrator is one of the major characters, but in Hemingway's day, it was just as likely that the action and central characters were filtered through the viewpoint of a minor character. (Think of Nick Carraway in *The Great Gatsby*.) So Hemingway might just as easily have narrated this scene in the first-person perspective of Robert Wilson, the macho expedition leader who would never run from a fight:

I busied myself cleaning my rifle as the cook and personal boys carried Macomber through camp. He was making like the great white hunter, but the pained look on his face told me that he was actually considering telling the truth. But they deposited him in his tent and came out still pleased with his success. Well, they'd been with me too long—they thought a big man with a big gun had to have courage.

The gun-bearers knew better. They exchanged furtive glances, and I had to speak sharply to them. Couldn't have them being disrespectful to the paying clients, could I? Even if the paying clients deserved no respect.

Macomber's lady walked into the tent. She had a fine walk, and I stopped working to watch her rear disappear through the tent flap. She deserved a real man. I ought to make sure she got one.

You'll notice this is very much a process of revision. Some writers can identify immediately and deeply with a character so that they need no reminders to channel the POV. But most of us will need to add bits of sensory detail, thoughts, and emotions filtered through a particular POV as we revise a passage. Notice the closer we get, the longer the passage gets. That's one hazard of focusing POV, but the passage is much more interesting and purposeful once we "channel" the scene through the character.

FINDING YOUR STORY PERSPECTIVE

1. Jot down a paragraph or so summarizing the story you're working on.

2. Is there a single central character (protagonist)? Or a couple of central characters? Or a host of them? Jot down the names or other identifiers of all the major characters whose perspectives you might want to explore.

3. Next to each name, write a word or two that gives a hint to that person's perspective. For example:

   Francis: ashamed, disappointed
   Mrs. Macomber: expects too much, romantic
   Robert Wilson: arrogant, poor

4. Pick up a published novel you enjoy but don't mind writing in. With a highlighter in hand, read through a scene and highlight any word or phrase that tells you you're in a particular character's head—not dialogue (which could be heard) but thoughts (*he wondered what the crowd was looking at*), feelings (*she was losing hope of ever finding Timmy*), and perceptions (*his hands grew numb*). At any given moment, stop and think: Whose experience am I sharing?

That's the POV character. You might need two or three different colors of highlighter, depending on how many characters have a viewpoint in this scene. After analyzing a couple scenes, you will have trained your mind to pay attention to POV "signals" like the thought-emotion words, and perceptions that can only be experienced by one character.

5. Now print out a scene from your own story, and try the same highlighter exercise. Highlight words or phrases that tell you whose head you're in. Then wait a day and read over the same scene. If it had to be in only one POV, whose POV would you choose? What would you have to change to keep the scene entirely in that POV? Now try recasting that scene from yet another POV. What would you have to change? Go beyond words and phrases here. What would a different but unified perspective—say, the perspective of the foot soldier instead of the general—require?

POV CHOICES AND WHAT THEY COMMUNICATE ABOUT YOUR STORY

2

You don't choose POV; it chooses you. Well, not exactly. But rather than conceiving a story with a desire to write in a particular POV ("I'm just dying to write in omniscient!"), think instead about the story you want to write and then determine which POV will help you best tell this story.

You are important here. The sort of novels you like to read and want to write is probably reflective of some aspect of your character, and that's going to affect which POV you find most comfortable for your story. I have a theory that visually oriented people tend to prefer multiple POV over single-third or first-person POV. They might "see" a story as the braiding of the lives of several different characters. Someone kinesthetically oriented, however, might prefer to tell this same set of events in the more directly active first person. If you can't imagine writing in first person, don't chose that POV just because you admire other first-person books similar to your project in style, tone, or theme. First and foremost, know yourself and get to know your story. Make your manner of writing the best way to tell that particular story.

POV APPROACHES AND THEMES

Each POV approach reflects a particular concern that has preoccupied fiction writers since the dawn of storytelling. These themes, if recognized, can deepen your story's own themes.

- First-person POV explores questions of persona and identity: What of myself do I reveal the world? What do I conceal? (Multiple–first person, by the way, adds the dimension of contrasting views both of the world and of the self.)
- Second-person POV explores the nature of identity construction: How does *you* compare to *I*?

- Objective POV explores whether there is an objective reality, apart from each of our own interpretations.
- Classical omniscient explores human society: How do we interact and why?
- Contemporary omniscient explores the conflict between our need for society and our need for freedom.
- Single–third person explores the issue of the interior life: How do internal needs and conflicts drive an individual's external actions?
- Multiple–third person explores the issue of perspective: What we see is very much dependent on where we stand.

These themes are not mutually exclusive. For example, if you use a contemporary-omniscient opening to a scene and then slide into single–third person or multiple–third person POV, the combination can help you explore the tension or balance between self and society.

This does not mean that these POV themes are the only ones that can be examined in your story. Rather, POV approaches evolved, in part, to explore these issues; your attraction to any particular method probably reflects your subconscious interest in the issues brought up by it. For example, if you are writing about a woman whose life is still being affected by her parents' early deaths, you might decide that single–third person POV will help you delve more deeply into her internal reality. Then again, if you are more interested in how a cold-case police unit investigates her parents' deaths, a single-POV focus might unnecessarily limit the narrative and action. A multiple-POV account could show the action from the characters who are most involved, while contrasting their different versions of reality.

As you build your own story, keep the central issues provided by POV in mind and let them enhance your own work. At the very least, make sure the POV approach you choose doesn't undercut the themes you are trying to develop.

Does Your Story Focus on the Group or Individual?

In addition to thinking about central themes, you should also consider whether yours is more of a "social novel" or a "personal novel." The social novel focuses on the interaction of a group or community, while the personal novel tightly addresses the experience of a central protagonist. As always with fiction, these are not hard and fast categories. Charles Frazier's *Cold Mountain* involves both the exploration of a Civil War town and the personal journey of a soldier trying to find his way home.

Social novels are more likely to use omniscient or multiple POV, so that we are privy to the understanding of several characters and their interactions. Personal novels are more likely to use a tightly focused single POV, whether third person or first person, so we can share the internal experience of the character.

Social and personal novels both appear in most genres. For example, the thriller genre encompasses both Robert Ludlum's *The Bourne Identity*, which follows an amnesiac spy's attempt to discover his past (personal), and Ian Caldwell and Dustin Thomason's *The Rule of Four*, which solves an ancient mystery while exploring the friendships and rivalries within an Ivy League academy (social).

It helps to consider whether you are more interested in the journey of one (or two) main characters or in the actions and interactions of a larger group. Since most genres allow both types of novels, make sure you're not undermining your own purpose by, for example, using too many viewpoints in what is meant to be a deeply personal psychological thriller, or, conversely, sticking too tightly to one POV in a novel that's meant to describe the workings of an entire culture.

WHO'S HEADLINING?

Your POV choice can also affect the name of your story, as the focus of the story is often reflected in the title: *David Copperfield* promises a much more personally focused Dickens novel than *A Tale of Two Cities*. Two books in Stephen King's The Dark Tower series provide another good contrast. The first is called *The Gunslinger*, and it's very much concerned with a man who fights alone and ends up alone. The second book, however, is called *The Drawing of the Three*, which suggests the protagonist's new recognition of his need for allies and the building of his little army. Before you title your story, ask yourself: Is it the character or group that deserves top billing?

One or More Than One?
Genre Considerations and POV

Your choice of genre will greatly affect your POV, and your approach to POV may influence an editor's opinion about how to market your work (as a particular genre, as general fiction, or as literary fiction). The boundaries between genres might vary depending on historical period—a "romance" today doesn't mean what it did to Chaucer—but most contemporary fiction falls into one of these genres: mystery, detective, suspense, science fiction, fantasy, romance, horror, Western, thriller (legal and medical), adventure, or literary.

POV is infinitely variable, and you must choose the approach that works best for your story. Some books do stick very close to a single-protagonist POV, but most novels are filtered through more than one character's viewpoint. There's no rule that dictates you must use only one POV, even in first-person narratives. But while there's no real "formula" for writing popular fiction, each genre has a distinct purpose, set of conventions, and boundaries that readers understand and expect. These genre expectations, which are based in the experience readers want from these novels, may affect whether you use only one POV in your book or many.

For example, many mysteries are told entirely in the POV of the "sleuth" (using first person or a very close single–third person) so that the readers get only the information available to the sleuth. Part of the reason readers like mysteries is because they can compete with the sleuth in solving the crime; as result, they don't want to know anything extra that might "leak" through another POV character. On the other hand, in romance novels, most readers would feel cheated if they didn't get into the heads of both the hero and heroine, as a romance requires both of these viewpoints in order to get the "full" story of how the couple comes together.

Usually, literary and historical first-person novels are told through only one POV, but authors have also experimented with sequential multiple-first person, where one character might have his say for a hundred pages, then another character might have her say, or narrators might alternate chapters. Susan Howatch's multigenerational family saga *Cashelmara* is a good example of sequential-multiple first-person POV, and William Faulkner alternated narrators in *As I Lay Dying*, the story of the Bundren family's pilgrimage to bury their deceased matriarch.

If you're writing popular fiction or using any of the traditional storytelling structures (like quest or Gothic or romance), you'll need to understand tradition, particularly when it comes to approaching POV. As always, if you're writing a particular type of novel, read widely in that fictional area and figure out what's conventional, what is unusual, and what is rarely, if ever, done. It's helpful to study novels in your chosen genre to see the variety of choices and how each choice might fulfill the author's purpose in the novel. But you might also look for the elements that don't work—when a glimpse into the twisted mind of the villain provides laughs rather than thrills, when you figure out the mystery too early because the author let too many clues drop in that secondary character's POV, when time travel is explained by a twenty-third-century engineer who can't possibly know how ignorant we twenty-first centurians are.

You don't have to stick with what's conventional if you sincerely feel your approach is better for the story, but think it through before you do something groundbreaking in that type of work—say, second person in the traditionally first-person detective novel. Readers and editors are willing to experiment, but they also have an appreciation for the conventions of the story type, which have proven their effectiveness for many years. Because POV has such a comprehensive effect on how the story is experienced, always consider the effect on the readers as you make choices.

The following is a breakdown of the major story types and some challenges and conventions you should consider before choosing a POV for your novel.

Crime Novels: Private Eyes, Mysteries, and Thrillers

The *private-eye/detective novel* has traditionally been told entirely in the first-person voice of the detective. The purpose of the tightly focused POV is to allow the reader to follow one person's interpretation and investigation of a case. The first-person approach also lets the protagonist's voice convey the narrative, and private-eye voices are usually intriguing, another genre tradition. In fact, ever since Raymond Chandler's sardonic and cynical Philip Marlowe solved his cases out loud, readers have expected detective novels to offer not only satisfying plots but also compelling P.I. characters.

I suspect the private-eye first-person POV convention is one of the most rigid in popular fiction today, although there are occasional variations. For example, Robert Crais will intersperse third-person secondary-character scenes with the more traditional first-person scenes of detective Elvis Cole. That allows him to reveal events and motivations that his detective doesn't know. Other authors have done most of the story in first-person narration by the private eye but used third person (or another first-person perspective) to offer a glimpse into the villain's head. But readers still enjoy private-eye novels as much for the private investigator's voice and personality as for the mystery; so if you're interested in writing detective fiction, work on getting to know the central character's POV and developing his unique voice.

There are alternatives for crime-fiction writers who prefer the third-person POV. The *mystery novel* has traditionally used a tightly focused third-person narrative, concentrating on the viewpoint of the "sleuth." But the sleuth's voice isn't as central to the experience of a mystery novel, which focuses on plot, as it is in a detective novel, which asks the reader to focus both on the crime and the person solving it. (Notice that even the names of the subgenres—*detective* and *mystery*—suggest what their relative focus is: the puzzle solver or the puzzle.)

The essential element of the mystery genre, the one most important to the author, is that both reader and sleuth have access to the same essential information, and this is ensured by POV control. Some mysteries offer occasional omniscient passages (such as a scene when the body is discovered), but with the assumption that the sleuth also has access to the information revealed to the reader in those passages. Additionally, I have read mysteries with passages in the POV of a minor character, but where the information provided isn't essential to figuring out the puzzle (such as the victim's last moments before the murder). The author's most important task in a mystery novel is to use the sleuth's perspective to create the puzzle while leaving enough distance for the reader to jockey for the solution.

Cozy mysteries, however, often use a first-person narration by the amateur sleuth. "Cozy" makes these books sound very sweet, but there's a paradoxical form of sociopathology in cozies that you seldom get in third-person POV. The sleuth is usually only peripherally involved with the victim and is therefore detached from really caring about the death. (Indeed, the victim is often unlikable, the town bully or gossip.) First-person narration might be the only way to draw the reader close to a sleuth who thinks of murder as a game and murderers as competitors.

The *thriller* or *suspense novel*, on the other hand, has the purpose of not only providing a puzzle but also a vicariously scary experience. To achieve this sort of thrill, these books usually focus on the "victim," the person being stalked or threatened. But they'll also often provide a glimpse into the villain's mind in order to give more sense of her psychology. These passages in the villain's POV can sometimes reveal her identity or at least give clues that allow the reader to guess. In other books, the author will go to some lengths to disguise the villain's identity even while using that POV; you'll see a lot of first-person villain passages, as that avoids telling if this person is a *he* or *she*. Occasionally, an investigator's POV will reveal the process of tracking down the villain (though notice in a thriller, the investigator often fails or ends up dead, and the potential victim actually resolves the problem). The author's primary POV challenge in a thriller is to use the victim's perspective to create a growing sense of menace and terror, and to portray the villain without diminishing the threat with too much familiarity. Third-person (often multiple) POV is common in thrillers, especially in stories that have several settings and simultaneous action.

Legal and medical thrillers are also concerned with crime, but they are more likely to examine the intersection of individuals within the greater society (in the court system or the medical establishment). Often, these stories use the viewpoints of several characters—for example, a nurse, a doctor, and a patient; or a victim, a defendant, a prosecutor, and a defense attorney. The multiple POV approach gives a more expansive and comprehensive perspective that reflects the institutional conflict of law or medicine. The author's primary POV task in these books is to identify and stick close to a central protagonist while fleshing out the narrative with other perspectives.

Emotion Novels: Horror and Romance

Crime stories usually provide an intellectual experience, pitting the reader against the villain to discover the solution to the crime. But another type of novel aims to create an emotional experience, which is facilitated by POV. *Horror novels* create both a sense of personal terror and an overall awareness of evil. Stephen King often uses a contemporary-omniscient POV, tightly focusing on a single character once the scene is launched. He has also used a single–first-person narrator for an entire book, creating a bond with the victim. Dean Koontz is known for his tight, almost claustrophobic passages from the viewpoint of either a terrified victim or a deranged villain. At the same time, horror is the genre most likely to use some form of omniscient to help replicate the looming dread of a supernatural entity and the foreboding atmosphere that hangs over the characters themselves.

Romances provide a different sort of emotional experience that allows the reader to participate in a couple's journey to love. These books typically have two protagonists, the hero and the heroine, and the narrative is usually told entirely or almost entirely in these two viewpoints. Occasionally, especially in historical romances, there will be an omniscient narrator at the beginning of scenes, but it's unusual these days to see an entire romance in that distant viewpoint. Both multiple POV (more than one per scene) and single POV (one per scene) are common in romance. Since the romantic plotline follows the growing compatibility between these two people, crosscutting from one POV to the other is often used to compare and contrast their understanding and interpretation of events. Romances sometimes have an external plot that might take the form of a mystery or a quest, but the focal plot will probably guide you to a tighter focus on the POVs of the hero and the heroine. The major challenge in writing a romance is creating distinctive POVs so that both the hero and heroine come across as intriguing, sympathetic individuals.

Romance is an element of the large category of novels marketed as *women's fiction*, a niche that is hard to define but includes novels that are more likely to appeal to female readers. They can have male protagonists (like Susan Howatch's books) and violence and murder (like Tess Gerritsen's thrillers), but generally there's more emphasis on relationships and personal journeys than in books aimed at men. The more character-focused women's novels generally use a tightly limited third-person or first-person POV. But many works of women's fiction, like those written by Jan Karon and Debbie Macomber, are more community-based and use multiple or contemporary-omniscient POV to show a small group's interaction. These community-based novels are often shelved as general fiction rather than romance.

Men's Fiction: Western and Action-Adventure

Just as there's a category of novels aimed specifically at women, there are two genres aimed at men. (Of course, women read men's fiction and vice versa; it's a matter of the target market.)

Western is an American genre (though it has had some popularity in Europe) that mythologizes the ethos and events of the Old West. Even before the Old West was "old," authors were writing dime novels featuring cowboys and ranchers and the grand vistas of the Great Plains and Upper Rockies. These earliest Westerns treated cowboys as emblems of manly virtues, rather like medieval knights, but the great author Zane Grey focused more on the unique American geography and experience. He often used a contemporary-omniscient POV to emphasize the epic scope of the frontier and the themes it inspires—nature, God, and human heroism. Louis L'Amour continued the exploration of the frontier but focused more on the Western man in interaction with his environment and community, moving closer to single–third person. New Westerns, such as those by Mike Jameson, use a deep third to create an even tighter focus on the individual in conflict with the land and its people. But some Western authors (like Tabor Evans) have returned to omniscient for a more ironic view of the Western myths.

Action-adventure, like the Western, has in some ways been co-opted by Hollywood. Where horror and romance stories, for example, seem best embodied in words and books, the vast vistas of the West and the explosive clashes of action plots might have been designed for cinematography. But, as with the Western, the action-adventure still has a novel market. There are two basic kinds: the big techno-thrillers (like Tom Clancy's novels) and the shorter "special-ops" books that are either standalone or belong to a series (like Warren Murphy and Richard Sapir's The Destroyer or John F. Mullins's Men of Valor). The action-adventure genre might seem to be a successor to the Western (both deal a lot in guns), but the Western—traditional and contemporary—is inextricably tied to the setting and themes of the American frontier, and so follows the slower rhythms of an earlier time. The action-adventure genre is, in contrast, hyper-modern, often concerned with state-of-the-art technology and tomorrow's headline news. These novels are usually fast-paced and detail-oriented, with a greater emphasis on narrating *what* and *how* rather than *why*.

Techno-thrillers are aimed at an audience that values precision and detail (often military enthusiasts), and the POV approach, therefore, is usually more traditional. These books tend toward a comprehensive, even exhaustive approach to describing and explaining technology and processes, and, as a result, most are in a contemporary-omniscient POV that facilitates the narration of a large cast over several central settings. The shorter special-ops books usually focus on one adventurer or a small team, and the POV is tightly focused on one character at a time. Because these stories appeal to a technologically savvy, mostly male audience, often the prose is edgy and clipped. The narration means to create the visceral experience of danger and excitement, so the POV, though deep into one character, is more physical than emotional. The POV challenge in these books is to give the narrator such an authentic voice and perspective that he can explain complex technology and intricate plots while still propelling the action forward.

Speculative Fiction

Science fiction and *fantasy* have an eclectic mix of POV approaches. Although they often get lumped together as "SF&F," they are two very different genres, and the POV purposes vary because of that. Science fiction might employ faster-than-light travel, but otherwise the genre tends toward realism or even naturalism, often focusing on the scientific or social aspects of life in the future. (Science fiction is one of the few genres, by the way, with a thriving short-story market.) There is limited single POV (sometimes throughout the entire novel) for the novels that follow one character, and multiple POVs for the more epic novels with several settings and a large cast. First person is rare, though getting less rare in the "Me Millennium."

Science fiction writers face a challenge in explaining an alien world or as-yet-uninvented technology to readers, using the POV of characters for whom all this exotica is nothing new. This is also a genre where many readers are Web savvy and have come to expect more innovation than is generally found in print, such as hypertext novels with elaborate graphics and maps. This is the popular fiction genre where you're most likely to see experimental narration, such as Robert Silverberg's *Sundance*, which starts in second-person POV (itself very experimental), moves into third person, and then shifts into first person. The thriving science fiction short-story market allows more experimentation than seen in most novel-oriented genres.

In some ways, fantasy resembles the historical novel more than it does science fiction. Both fantasies and historical novels have to do a lot of "world building," explaining this setting to the reader who lives in a different world. Most fantasies are set in a world that technologically resembles the Middle Ages, however advanced the culture is socially. (You seldom see a hero in a fantasy novel attacking the dragon with a tank, after all.) The common POV approach for fantasy also resembles that of historical novels, a mix of omniscient and third person (single or multiple), which allows both a comprehensive worldview and a tight character focus. The challenge of fantasy novels is to create identification with characters who might have gifts few readers share, like magical powers or telepathy.

General Fiction

This is a generic description, just as indistinct as the category itself. *General fiction*, also called *mainstream* or *contemporary fiction*, is a marketing term, not a literary term. Basically, it refers to those novels that appeal to the broadest possible audience and are often shelved in bookstores and libraries apart from genre novels or literary fiction. They may contain elements of one or more genres, but they do not adhere as strictly to any set of genre conventions. Also, they may contain themes or characters that publishers and booksellers feel could appeal to more readers than any single genre audience. Some novels with a genre structure are considered general fiction because they are "bigger"—longer in length and more epic in scope. They often span a greater period of time than the more tightly plotted genre novels. Examples would be the mysteries of P.D. James and the romances of Nora Roberts. In this category, you'll find most bestsellers, many of the earlier "Oprah books," and many women's fiction novels.

General fiction can be tragic or comic, a family saga or a war drama, an old man's reminiscences or a young mother's diary. So the POV approaches in these novels will vary according to the author's judgment on which method will work the best. You'll seldom see experimental POV (like second person) in general fiction, as that choice would put the emphasis not on the story but on how the story is told, and with general fiction, story is more important. Multiple POV is also relatively rare, but first person is very common, as is single–third person. Omniscient is more common in general fiction than in genre fiction because general fiction follows a more classical form and tone.

The purpose of general fiction is a well-told story, without strict genre conventions. So if you're writing general fiction, your guideline is only that: Choose the POV that best suits the story. The primary consideration is the relative tightness of focus. Personal novels like Marek Halter's *Sarah* would probably benefit from the intimacy of single-third or first-person POV. Social novels like *The Bookseller of Kabul* by Asne Seierstad will convey more about the featured culture through an omniscient approach.

The challenge in writing general fiction is choosing from a wide variety of POV options for the one that best suits this story. Since there are no conventions to adhere to, it's not unusual for general-fiction writers to learn by trial and error. This is a large and varied category of fiction, but that doesn't mean anything goes. General fiction is all about story, and POV is the most important way to enhance readability.

Literary Fiction

Literary novels defy an easy definition, but generally speaking, they don't fit into the traditional storytelling genres, and they get creative with language or style and may be narratively experimental. Their plots often seem secondary, but this might be by design, as they frequently focus on how seemingly trivial events transform the characters in unpredictable ways. Some literary fiction, like Vladimir Nabokov's *Lolita*, uses the journey motif to show the deadening or maddening effect of modern life on the ability of characters to grow and change.

The term *literary fiction*, incidentally, is usually used only to define post-WWI fiction. Anything from an earlier period is simply considered "literature"—Dickens, Austen, et al—even though those themes and structures are more likely to be found now in popular fiction. It's the experimental nature of literary fiction that breaks away from its influences, while popular fiction follows the traditions of earlier eras. Most literary novels, following the modernist custom (à la James Joyce), have a tightly focused POV, either first person or third. But they seldom stop there: Good literary novels use POV to explore hidden aspects of story and character, to innovate in prose passages, and to cast doubt on the veracity of the narrative itself. (We'll talk more about the "unreliable narrator" in chapters four and seven.) Narrative experimentation often involves experimenting with POV. Joyce told his stories through a third-person POV so internal it replicated the chaos of a troubled man's thoughts. This type of narration even got its own name: stream of consciousness.

While the stories in this category vary widely, some factors remain constant. You will catch a literary editor's attention with more experimental ways of telling your story, deeper immersion into the internal workings of a character, or strikingly inventive prose and imagery. All of these will require a particular attention to how you use POV as a narrative element, so as you draft, think about *how* you can tell this event in an innovative way.

Postmodernism: "This Book Isn't True"

Postmodern novels, a subgenre of literary fiction, are even more experimental. While the aim of most traditional novelists is to make you forget you're reading a book, to subsume you into this experience with a "suspension of disbelief," postmodern novels keep reminding you that this story is an invented experience. They use metafictional techniques to undermine the traditional logic of the narrative by juxtaposing events, providing ambiguous endings (John Fowles's *The French Lieutenant's Woman* has three alternate endings, one of which features the author as a character), inserting seemingly irrelevant details (Thomas Pynchon's speculation on JFK's excrement in *Gravity's Rainbow*), and using academic devices such as footnotes and professorial commentary (David Foster Wallace's extensive footnotes in *Infinite Jest*).

You might think anything goes as far as POV in a postmodernist novel, but, in fact, postmodern POV, like the other narrative elements, should serve the purpose of the experiment, even casting doubt on the value or truth of the story. A more traditional novelist might juxtapose two characters' versions of the same event to challenge the reader to determine for herself what the truth is. But a postmodernist might jumble up POV passages to assert that there is no objective truth at all, and indeed, the search for truth is futile (as in Robert Coover's famous short story "The Babysitter").

The postmodernist tradition is difficult for most writers to work within; we actually believe, naifs that we are, that truth can be found in fiction if not in reality. But if you're more skeptical of the fictional experience, if you distrust eternal verities and feel more comfortable with artistic relativism, then go for it. Just remember that your motto should be "This book is a lie," so your POV approach should cast doubt on the credibility of your story—just the opposite of the usual POV task.

When in Doubt, Read

While I have broken down and summarized the major fiction categories for you, there is no substitute for reading other works in your target genre and seeing what they do and how they do it. Your book will be individual, but its impact will depend in part on how it connects with and reacts against other books the reader has read.

EXERCISE

WHERE DOES THIS STORY FIT?

Think about your own story and jot down answers to these questions:

1. Does your story fall into a certain genre or type of book? For example, is it a mystery or a science fiction novel, a romance or a Western? Or is it a quest story, an epic, an adventure, a coming-of-age story, a family drama? There are many different types of stories, and sometimes the genre has an influence on your POV choices. If you can determine the genre or type of story, glance through a few books in that category to see if there's a discernible POV approach. (For example, most detective novels are in first person.) Don't worry if you don't find one.

2. If you can't characterize your story as a particular type, can you name a novel or two that resemble your story? (For example, if you're writing a gritty book about the Civil War, you might think it resembles *Cold Mountain* a bit.) Check out those similar books and see what sort of POV approach they take. Again, this doesn't mean you have to write it that way, but it gives you a sense of what others have done and a chance to evaluate how the approach works.

3. What sort of experience do you hope a reader will have with your story? Try to be specific. "I want chills and thrills and laughter and tears and awe at my great prose!" won't get you anywhere. "I want the reader to be frightened by my villain and relieved when he's caught, but understand why he did it" is more specific, as is "I want my reader to vicariously enjoy the growing love between my hero and heroine," or "I want my reader to puzzle through the

mystery but not be able to solve it," or "I want the reader to get to the end and be confused by the ambiguity of the resolution."

TOOLS, NOT RULES

Start thinking of POV tools, not POV rules. I don't agree with supposed hard-and-fast rules like "never change POV in the middle of a scene" or "always put the viewpoint in the character who has the most to lose." POV has to be author-controlled, with the intention of producing the best experience for the reader. Each author might come up with his own rules, but those might not be right for another writer or for another book.

"No rules" doesn't mean anything goes, however. Most authors don't get it right the first time and won't achieve that great reader experience without rethinking and revising. There are lots of different approaches to different writing situations, and different authors presented with the same situations can make different and equally valid POV choices, depending their purposes. For example, you might always go for the most intense emotional experience, so in a scene where a woman learns that her lover has betrayed her, you might go into her clearly emotional POV. On the other hand, I like to give the reader more of an experience in doubling—in being both the participant and the observer in an event—so I might be more inclined to use the POV of the betraying lover who doesn't yet know he's been found out. The reader, then, would be able to participate in the lover's guilty secret, while observing the woman and trying to imagine what her suddenly unusual behavior is indicating.

Both of these are good purposes that will lead to a vivid reader experience. The difference in purpose explains why two writers can write "a betrayal story" and each do it differently—and why one writer can shift POV from betrayed to betrayer in the middle of the scene and make it work, while another sticks tight to the betrayer's POV and makes that work, too.

I'd better confess my own bias. I am a purist; that is, in general, I use only one POV per chapter (single–third person). I know I'm stricter than most. Even most purists change POVs from scene to scene, and I have done that. But mostly I stay in one per chapter; that's about twelve to fifteen pages and one to three scenes. I like to present one person's perspective in its entirety and show the whole event through that person's POV so the reader gets to know the inner workings of that mind. I do make sacrifices to maintain this intimacy, but I've learned to work around most of the limitations. I am a writer who gets most creative when I'm most restricted, and a strict POV approach fires my imagination.

But this is a personal preference, what works best for me. I think other POV approaches are also valid. No rules! So even though I'm pretty strict with my own writing, I won't be trying to persuade you to join my particular POV camp in this book. Rather, I'll offer guidance on how to decide what works best for you and your story, and how best to exploit its potential to develop character and convey information.

3

POV AND THE ELEMENTS OF STORY

POV is the individualizing element of your story. Through POV, you can shape every other element to reflect your particular purpose and the unique perspective of the characters. No matter how conventional your plot, POV can help you make the narrative, the information, the descriptions, the scenes, and even the language fresh.

But you do have to learn two rather contradictory techniques: analyzing your story and intuiting your characters.

NARRATIVE PURPOSE AND POV

Of all the fundamental elements of fiction, "narrative" is where POV can most individualize a story. Narrative is how a story is told, the process of recounting a plot's action. It's not equivalent to plot, because it's not necessarily a chronological rendering of the events. And while plot can be explained in summary, narrative is told in scenes, in a description of the action, reaction, and interaction of characters.

For example, the plot of The Odyssey could be summarized as: After the conquest of Troy, Odysseus offends a powerful god, is punished with privation and exile, and finally escapes and gets home, only to find he must seize his castle and wife back from the men who have taken over his kingdom. But the narrative doesn't follow this linear structure: It starts in the middle of the action—when Odysseus escapes from captivity—and backtracks in time to tell how he got into this fix; then it plunges forward to chronicle his return home.

POV choices can affect narrative not only because each character has his own perspective on what the story's action means but also because all characters might not experience the same events. You can see this effect more clearly in drama precisely because most of the obvious parts of POV (the narrator's word choice, perception, and knowledge) are stripped away, making paramount the selection and priority of events, along with the dialogue of the characters. So the narrative of *Hamlet* would be much different if the story were told from the POV of two minor characters, as Tom Stoppard demonstrated in his play *Rosencrantz and Guildenstern Are Dead*.

In the twenty-first century, when it seems as if all stories have already been told, how a story is told becomes of supreme importance. Spend some time thinking about how you can tell your story in a way that gives the reader a different, yet fulfilling experience. This is especially important if you're retelling a classic plot or working out an old puzzle like a locked-door mystery. Make it fresh for the reader through a new approach to the narrative so it doesn't replicate earlier versions. Great plots actually benefit from reinvention.

Think of *The Odyssey*'s plot, which inspired John Keats's sonnet "On First Looking into Chapman's Homer," Alfred Tennyson's poem "Ulysses," Derek Wolcott's epic poem "Omeros," James Joyce's stream-of-consciousness novel *Ulysses*, Charles Frazier's Civil War romance *Cold Mountain*, and the film *O Brother, Where Art Thou?*, among others. Each borrows some elements from the traditional plot, but tells the story in a new way. Wolcott's protagonist, for example, is a lonely Caribbean fisherman, while the film's hero is a slick-haired, silver-tongued Depression-era grifter. Joyce's *Ulysses* uses a stream-of-consciousness narrative to explore the inner chaos and order of characters, while *O Brother* uses songs to convey character values and deceptions.

As you start to write or rewrite your own story, don't stop with assembling the plot. Consider how you're going to narrate this story, and what that means for the story. For example, if you are going to stay in one person's head, what's unique about that experience? What does this person bring to the story in terms of knowledge or lack thereof? What is her agenda? What is she trying to accomplish (such as vindication, redemption, or acquisition of knowledge)? How are those characteristics going to change this narrative?

A narrator's motives maybe be more obvious and important to the plot in single POV, whether first person or third, but if your scope is wider—if you're working with a larger cast of POV characters or with an omniscient narrator—you'll still need to consider each character's angle. For instance, if you're using multiple POVs, what connects them together? Maybe all or most of them are connected to a certain place or event—a crime that rocks a small town, for example. Are you planning to show different versions of the same event or how different people are affected differently?

Every Narrator Has an Agenda

The agenda of the POV character will form the narrative by shaping his actions and reactions. Hamlet, for example, is the most reluctant of avengers and has a need for certainty before he acts. He regards every event, from the appearance of his father's ghost to the prayers of Claudius in the chapel, as evidence he must sift through before making a decision. Hamlet's narrative, which has the purpose of determining whether or not he should take vengeance, will be shaped much differently than the narrative of Macbeth, who is more the "act first, think later" type. Hamlet takes most of the play deciding whether to "answer the call to adventure," while Macbeth answers it early on (killing Duncan in Act II) and then spends the rest of the play dealing with the consequences.

Who your POV characters are and what they're trying to accomplish should also influence how the story develops, even if the plot events are identical. Just think what *The Great Gatsby* would have been like if Gatsby were the narrator instead of the callow observer Nick. What events would Gatsby have highlighted, and which would he have left out? Which events did he witness that Nick didn't? How might Gatsby's adored Daisy have been presented in a more positive light?

Imagine if the Sherlock Holmes stories had been narrated by Holmes, instead of by Dr. Watson. Holmes might have tried something sneaky in his narration, making the story even more of a puzzle. Or he might have spent whole pages informing us about some obsession of his—the ashes of 140 different varieties of pipe, cigar, and cigarette tobacco, say—rather than sticking to the action as the more reader-savvy Dr. Watson does.

Using Distant Narration as a Reader Stand-In

Usually the narrator is a major character, often the protagonist of the plot. But occasionally, especially in short stories, authors use a narrator who is somewhat removed from the center of the story. For example,

Herman Melville chose a common seaman to narrate *Moby-Dick,* not Captain Ahab. And Dostoyevsky used an obscure provincial official, not the central character Stavrogin, to narrate *The Possessed.* Faulkner used a boy who wasn't even born during the time of the plot to narrate "A Rose for Emily"; he is reporting what he has heard from older neighbors. This approach is a little old-fashioned (popular in the nineteenth century especially) but it can certainly work, particularly when the author wants an "everyman" perspective on an unusual character. (Ahab is an insane monomaniac; Stavrogin is a nihilist; Miss Emily is a dangerous recluse.) Theoretically, the reader can more easily identify with an Ishmael than an Ahab and is better able to understand his POV.

In these cases, the narrator functions as a reader stand-in, observing the action without too much participation. He is not the protagonist, and though he might be changed by the events, he's not in charge of the action. If you're unsure about letting your protagonist tell your story, think of a nonprotagonist narrator as you would the color commentator on the sidelines narrating Tiger Woods's tournament play. He has a unique and instructive perspective on events, maybe even an emotional response (envy, resentment, awe, willing or unwilling admiration). If you can't make this perspective matter, you might as well let Tiger tell the story.

Modern readers usually prefer to be closer to the main character than to an outside narrator. Now we're more open to exploring the unique POV of the eccentric Holmes-type character; a contemporary example would be Christopher, the young autistic sleuth in Mark Haddon's Holmes-inspired novel *The Curious Incident of the Dog in the Night-Time*:

> It was seven minutes after midnight. The dog was lying on the grass in the middle of the lawn in front of Mrs. Shears' house. Its eyes were closed. It looked as if it was running on its side, the way dogs run when they think they are chasing a cat in a dream. But the dog was not running or asleep. The dog was dead. There was a garden fork sticking out of the dog. The points of the fork must have gone all the way through the dog and into the ground because the fork had not fallen over.

But keep in mind that even if modern readers are more willing to follow the lead of a narrator who's a bit more whimsical or unconventional, the voice you give that narrator must be believable and compelling. Fans of *The Curious Incident* embraced Christopher because his narrow world-view and deadpan delivery were intriguingly different from their own; his narration offered them a glimpse into the brilliant but complicated mind of a young boy with autism.

Writing Inside the Frame

Most novels take the conventional approach of presenting a story without making a big deal about why this story is being told. But some authors, especially those interested in experimenting with postmodern fiction or metafiction, like to conceive of a "frame story," an overarching story that contains another story (or stories), unifies them, and provides some kind of reason or explanation, such as a botched murder investigation couched in a retrospective police report, or the story of two lonely people and their unconventional romance told through the transcripts of phone sex conversations.

The frame story concept dates back to ancient Sanskrit epics. One of the most famous frame stories is the popular *One Thousand and One Arabian Nights,* wherein a young bride must tell a story every night to stave off execution. Other famous frame stories are Geoffrey Chaucer's *The Canterbury Tales* and Giovanni Boccaccio's *The Decameron* from the Middle Ages, in which a group of people each tell their own tales.

The frame gives a unique shape to the POV approach, first because it makes clear the agenda of the overarching narrator and the purpose for the storytelling, and then it encapsulates the interior narrative(s). There are actually two stories, with two POV approaches, to consider: the one in the frame and the one in the story within the story. Usually, the frame is introduced in the first scene and established quickly. For example, the film *Citizen Kane* starts with Kane's last word—"Rosebud"—as he dies, and a young reporter getting the assignment to figure out what that meant. Then, the second story begins (the interviews with those who knew Kane).

If you go the frame route, remember to close the frame. The reader will need some resolution to feel the overarching story is complete. The "frame issue" doesn't have to be fully resolved, but at least close off the narrative by returning to the frame story and ending it somehow, as *Citizen Kane* ended ironically with the burning of the sled that would have answered all the reporter's questions. Edgar Allan Poe's "The Cask of Amontillado," which began with Montresor confessing to burying his rival alive, ends with him smugly averring, "For the half of a century no mortal has disturbed [the body]. In pace requiescat!"

The frame is still an unconventional method, but it reminds us that we writers need to think about the purpose of each narrative. The different narrators' objectives will help us select which events to portray and when.

Types of Frames

The popularity of *epistolary novels*—novels that take the form of letters or other documents such as journal entries—rose during the early-novel era with works such as Samuel Richardson's *Pamela* and Daniel Defoe's *Robinson Crusoe*. The fact that this form has revived recently with works like Helen Fielding's *Bridget Jones's Diary* attests to the power of the frame novel. I remember Bel Kaufman's book *Up the Down Staircase,* published in 1965, was made up entirely of interoffice documents sent and received by a novice teacher—notes, memos, letters, exams, written reprimands—and after more than forty years, that format still seems revolutionary. This type of frame story is appealing because it offers a voyeuristic glimpse into someone else's life, and it adds another narrative layer to a work of fiction. (More on epistolary novels in chapter four.)

Many stories have benefited from an *"as told to" frame*, where one character tells a story to another for a specific purpose. Steven Pressfield's *Tides of War* tells the story of the Athenian traitor Alcibiades through the perspective of his murderer. Emily Brontë's *Wuthering Heights* has a peripheral character narrating the story to an interested but uninvolved listener. Vladimir Nabokov's *Lolita* is told in a confessional style, as the case notes of a psychiatrist who has interviewed the main character. This frames the story around Humbert Humbert's first-person narration, and lets us know that he is jailed for the murder of his rival. "The Cask of Amontillado" also features a murderer, who late in life (perhaps on his deathbed) confesses the crime.

Another trend is the *faux academic treatise*. This type of frame started with Nabokov's *Pale Fire*, wherein a pompous professor edits, catalogs, and footnotes the epic poem of a colleague. The irony is that the reader is aware that the colleague's poem is about his daughter's suicide, while the editor/professor assumes it's all about himself. Susanna Clarke's bestseller *Jonathan Strange & Mr. Norrell* provides a history of magic in the Napoleonic

Wars, complete with erudite footnotes referring to previous (invented) histories of magic.

You don't have to go with a radical format to make use of a frame to help organize your story and make your characters' perspectives and motives more apparent. Again, there's no need to abandon the standard novel format, but just spend a moment imagining frames and the stories they could tell.

EXERCISE

CONSIDERING NARRATIVE PURPOSE

Think about your own story, and answer the following questions:

1. As the writer, what would you say is your purpose for telling this particular story? (For example, to make the reader laugh, to present and solve a locked-door mystery, to show how tragedy affects not just a family but a whole town.)

2. Now consider your major characters, or the ones whose POVs you might be highlighting. What plot aspects would give their POV a unique perspective (e.g., determined to get revenge, desperate to escape death, hiding a secret)? What is their purpose in narrating the event?

3. How might your major characters' agendas shape the narrative differently? Whose agendas are conflicting?

4. If you're interested in postmodernism, metafiction, or cutting-edge fiction for the Web, what "entry" does your story give for some experimentation? Make sure you consider the logic of using experimental devices. (If you see your story as a transcript of a long interrogation, for example, that's going to limit your narration considerably.) What are the limitations going to be, and what will your reader get out of that constraint?

SEE AND BE SCENE

Stories—whether they take the form of novels, short stories, films, or plays—almost always develop through a sequence of scenes. A *scene* is a unit of action and interaction taking place more or less in real time and centering on some essential event of plot development.

The important elements of a scene are:

- *Action*: Something is happening! There is movement and progress and change during this time. Where there is action, there is conflict or risk of some kind.

- *Interaction*: The POV character is interacting with other characters and the environment. This will cause sparks. The interaction will force more action on the POV character.

- *Real time*: A scene usually takes place in a continuous span of time with a starting point and an ending point. This sounds basic, but it's essential. Unless the reader sees the action unfolding through the real-time perspective of a POV character (that is, not in retrospect or summary), she will lose that important sense that this event is really happening.

- *Event*: Every scene should center on an actual event, something that *happens*—not a dream, not a flashback, not a passage of introspection. A character is doing and experiencing something, not just in her mind, but in the external reality of the story. That can mean she's taking an action, discovering a secret, encountering another character, having a conversation, creating something new, enduring a trauma. You, as the author, should be able to identify what event has taken place in this scene. (If you can't, your readers definitely won't.)

- *Plot development*: Events are important because they are concrete and have consequences. Most important, they have an impact on the plot. Events and scenes should cause a development in the story and some sort of change for the POV character.

Think of each scene as a ministory, with:

- a beginning (Character enters scene with some goal or agenda.)
- a middle (Character tries to attain goal and encounters obstacles.)
- an ending (Character either achieves or doesn't achieve goal, or something else happens: a disaster or surprise she didn't plan on.)

POV is important in scenes in order, first and foremost, to provide the reader with a way to experience the action close up, through a character or characters experiencing the action. But POV also lets the characters establish goals, if only in their own heads, and react mentally and emotionally to the obstacles.

This is why POV is usually defined by scene—that is, if you stick to one character POV throughout a scene, that's single POV, and if you go with more than one POV in a scene, that's multiple POV. Here are the most common scene-POV structures:

- *First person*: Almost inevitably, first-person POV in a scene is the only POV. This narrator controls the entire scene, describing the setting and action through her particular perspective and in her own voice. Other scenes might be told through someone else's narration, but within this scene, there is only one *I* telling the tale.

- *Second person*: Second-person POV is a very complex approach, and very rare. As you're writing, ask yourself: Is this really a second-person POV (in which case the narrator will probably be *you* throughout the scene), or is it some disguised form of *I*? Sometimes a first-person narrator, encountering a particularly sensitive issue, will distance himself by referring to himself as *you*. For example: "You try and try, but no matter how much love you give, she doesn't love you back." But that's just a passage of disguised first person, not true second-person POV. Usually, second person, done logically, is the only POV in the scene.

- *Classical omniscient*: In this traditional POV approach, a narrative persona controls the narration of the scene. It might be an actual author stand-in who has a comprehensive knowledge of the events, like the Lemony Snicket narrator in the A Series of Unfortunate Events children's book series. Or, it could be the detached presence you often find in Jane Austen's scenes that comments ironically on the characters. Usually, the omniscient narrator starts each scene with an overview of the setting and situation, or a comment about the characters. Then, within the scene, the narrator "dips into" the minds of characters as needed.

- *Contemporary omniscient*: Contemporary-omniscient narration lacks the narrative persona of classical omniscient but still can present the setting and situation comprehensively. The most common technique is to start in contemporary omniscient, narrow into one character's POV for a passage, and then return to contemporary omniscient before switching to another POV. Both forms of omniscient are helpful in corralling large casts or several settings.

- *Single-third person*: This keeps the scene entirely in one character's POV, viewing the action and setting through the filter of this person's perspective. In deep third, a variation of single third, the POV character provides the narrative voice, so that the narration sounds as if the character is telling the story, like first person only with third-person pronouns. This approach gives an intimate exploration of one person's understanding of reality.

- *Multiple-third person*: In this POV, the narration of the scene switches from one character's POV to another as needed. The "as needed" is key to controlling multiple POV, which can easily devolve into head-hopping (the indiscriminate shifting between POVs). Done right, multiple-third person juxtaposes characters' perspectives to create a collage of reality. The point at which the switch to a new POV takes place tells the reader what the connection or disconnection is.

All these POV approaches will be described in greater depth in Part Two.

FILLING IN THE BLANKS WITH POV

Exposition is another element that will be affected by POV. *Exposition* is explanation. It's the little interruption of an event's narration to explain some piece of information the reader needs to understand the passage or story. Exposition can be broken into three general categories:

1. information about the setting, including historical information
2. information about some process or condition
3. information about the background or history of the characters

Here is a "world-building" passage from the opening of *The Holy Thief* by El-lis Peters, a medieval-era mystery, that quickly clues us in on the rigid beliefs of the time and even a bit of religious history:

> [Geoffrey de Mandeville] was an unabsolved excommunicate. Not even a priest could help him, for in the Midlands council, called the previous year by Henry of Bloor, Bishop of Winchester, the King's brother and at that time Papal Legate, it had been decreed that no man who did vio-lence to a cleric could be absolved by anyone but the pope himself, and that not by any distant decree, but only in the pope's presence. A long way from Mildenhall to Rome for a dying man in terror of hell-fire. For Geoffrey's excommunication had been earned by his seizure by violence of the abbey of Ramsay.

This passage lets us know that the worst fate that can befall a man in that era is excommunication, but it also hints at the sacking of the Ramsay Ab-bey, which will lead to the story's events.

In *Moby-Dick*, readers didn't much mind pages and pages of exposi-tion about whales, sailing ships, and the North Atlantic. (Or they just skimmed them, as I always did!) But readers now tend to want more story and less lecture. They still want to know about the different types of whales and how Captain Ahab charts his course; they just want it integrated within the story itself. The best way to do this is to sneak it in through smaller bits of information. Think paragraphs rather than pages, phrases rather than sentences. And whenever possible, insert the information through the narration of the POV character.

If you do this subtly, the reader will pick up the necessary facts without losing track of character or story. Describe the war-torn landscape through the eyes of a soldier, and the history of the battle through his memories. Or instead of writing, "Registration at Meir College was always complex and frustrating," build a scene around the student character actually register-ing for classes and encountering the sorts of obstacles registration typically brings. Try to bring in the necessary facts through the POV of a character.

But what are the necessary facts? Who, where, when, what, and how—that's a good start. One good way of discovering what a reader needs is to ask a reader. Write a scene and then hand it to a friend to read, telling him to jot down any questions he has.

Exposition can be especially tricky when you're trying to set up the context of the scene, what the reader needs to know to understand what in the past of the story (the backstory) will be causing the coming events. Here's an example of well-done exposition from *The Wolves of Calla* by Stephen King:

> Tian was blessed (though few farmers would have used such a word) with three patches: River Field, where his family had grown rice since time out of mind; Roadside Field, where ka-Jaffords had grown sharproot, pumpkin, and corn for those same long years and generations; and Son of a Bitch, a thankless tract, which mostly grew rocks, blisters, and busted hopes. Tian wasn't the first Jaffords determined to make something of the twenty acres behind his home place; his Gran-père, perfectly sane in most other respects, had been convinced there was gold there. Tian's Ma had been equally positive it would grow porin, a spice of great worth.

Here, in deep third, Tian expresses what he knows: that the setting of the scene is a world of farmers barely above the subsistence level, that a farm field in this place is called a "patch," and that twenty acres is a typical size. We know it's not our own world because of a few alien words and the referral to Tian's family not as "the Jaffords clan" but as "ka-Jaffords." See how subtly an important cultural fact is slipped in, that land and the family name are not automatically passed from father to son, but, rather, stay in the bloodline from grandfather to mother. The question of why Tian inherited this instead of his sister provides one of the main subplots of this scene. We also learn background about Tian, about his mordant sense of humor, and about his rueful recognition that he inherited not only the family land but also the family obsession.

The first page of a scene allows a great deal of flexibility. That's where you can anchor the scene in time and place. Exposition here, at the start of the scene, is easily absorbed and accepted, as the reader is seeking to make sense of where he is in the story. So consider making good use of the first few paragraphs. No matter what POV approach you're using, think about what the reader needs to put the scene's action into context and what tone and POV approach you want to establish. Linguist Paul Simpson suggests that a good way to start a scene is to imagine how it would be filmed—where the director would set the opening shot, who or what would be included in it, and what action the camera would zoom in on. The initial views in a film scene are called "establishing shots" for a reason: They establish what is important or what will lead audiences to ask what's important. Imagine filming a scene with a cop returning to her precinct, the camera focusing on her as she walks in and looks around, sees the same old decrepit building, and then, slowly, smiles. Now imagine writing that in narrative prose, as J.D. Robb did in *Rapture in Death*:

> Three weeks hadn't changed Cop Central. The coffee was still poisonous, the noise abominable, and the view out her stingy window was still miserable.
> She was thrilled to be back.

This scene opening tells us when (three weeks after the POV character was exiled), where (Cop Central), what (her office homecoming), how (conditions still terrible), and who (the woman cop). The final line places the scene squarely in the perspective of the woman cop by using "she" and an emotion (thrilled).

While context-setting should probably come early so the reader can make sense of the scene, you might make a list of other revelatory facts and start looking for places inside the scene to place them. For example, you can sneak in exposition through the action or thoughts of the POV character. Science-fiction writer Jo Walton calls this "in-cluing," which is "the process of scattering information seamlessly through the text, as opposed to stopping the story to impart the information." The trick is to do it discreetly without calling attention to the information itself, allowing the reader to figure out the meaning through context. Here's a skillful example from *Master and Commander* by Patrick O'Brian:

> Jack came blinking on deck as the first cheer roared out, a shattering wave of sound at twenty-five yards range. Then came the *Amelia*'s bosun's pipe and the next cheer, as precisely timed as her own broadside: and the third. He and his officers stood rigidly with their hats off, and as soon as the last roar had died away over the harbour, echoing back and forth, he called out, "Three cheers for

the *Amelia!*" and the Sophies, though deep in the working of the sloop, responded like heroes, scarlet with pleasure and the energy needed for huzzaying proper—huge energy, for they knew what was manners. Then the *Amelia*, now far astern, called, "One cheer more," and so piped down.

It was a handsome compliment, a noble send-off, and it gave great pleasure ....

Here, we are given a glimpse into an unknown world's rituals and traditions: how nineteenth-century warships saluted another ship that had come home victorious. It does not seem like an "info-dump" because the information is integrated into Jack's actions (coming up on deck, doffing his hat, calling for a reciprocal cheer). We also get some sense of Jack's gratitude at this generous recognition by his fellows—he has finally made it—and his need both to involve his crew and to reciprocate.

One purpose of exposition, especially in science-fiction and historical novels, is to define important terms that the reader might not understand. One way is simply to equate the unfamiliar word with a more understandable term, as Herman Melville has done here in *Bartleby, the Scrivener* (emphasis mine):

The nature of my avocations for the last thirty years has brought me into more than ordinary contact with what would seem an interesting and somewhat singular set of men, of whom as yet nothing that I know of has ever been written: I mean the *law-copyists or scriveners*.

But you can also use the opportunity of definition to provide context for the world of the book and the internal feelings of the POV character, as is the case in this example from *Master and Commander*:

The first thing he did [on being promoted] in point of fact was to cross the road to the naval outfitter's and pledge his now elastic credit to the extent of a noble, heavy, massive epaulette, the mark of his present rank—a symbol which the shopman fixed upon his left shoulder at once and upon which they both gazed with great complacency in the long glass, the shopman looking from behind Jack's shoulder with unfeigned pleasure on his face.

We might not know exactly what an epaulette is, or why he gets only one on his left shoulder (later we find out that the second comes with a higher rank). But we know that it pleases him, and that his pleasure is so great it's reflected by the shopman. It's the POV of the character that gives simple facts life and meaning.

One trick is to use single words and short phrases to insert necessary exposition into the thoughts of the POV character. Granted, most of us don't think about what we already know, but little quick bites of information go down easier, especially if you filter them through the character's normal mode of expression.

For example, maybe you think the reader needs to know that Millie is your character's aunt. In omniscient POV, which allows a more conventional information transfer, you might just say, "Mike called Mildred Henderson, his aunt." In third person, "Mike called his Aunt Millie." In first person, "I called Aunt Millie." In each of these, you convey the necessary information that Millie is Mike's aunt in a way that will seem natural to the reader—more formal in omniscient, more colloquial in third person and first person.

Adjectives are helpful, too; for example, you might write, "The light poured in the windows," but if you want to tell what time of day it is, add an adjective: "The morning light" or "The afternoon light" or "The moonlight." Just remember, in-cluing will work better with almost any POV approach than info-dumping. Small bites, not big chunks, will go down easier.

GETTING INTO CHARACTER

To descend into a character's POV, it helps to become that character, if only for a moment, to get into that person's body and mind. This is understandably difficult because there's a certain relinquishment of self involved in entering the POV of another person. That is, it's easier to decide to write about how you feel as a parent of children who participate in organized sports than it is to create a character, like a Little League coach, with his own views. The best fiction has characters who are separate from their creators, and POV gives you a chance to demonstrate that.

I suspect this ability to enter into the thoughts and feelings of another person comes naturally to some people—particularly actors, psychologists, and some writers. The rest of us have to work at it. We have to use our imagination and empathy to transcend the borders of self and enter someone else's mind.

Here's what I do, and I do this quite consciously: I call it "sitting in the character." I actually sit down, close my eyes, and let myself relax so much that I end up slumping a bit. Then I take a deep breath and think about the character I want to "enter." It helps to have a scene in mind, something this character is witnessing and experiencing. Then I imagine, from the inside, how this person is reacting to the event. I try to feel both the inside (emotion and thought) and the outside (the fictional environment), but always from the character's perspective. For example, here's a excerpt from *Fledgling* that shows author Octavia Butler channeling or "sitting in" the character of a newly awakened vampire:

I awoke to darkness. I was hungry—starving!—and I was in pain. There was nothing in my world but hunger and pain, no other people, no other time, no other feelings.

It hurt to move. It hurt even to breathe. My head pounded and throbbed, and I held it between my hands, whimpering. The sound of my voice, even the touch of my hands seemed to make the pain worse. In two places my head felt crusty and lumpy and ... almost soft.

And I was so *hungry*.

The worst was, no matter where I looked, there was no hint of light. I couldn't see my own hands as I held them up in front of me. Was it so dark, then? Or was there something wrong with my eyes? Was I blind? ...

Then I heard something coming toward me, something large and noisy, some animal. I couldn't see it, but after a moment, I could smell it. It smelled ... not exactly good, but at least edible. Starved as I was, I was in no condition to hunt. I lay trembling and whimpering as the pain of my hunger grew and eclipsed everything.

Notice this passage starts out setting the scene and situation: "I awoke to darkness. I was hungry—starving!—and I was in pain." But these sensations come entirely from within the character. The author's perspective isn't there at all. Presumably, Butler knows if this is a forest or a seashore, a city alley or neglected country lane. But she retreats and lets the character give a limited perspective. (See what I mean about "relinquishment of self"?) Most intriguingly, this takes place at night, so Butler limits how much information is conveyed for the most prominent of the human senses—sight—and forces the character to learn her surroundings through her other senses. This lets the reader feel along with the character, deepening identification and enlivening the experience.

Understanding comes only after the experience, and Butler shows the character evaluating her perceptions and drawing some conclusions. She keeps focused on the interior experience of the character. The vampire, above all, is hungry. An author might forget that, but a character cannot; so in this passage, the perceptions are all filtered through the need to eat. This is used to create intentionality in the character—a goal: to catch and eat the animal.

The author "sits in the character" to create the opening of the scene. Most of us won't transfer our channeling directly onto the page; rather, we will use what we experience for both setting details and deepening understanding of the character's way of perceiving.

This exercise isn't easy for me. I'm profoundly nonvisual, so much so that I ordinarily never "see" a scene. As such, I have to remind myself to look around to notice if it's day or night. I find myself (like Butler's awakening vampire) starting with tactile input—the pain, the hard ground—then using that as a route to the other senses, then inward to the thoughts and emotions. When I write a scene I've first experienced through the POV character, I try to capture a few specific elements revealed by this exercise: the vivid experience of the setting— the dry, dead leaves against her hands, the smell of the animal—and her feelings and needs. I know I'll also keep that running internal commentary when my character is evaluating her own situation.

But I don't have to transcribe my "in character" notes into my story unedited. I can rearrange the perceptions for greater drama. For example, I might have her try to determine if she really is blind or just in total darkness, and if she's inside or outside. She is hungry and exposed, so her focus will be mostly on survival and what she needs to learn about the setting to ensure that. That will anchor the reader in the setting, which is necessary to set the context of the scene. Then, when she's got enough information to know how to protect herself, I might expand to include her thoughts and feelings, perhaps ending the passage with her shame at giving into her carnivorous appetite. This will show more about her as a person, what she values about herself, and what she fears she might become. (More on this sort of narrative shifting when we discuss the levels of POV in chapter ten.)

Try to "sit in" a character, record what you experience, and generate sensory and internal information for writing scenes. If this sounds too touchy-feely for you, that's exactly why you should try it! Break through that resistance and enter the mind of another person.

Interviewing the Character

If you try to channel a character and it doesn't work for you, I also use another technique that gives me the character's perspective, but at one remove: I'm not in the character's body and mind, but rather sitting across the table taking notes as I "interview" him. I ask leading questions and record the answers in the character's first-person voice.

When I interview a character, I'm aware that I'm making up this person. But rather quickly, if I use that character's first-person voice, it's amazing how the character takes over, even a character I don't know well. The advantage of this technique is that you almost "channel" the character. The character (or your subconscious construct of him) takes over and starts directing the answer. (Trust me on this; just let go, and it will happen.) You get a sense of his voice, as well as his attitude, and you can even direct him to describe the setting and sensory experience. In fact, in my character-development classes, I use precisely this interview technique to help students get to know their characters better. This method taps into our subconscious empathy for other people and our experience of how others think and feel. It's a bit more directed and distanced than the "sitting in" technique, but it can generate the same "inside and outside" perspective.

Try interviewing a character. You might end up with three pages of his answers, some of which you can use in your actual narrative. You might find new incidents that will add to the scenes in the book.

When I was working on my story "Allegra" for the novel *Lessons in Love*, I'd never even considered that Allegra must have written her husband, Nicholas, dozens of letters when he was away fighting the war, and that he would have saved them, until I interviewed Nicholas. What turned out to be the catalytic event for that section of the book—his finding and reading the letters—came directly from his account of his experience. It's almost eerie.

Even the prose of the interview answers, with some modifications, can go into your scene. Here's an example: Nicholas is a soldier who returned from the war to a wife he hardly knows. Months later, he's still distracted and disoriented, and she has given up trying to reach him. He doesn't really wake up to her unhappiness until she's left him for a few days. I start with an unthreatening question ("How old were you when you married Allegra?"), and then, when I have the poor fellow relaxed, I get more intrusive. It's almost like I'm hypnotizing him. I'm also going to ask him to describe the exterior—where he was, what he saw, what he heard—so that I can use that to write the setting details later.

(Yes, I'm entirely aware that Nicholas is a figment of my imagination. It's not crazy, it's the process of writing fiction, so don't feel silly. We have to be able to know we're inventing these people but still let them become themselves. It's rather like parenting.)

So finally, in answer to my prompting, "How have you gotten along with your wife since you came home from the war?" Nicholas said:

> Sometimes it was annoying to have her keep asking what did I want to do. Did I want to redo my father's study? Did I want to buy a few more mounts for the stables? Did I want to go to London for the season? Did I want salt on my eggs? Did I want to hear that new sonata she'd learned? Did I want to have another child? Did I want to be alone? That's all I remember, really, all those questions. I reckon she wouldn't have asked them, if she didn't want to know. But I was supposed to say yes or no, when ... when I didn't really have an answer. So sometimes I said *yes*, and sometimes I said *no*, and she'd go off and do what she thought was best anyway. So I remember she asked me, do you want me to go, and I said ... I don't remember. Yes or no, one of those two.

You can probably see how easy this would be to "translate" into a first-person narration, but it's also helpful for third-person passages. Use the sensory details to embellish the relevant parts of your story, to add description from within the character. Use the emotion to give the reader an understanding of why he behaves as he does. And use the voice to give a sense of immediacy and clarity to the characterization. Here's how the above answer translated into the actual book:

> She had so many questions, that's all he remembered from that blurred time. She kept asking what did he want to do. Did he want to redo his father's study, did he want to buy a few more mounts for the stable, did he want to go to London for the season. Did he want salt on his eggs. Did he want her to play him that new sonata she had learned. Did he want another child. Did he want to be alone.
>
> He was supposed to say yes or no, when he didn't have any answers. So sometimes he said yes, and sometimes he said no, and he must have given the wrong answer, because one day he came back from the garrison to find himself alone.

You won't have to do this exercise for every event in the book. Once you get a sense of a character's POV, you won't ever lose it entirely. It's as if that channel is open in your mind, and you just have to make the decision to switch to it when appropriate, letting the character's own perspective on each event dictate the narrative.

PUTTING POV ON THE PAGE

For a lover of stories, it's very interesting to get to know the character deeply with these exercises. But the reader is going to benefit most if you actually *use* these insights to craft how you write scenes. How you accomplish this might depend on whether you draft a whole scene at once, or just sketch it out and add detail later. If you generally do one major draft of a scene, then before you write it, spend a bit of time thinking about how the main character would perceive, think, and feel. Then start to write, forcing yourself to get into her POV early. Try starting deep in her head, with a line of introspective thought or feeling—something like:

> Carrie was humming happily to herself, walking in the warm June sunlight, still tasting the chocolate mousse she had for lunch, when she turned a corner and saw her boyfriend's car parked in front of the old Angleton mansion. He was in there with some slut. She knew it. And she was going to get him for it. Gathering her courage, she started up the steps to the old house.

Once you establish for yourself that you're in her perspective, you can write the rest of the scene from her POV, not your own.

But if you're like me, and you just sketch a scene first, you'll have to later add in all the intriguing details and asides that make this clearly her scene. I get pretty clinical about it, reviewing the passage sentence by sentence, adding in texture, thought, and emotion as I go. Then I'll usually go back and reorganize so that the narration progresses logically; that is, in the case above, her perception is followed by realization and then by emotion and then by decision and action.

Here's a sketch scene:

> There was no answer to Carrie's knock, but the door was open an inch or two. She pushed at the front door and called out, but no one replied. The hall was dark and full of furniture. Beyond that was another door. She turned the knob, and walked into a kitchen, where a dead body was lying on the floor....

This passage wouldn't be so boring if "she" was a real person who let us have an idea of what's going on and what it feels like:

> There was no answer to Carrie's knock, but she couldn't help but notice that the door was open an inch or two. It was a Gothic sort of door, ornately carved with grinning gargoyles along the outer edge. Carrie hesitated there, contemplating her options. She could just turn and go home and pretend that she hadn't seen her no-good cheating boyfriend Jonny sneak in here after some woman .... Or, she could go in after him and prove to herself that he wasn't worth keeping. It would be easier, she thought, if this old place just wasn't so spooky. Trust Jonny, with his horror-film addiction, to choose a monster mansion like this for his love nest.

Don't be a coward, she told herself, and shoved the door open. She breathed in the must of neglect. For a moment, she couldn't see anything but ominous shapes in the dark hall, then her eyes adjusted to the dark and the humped outlines revealed themselves to be dustcloth-covered furniture. No sign of Jonny. The loser had probably heard her knocking and run out the back way. She threaded her way through the hall between the abandoned chairs to a door that looked like it went to the kitchen.

She was right. When she pushed open the door, her flashlight revealed a forties-style kitchen and a dead body sprawled facedown on the linoleum. Her heart stopped short and she covered her eyes. What would be worse: to look again and find it was Jonny, or look again and find it was Jonny's cheat-mate?

You can see how much more we learn from the narrator's perspective: her goal (to find her cheating boyfriend), her motivation (to give herself reason to break up with him), her dominant emotions (anxiety and dread), and something about the way she thinks (she's analytical and self-aware). In other words, we have a real character encountering a real event in an individual way. Anyone can find a dead body; the tighter POV makes this unique to this character and her experience. After all, that's the real story: not just what happens, but how it affects the characters.

If I were to mark every word or phrase that showed this was in Carrie's perspective, it would be overkill. Most of the passage is filtered through her perceptions, thoughts, and emotions. I'll list only a few:

- *... she couldn't help but notice ...* This shows not only that she notices, but she's trying not to notice it.

- *She could just turn and go home and pretend ...* We're not just presented with her decision or action. She's actually running through the options in front of us, making the decision as we read.

- *Trust Jonny, with his horror-film addiction ...* This "info bite" shows her unique knowledge of the other character.

- *Don't be a coward, she told herself* ... This uses mental dialogue to let us hear precisely what she is telling herself. "She told herself not to be a coward" would have worked, too, but the direct "quote" is deeper into her psyche and more immediate. We're in her head and hearing the words she thinks to herself. We can almost hear her voice. (Note that the *she told herself,* like *she thought* or *she mused,* is used conventionally as a POV tag; otherwise, the reader would be confronted with that first-person present-tense line, *Don't be a coward,* without any context. *Is she talking to me?* the reader might wonder. After all, stranger things have happened in narration. Just the tiny tag line of *she told herself* is enough to make it clear that this is inner dialogue. With that tag line, also, I don't need to use quotation marks or italics to indicate thought.)

- *She breathed in the must of neglect* ... That's her sensory experience.

- *Her heart stopped short* ... That's her physical and emotional reaction to what she discovers.

Just open yourself up to the character's perspective, and remind yourself to consider what she'd be thinking, feeling, and perceiving at every moment. Use only as much as you need, of course, but keep checking in on her perspective.

EXERCISE

FREEWRITING IN A CHARACTER'S VOICE

Freewriting is the best way to interview a character. Set a timer for three to ten minutes, compose a question, and then write freely about it. *Use the first-person voice of this character!* Don't edit yourself, just write down whatever your subconscious sends you, without regard for spelling, grammar, or organization. Often, it's the digressions from the subject that provide the most fascinating insights.

You'll want to customize your interview, but here are some sample questions that might get you started:

1. So [name], how did you get into this mess?

2. What is it you want? Why do you want it so badly?

3. How did you feel when [fill in the blank with some event] happened?

4. Why are you so upset?

5. Can you tell me about this place you're in?

6. What are you going to do next?

ANALYSIS PARALYSIS

Some writers don't like to analyze all this. They'd rather go with instinct, letting the gut decide whose POV to use and when to switch. All this analysis might paralyze them and make them feel like this is a mechanical process, not a creative one.

I know what analysis paralysis feels like and what "creativity" feels like. Sometimes I write a scene in a white heat of inspiration, and the process feels so rewarding, so "gut right," that I can't help but believe the scene itself is pretty nigh perfect. But even then, I usually analyze the scene, if only to figure out what I did right. There are times this analysis leads me toward a conclusion that makes my gut rebel: complete revision. (This is hard on the digestive system! I'm working on figuring these things out *before* I've invested days in drafting the scene. Some of the exercises in this book come from my quest for a more efficient writing process.) Painful as this is sometimes, I'm an analytical sort of person, and I don't see analysis as destructive because, after all, once I know all my options, I can always choose to go back with the one I went with instinctively.

I seldom do go back, however. And often I find that my resistance to analyzing is rooted in a fear of what I'll find: that the scene really doesn't work, that it needs to be reconceived, that I can't rely on my instincts. Once I push past that fear, I can be more objective about the scene in question, consider the questions I probably should have considered before I started writing, and determine my purpose and my methods. I realize that, in fact, I do have some ability to diagnose problems and fix them, and thus provide the reader with a more vivid and powerful experience. At these moments, I feel more in control, more like an author and not just a writer.

part two

building your
STORY

FIRST PERSON

4

If you're considering writing in first-person POV, keep in mind that the use of first person is more restricted by market than the other choices. Contemporary omniscient, multiple, and single-third (and the combinations of them) are common to almost every kind of fiction, and none of them will raise editorial eyebrows as long as they're done well.

But first person tends to be restricted to short stories, detective novels, literary fiction, mainstream (usually women's fiction) novels, and the recently revised genre of Gothic novels. (Stephen King usually writes in a contemporary-omniscient-dominated third person, but when he chose to do what he called a Gothic romance, *Bag of Bones*, he chose first person.) You also see it occasionally in young-adult fiction (geared toward readers ages 12–18) and less often in children's books.

It's not that first person won't work in other types of books, but many editors and readers feel it is limiting; they don't like being confined to one person's head for a whole book. On the other hand, many readers love first person and find it more natural and readable than third person. "It's like someone sitting down beside me and telling me a story," one reader told me.

You might think this would be the easiest POV approach—just a matter of letting the character tell the story. But take it from a writer who is struggling with it now: It's much harder than it looks! In this chapter, I'll explore the challenges and special considerations of first-person POV so you can spend less time wrestling and more time writing.

FIRST-PERSON BASICS

First person has unique advantages, which I will explain in the sections that follow. But for now, here's a quick rundown:

- Intimate perspective increases reader understanding of one character (the narrator).
- Tight focus deepens reader identification with the narrator.
- Narrator's voice can be more colorful or distinctive than those of less intimate narrators.
- Narrative deception leads to more potential intrigue.
- Certain genre expectations (such as those in detective novels and women's fiction) have trained their readers to appreciate first-person narration.

However, every advantage becomes a disadvantage if the first-person narration isn't handled well or is inappropriate for a particular story. Consider the following:

- Confinement to one character's perspective can be restrictive.
- Claustrophobic focus can lead to antipathy toward narrator.
- An overbearing narrative voice can become annoying; a bland one can be boring.
- A straight-on direct plot treatment wastes the potential of first-person narrative.
- Some readers, particularly in certain genres, will resist first person.

Spend some time thinking about your story in terms of these pros and cons. Are you looking for a voice that's more intimate and distinctive, or does your plot require a little more narrative flexibility? Read on to understand how first person affects the key elements of your story.

BUILDING YOUR STORY IN FIRST-PERSON POV

First-person POV in the twenty-first century is not bound by its previous limitations. You can have several first-person narrators in the same story, or you can alternate first person with third person. You can use a separate frame to enclose the first-person narrative, or have the first-person narrative be the frame enclosing a conventional third-person story. You can make the story itself a frame, an exchange of letters, for example, or an extended journal entry.

You can do almost anything, but that doesn't mean you should forget the central purpose of first person: to bring readers into the mind of another person and to allow them to experience the thoughts, feelings, and perceptions of another. There are plenty of good first-person stories to serve as examples. Just remember that the effect a first-person narrative has on the reader is profound. As a result, your responsibility as the author is also profound. You must give the reader a reason to suspend his ego enough to let someone else be *I*. Following are some points to consider as you craft a first-person POV.

The Scope of the Story

First-person stories are usually limited in time and space, because so much of the action is seen through the eyes of one narrator. Most first-person novels follow this one person through a psychological journey (as in many women's fiction and literary fiction) or through an external quest (as in detective novels), with every scene told from the perspective of the narrator.

But some authors have taken this seeming limitation as a challenge, using variations of first person both to give the deep intimacy of a single perspective and to broaden plot possibilities of multiple perspectives. William Faulkner was the pioneer here, experimenting with sequential first person in *The Sound and the Fury* (three sections by separate first-person narrators, and a fourth section in third person), alternating first person in *As I Lay Dying* (chapters of varying lengths in the perspectives of a dozen narrators, some repeating), and omniscient first person in "A Rose for Emily" (told by a young narrator from the perspective of an entire town, as if he's telling a story he has heard many times from older relatives). These techniques are all in use today and can be adapted for many "bigger picture" stories.

For example, in *Middlesex*, Jeffrey Eugenides uses omniscient first. The narrator, a middle-aged "middlesex," or hermaphrodite, tells his own story. But he also tells his family's story, going back several generations, as it was told to him. The narrator never disappears; even in the historical sections, stories are filtered through his "ears." Consider the following passage:

> [My mother] didn't surrender until after Japan had. Then, from their wedding night onward (according to what my brother told my covered

ears), my parents made love regularly and enjoyably. When it came to having children, however, my mother had her own ideas. It was her belief that an embryo could sense the amount of love with which it had been created. For this reason, my father's suggestion didn't sit well with her.

If your story involves centuries and continents, consider a more distant third person or a complex multiple-first person, perhaps with different story lines narrated by different characters.

There's no doubt that a big-scope book is going to be hard to handle in first person, and you might end up sacrificing that intimacy. You need good reason (and a good plan) for building a multigenerational family saga or globe-trotting thriller in first-person POV. Some advice:

1. See how other authors have handled this sort of project. Iain Pears, in *An Instance of the Fingerpost*, wanted to present several perspectives on the murder of an Oxford don in order to heighten the mystery and show that "reality" isn't an exact entity. He chose the "Rashomon" technique (named after a film, actually) of sequential first person from four eyewitnesses. Michael Gruber, in *The Book of Air and Shadows*, uses a frame story of a first-person narrator, writing his story to implicate those who might murder him, around a more standard third-person narration. Using such models can show you the possibilities and the pitfalls, and also how to deal with plot problems the POV choice might bring.

2. Scenes are the basic unit of POV. So once you have chosen a narrator and developed a plot, outline the story in projected scenes on a storyboard or posterboard. Make note of the central event, setting, and time, then list the characters who will be there to experience and witness the event. If the chosen narrator isn't there on the scene, consider how you will transmit the information to the reader. A sample scene plan from Eugenides's *Middlesex* might have looked like this:

Scene 3: Spring 1959, right before narrator Cal's conception; parents' home in Detroit.

Central event: Dad thinks he figures out a way to have sex that increases the chances of conceiving a girl.

Narrative possibilities: Dad or Mom can later tell Cal this so that he reports it in dialogue. Or Mom can write it in a letter to her own mother, and Cal can read it later. Or Cal can speculate about this and "conceive" the scene based on what he knows of his parents, which might work if Cal admits that he's making this up. This is literary fiction, so I think the reader could accept the last one: Cal inventing the scene but arguing it's plausible.

3. Consider using an intriguing frame that allows methods beyond simple first-person narration, such as the protagonist reading a set of letters or a diary from an earlier time, or an older person recounting the history to the narrator. Faulkner, in "A Rose for Emily," has the narrator recount a story he has heard from older townspeople so often that he can put himself in the scene, even though he hadn't been born yet. The first-person narrator is a stand-in for the whole population of the town.

4. You can also try using multiple first-person narrators. (See "When First Person Is Not the Best [or Only] Person" on page 84 for more on this alternative plan.)

Narrative Purpose and Agenda

First-person POV should be limited to a narrator who is telling *this* story in *this* way for a reason. Maybe she wants to persuade the reader, or she wants vindication or justice. As you begin to build your story, think about how the narration can fulfill the narrator's purpose. (If you are going with multiple-first person, every narrator will have a separate purpose.) Then construct the story to present and execute that purpose. For example, maybe you choose to craft a story frame that furthers the narrator's agenda, such as a long letter meant to seduce the recipient, or a legal brief alleging libel. (More on the story frame in "Why Are You Telling Me This?" on page 101.)

Next, consider the narrator's journey, both in performance of the purpose (seduction, vindication, solution of the mystery) and in fulfillment of some inner need. In a first-person narration, there are usually two actual plotlines—the external purpose-driven plot (Does the character achieve the goal?) and the internal need-driven plot (What does the narrator reveal about herself—what deception, what secret, what loss?). It might help to outline the external plot, pick out the major scenes, and sketch out how the narrator will present each.

How the narrator relates each external scene should alert the reader to the internal plot. The narrator might never come out and say, for instance, "I feel guilty about my mother's death," but the reader should be able to intuit that from the way she narrates—what she says and doesn't say (in both dialogue and exposition) and how she reacts to the people and situations she encounters. The end of a successful story should have some resolution of both the internal and external plots.

Who Is This Narrator?

The conversational aspect of first person can allow for early establishment of narrator attitude through the self-introduction. There's a practical reason to do this: it quickly establishes the narrator's name, which might otherwise be difficult to sneak in. But it also can give the reader more sense of the person who will dominate this story. Think about how your narrator would introduce herself to the reader, and make that introduction give an initial glimpse of the narrator's self-image. For example, your narrator might define himself by his profession or role in the story, as this POV character does in *Storm Front* by Jim Butcher:

> My name is Harry Blackstone Copperfield Dresden. Conjure by it at your own risk. I'm a wizard. I work out of an office in midtown Chicago. As far as I know, I'm the only openly practicing professional wizard in the country. You can find me in the yellow pages, under 'Wizards.' Believe it or not, I'm the only one there.

Notice how Dresden starts with his name (composed of the names of famous magicians) and then challenges the reader to "conjure by it," thus simultaneously setting up the motif of magic and undercutting it with his self-deprecation. (After all, it's just a job like any other; he's even got a Yellow Pages ad.)

Self-Deprecation

Self-deprecation by a first-person narrator aids in reader identification. This trait is so common in narrator introductions that it has become a convention in first person. Another narrator, the Roman private eye Falco in Lindsey Davis's *Scandal Takes a Holiday*, wants you to know up front that he's untrustworthy, which has the paradoxical effect of making us trust him more (What con man tells you he's a con man?):

> Just like old Brutus, any orator could say of us that Marcus Didio Falco and Lucas Petronius Longus were honorable men. And yes, the orator would make that claim with an irony even the most stupid mob would understand.

In *Watermelon* by Marian Keyes, a self-described "dumped wife" starts her account with an apology:

> I'm sorry, you must think I'm very rude. We've hardly even been introduced, and here I am telling you all about the awful things that have happened to me.
>
> Let me just give you the briefest outline about myself, and I'll save details like, for example, my first day at school, until later, if we have time.
>
> Let me see, what should I tell you? Well, my name is Claire, and I'm twenty-nine.

Claire's compulsive confession tells us a lot about her current mood and her own sense of unimportance. Stressing the narrator's relative insignificance helps mitigate what might otherwise seem arrogant—the act of demanding attention to her story with a first-person account.

Think of how you can use this convention to establish not just the facts about the narrator but the attitude, too. Dean Koontz's narrator in *Odd Thomas*, for example, shows a serious chip on his shoulder about something he hates—celebrities:

> My name is Odd Thomas, though in this age when fame is the altar at which most people worship, I am not sure why you should care who I am or that I exist.
>
> I am not a celebrity. I am not the child of a celebrity. I have never been married to, never been abused by, and never provided a kidney for transplantation into any celebrity. Furthermore, I have no desire to be a celebrity.

Try to self-introduce early in order to establish both the name and the attitude of your narrator. First-person narration allows you to accomplish directly what has to be woven into a third-person account, so make use of it. What do you want the reader to know up front about the narrator? And what would the narrator want the reader to know, even if it's not quite true?

Voice: Close, but Not Comfortable

Each author has a voice as unique as her fingerprint. But unlike the fingerprint, the author's voice can be enhanced, refined, modified, stripped, and polished. However, the first-person narrator, more than any other kind of narrator, has to feature a distinctive character voice, some particular way of telling the story or seeing the action. If a first-person narrator is neutral or bland, you're probably wasting the potential of first person and boring the reader by forcing her into very tight contact with someone talking nonstop, and in a monotone!

If you're committing yourself to a first-person narrator, get to know that character and create the voice. Think not only of how this person would sound, but how he would perceive the world around him and how his attitude, biases, vanities, and values would affect his interpretation of events. Here's an example from *The Code of the Woosters* by P.G. Wodehouse, a master of humor:

> He spoke with a certain what-is-it in his voice, and I could see that, if not actually disgruntled, he was far from being gruntled.

Here, the narrator, Bertie, is evaluating his friend's tone and coming to his own conclusion about what it means. But he's couching it in his own inimitable way, naively revealing both his verbal dyslexia ("what-is-it," rather than "I don't know what") and an amusing anomaly in the English language (You can be *dis*gruntled, but can you be "gruntled"?). We get a sense of a man who perhaps isn't very bright, but who thinks he's quite eloquent and is sensitive to the vocal tones of other people. Most important, his language and perspective are distinctive and intriguing. He's not just a "generic narrator" but someone quite specific.

You're probably already used to creating characters' voices because you do it when you craft their dialogues. First-person narration will generally resemble a character's dialogue but with a little more depth or texture. For example, a character's dialogue might show her speaking carefully, enunciating each word, using perfect grammar to conceal her lower-class origins. But maybe her internal narration will feature more casual diction, more slang, more color. The contrast will show us something about who she is, and it might make us wonder why she's projecting a different persona to the world. No matter who your POV character is or where she comes from, remember that one of the most important aspects of the first-person voice is *att-i-tude.*

Constructing Attitude: You Ain't Got a Thing If You Ain't Got That Swing

So what's attitude? It's the unique worldview of a person, mixed with his self-image, mood, and intention. Here's an example from John Mortimer's *Rumpole and the Confession of Guilt*, about a defense attorney in London whose own wife just called him an "Old Bailey hack":

> Hilda, I thought, had gone too far. I'm not exactly a hack. I've been at the work for longer than I can remember, and as is generally recognized down at the Old Bailey, there are no flies on Rumpole. After all, I cut my teeth on the Penge Bungalow Murders. I could win most of my cases if it weren't for the clients. Clients have no tact, poor old darlings. No bloody sensitivity! They *will* waltz into the witness-box and blurt out things that are far better left unblurted.
>
> I suppose, when I was young, I used to suffer with my clients. I used to cringe when I heard their sentences and go down to the cells full of anger. Now I never watch their faces when the sentence is passed. I hardly listen to the years pronounced and I never look back at the dock.

Let's examine each of the elements of attitude as demonstrated by old Rumpole.

Worldview

What is the narrator's view of the world? Is he optimistic or pessimistic? Naive or cynical? Suspicious or trusting? Does he view the outside world as a puzzle, a prison, an oppressor, a mark to be conned, or a lover to be seduced? Does he see life as a comedy or a tragedy? Does he have a political outlook or religious faith that colors his views?

Rumpole is a cynic but in the special sense of the failed romantic. Politically, he's something of a liberal, as he's protecting the rights of the accused, but he no longer has any idealistic illusions. Life for him is a comedy of the darker sort: "It hurts too much to laugh, but I'm too old to cry." He doesn't trust fate—or his clients. But he's always secretly hoping to be proven wrong. Look at his joking use of positive terms like "poor old darlings" and "waltz" to take the edge off his despair.

Self-Image

More than any other POV approach, first person explores a character's self-image. After all, he is defining himself in the way he's narrating this part of his life. He is presenting an image to the world and inadvertently revealing something of his inner self as he does it. When it comes to self-definition, what he denies is as important as what he declares.

With Rumpole, we see a man who struggles with a disconnect between what how he views himself and how the world views him. He thinks of himself as an expert with special skills and knowledge, but even his own wife dismisses him as a "hack." Somewhere inside, he worries that a hack is exactly what he's become.

More significantly, however, is his insistence that he doesn't care anymore what becomes of his clients, that he is hardened to their plights and feels nothing, especially not guilt, when they are sentenced. This actually sets up the story's *praxis*, or emotional action: Rumpole proclaims his hardheartedness early on but ends up taking a risk that a client really is innocent, winning the case. His actions in the story undercut his self-assessment. That's good; self-image, as revealed in first-person narration, is always more interesting when it's slightly wrong.

Mood

Rumpole is angry but trying to hide it—angry at his wife for calling him a hack, angry at himself for suspecting she's right, and angry at his clients for being stupid, guilty, and unsympathetic. Always jocular, he's filtering his anger through humor, hence the ironic "poor old darlings." At this point in the story, anger will create that edgy, steely attitude.

Intention

This can be tricky because the first-person narrator doesn't always seem to be aware that he has an audience. But with first-person narration, there's always some implicit intention behind the narrator's words in a particular passage. He's trying to explain or prove or hide something. In this case, Rumpole is trying to prove to the audience that he's hard now, that he isn't vulnerable to his clients' despair, that it's just a job to him. What's fun, of course, is that his very insistence on this point makes us realize that he's trying to convince himself.

Bringing It All Together

So how do you create attitude? First, you *discover* it. Think about who your narrator is and how he's feeling about the world and himself at this point. Freewrite in his voice—not the narrative of the story now, but, rather, answers to prompts like: "So, John, how are you feeling now? Why can't you be more candid about this event? What do you mean to have happen now?" Immerse yourself in his reality for a few minutes before starting to write his narration of a scene.

Then, as you revise, watch for the tone that your freewriting revealed, and see how you can enhance it without getting obnoxious. Here's an example of a conventional first-person tone, one of arch irony, from Elizabeth Peters's *The Last Camel Died at Noon*:

> To the readers who have encountered my distinguished husband in the flesh, or in the pages of my earlier works, it will come as no surprise to them that he reacted to the camel's death as if the animal had committed suicide for the sole purpose of inconveniencing him.

Everything in that passage, from the complicated sentence construction and the ornate language to the amused pride in her arrogant husband, creates that ironic tone, one that establishes a connection of shared superiority with the reader. That's great attitude, and while I can't say for sure, I'll bet you it didn't happen on the first draft. Learning to "revise in tone" is the mark of a sophisticated writer.

Get to know your POV character's overall worldview, self-image, and how he might change during the course of the book. At every narrative point, spend a moment or two thinking about his agenda and mood. Then let that perception guide your writing of his narration.

Tricks for Enhancing Attitude

There are also some specific tricks you can try to develop your character's attitude. One of my favorites is "the aside"—those snarky little comments that the first-person narrator makes, not in dialogue but inside his head. While this can be done in third person, too, it's more sassy and direct in first person. In fact, this alone is a good reason to use first person.

This technique is actually a controlled stream-of-consciousness POV. We're in the narrator's head, but the thoughts are in response to what's going on outside. It's not as claustrophobic as real stream-of-consciousness (and it's much more coherent), but it still has the freshness of real thought. It's almost a secret conversation because the narrator seems to assume that the reader will understand what the other characters aren't allowed to hear.

To avoid overwriting, use asides sparingly. Once you've established the voice with one or two of them, the rest should be used only to add meaning. Usually, these take place during dialogue, so mental comments are "aside" the actual spoken conversation. They might correct or amplify or reinterpret something said aloud. Their power is that the other character isn't privy to this information.

P.G. Wodehouse's Bertie frequently uses asides to explain himself, as he does here in *Thank You, Jeeves*:

> "Oh, I'm not complaining," said Chuffy, looking rather like Saint Sebastian on receipt of about the fifteenth arrow. "You have a perfect right to love who you like."
>
> "Whom, old man," I couldn't help saying. *Jeeves has made me rather a purist in these matters.*

The line in italics is the aside, addressed to the reader and explaining why Chuffy's minor mistake elicits such a correction from Bertie.

(Bertie is not known as a bright light of intellect, though he has a certain sophomoric linguistic capacity.) The humor comes from his focus on grammar rather than on his friend's annoyance and from the contrast between his slangy speech ("old man") and his ornate asides ("rather a purist in these matter"). The aside, more than his correction of Chuffy, tells us that he feels just a bit superior to his Jeeves-less fellows. Notice that even the quote tag has attitude; "I couldn't help saying" shows his sense that he must be reluctant about showing his superiority.

Here's one more example from Brian McGrory's political thriller *The Incumbent*, a particularly good in-your-face first-person narration. Jack Flynn, a newspaper reporter, is witness to an assassination attempt and returns a call from a beautiful FBI agent:

> Next, I dialed up Stevens. Ends up, she had left me her pager number, which was interesting. Even worried FBI agents don't give their home telephone numbers out to key witnesses whom they have an enormous crush on.
>
> Okay, so I made up the part about the crush. But it wasn't one minute before the telephone rang.
>
> "Jack, Agent Stevens."
>
> *Agent* Stevens. Isn't that precious beyond words? Perhaps I'd like to be identified herein as *Reporter* Flynn, or *Journalist* Flynn for all you National Public Radio types.

There's a lot of personality in this brief exchange. The narrator directly addresses the reader ("all you National Public Radio types"— and notice it's *you*, not *us*). He thinks in italics when he emphasizes a word. He uses slang like "ends up" and "okay" but also highfalutin legalese like "herein." He fantasizes about the crush. He doesn't mind ending a sentence with a preposition. (As a reporter, he wouldn't write that way in a newspaper article; that's the way he *talks*.) He mimics condescension with his "precious beyond words" verbal sneer. There's a real person here, a smart-mouthed secret romantic who doesn't appreciate elitism, even from a beautiful woman.

This sort of attitude is what makes first person so much fun to write and read. Now, of course, not every first-person narrator would be so sassy and casual. Jack is clearly a contemporary, urban man, and his asides reflect that: they're irreverent, a bit self-absorbed, but also self-amused. If the same conversation were being narrated by the dignified and erudite editor William F. Buckley, you can imagine how different the asides would be.

Later, Jack and the FBI agent are having dinner. This isn't a date; each is trying to pump the other for information about a presidential-assassination attempt. Jack's thoughts, however, stray again into forbidden territory:

> "I don't really know any journalists, professionally," she said. "I don't know if I'm supposed to do this, or if this is wrong, or what."
>
> You have a crush, I said to myself. You've developed a crush on me, and you don't know how to tell me. Just let it out. You'll feel better. Just let it all go.
>
> She said, "I wanted to ask you about that story you had in yesterday's paper that you ended up killing for the later editions."
>
> Oh, well.

Notice the cues that let us know we're in his thoughts: the present tense, the "I said to myself," the addressing her mentally as "you." And consider how barren the passage would have been if all we had was their dialogue without his anticipatory inner commentary.

The way to overcome the reader's instinctive resistance to "the *I* that isn't me" is a distinctive voice that is quite clearly the product of a unique character. With first person, it's essential to descend into the character and let him narrate the events in a particularly interesting voice.

Still, you must keep in mind that a successful narrative voice is one that is both memorable and natural, as there's a fine line between "unique" and "annoying." Imagine three hundred pages narrated by a Valley Girl, for example. In fact, what one reader might find fresh and contemporary, another might consider disjointed and vague. So a strong voice can be both a blessing and a curse, especially in the tight quarters of a first-person narration.

I, THE AUTHOR: FICTIONALIZING YOUR OWN LIFE

A brief note about fictionalized autobiography: This can be a problem in any POV approach, but is more acutely problematic in first person. If your story is based on an experience in your own life, especially a negative experience, consider avoiding first person altogether. You need to establish distance between yourself and the narrator, or there's a great danger that the story will come across as nothing but an exercise in self-pity. You'll be subconsciously favoring "yourself," that is, the narrator, and that preference will not escape readers. There's an old writer's maxim that the author has to be every character, not just one, and that's going to be much easier to accomplish if you write about events based on your own life in third person.

The Unreliable Perspective and Plot Twists

First person can offer some tantalizing plot possibilities. The very narrowness of the narrator's perspective can give subtle hints that things aren't precisely as they might appear, setting up a later plot twist. Here's an example from Poe's "Berenice" in which the narrator, Egaeus, who confesses earlier that he is afflicted with an obsessive-compulsive tendency he calls "monomania" that causes him to be both repelled by and covetous of his fiancée's teeth, approaches her coffin:

> The coffin, so a menial told me, lay surrounded by the curtains of yonder bed, and in that coffin, he whisperingly assured me, was all that remained of Berenice. ... God of heaven!—was it possible? Was it my brain that reeled—or was it indeed the fingers of the enshrouded dead that stirred in the white cerement that bound it? There had been

a band around the jaws, but, I know not how, it was broken asunder. The livid lips were wreathed in a species of smile, and ... there glared upon me in too palpable reality, the white and glistening and ghastly teeth of Berenice. I sprang convulsively from the bed, and uttering no word, rushed forth a maniac from that apartment of triple horror, and mystery, and death.

While this first-person narrator won't quite come out and admit it, he's just seen that his about-to-be-interred fiancée is inconveniently still alive. This passage—combined with his earlier exclamation that "I felt that [the teeth's] possession could alone ever restore me to peace..."—sets up the teasing suspicion that he is committing murder by omission. The final scene, in which Egaeus wakes up and discovers a box of bloody teeth beside him, confirms the reader's suspicions, and his attitude of befuddlement and surprise leading up to the vile discovery ("I had done a deed—what was it?") maintains the voice of the unreliable narrator.

Narrators Are Characters First

Since the first-person narrator has to perform the difficult task of *narrating*, sometimes the author forgets the narrator is a character, too. In fact, some authors get around this by having a noncharacter narrator. Dostoyevsky's narrator in *The Possessed* is an example; he almost never appears, except to tell the story. But that's a rather old-fashioned technique, as it distances the reader from the story.

Be aware of the narrator ceasing to be a character at crucial moments. Especially at moments of high emotion, there's sometimes a tendency to just narrate the action, without any checking back to see how the narrator feels or thinks as a character at this point. That works fine in third person, but it can just about ruin a first-person passage.

The narration should always be filtered through this person who has emotions, intentions, and values. If something emotional is happening, the POV character must react to it and not just narrate, unless, of course, emotional deadness is what you want to convey.

Here's an example from *Second Wind* by Dick Francis. The POV character is Perry, whose plane is crash-landing in the ocean during a hurricane:

I tried the radio again, to broadcast Kris's voice, and heard only Spanish, very faint. Space and time got jumbled. Thought became reduced for both of us to one idea at a time. My own mind clamped down onto the one reassurance that there was a life raft dinghy behind me in the passenger's cabin, and as airplanes didn't float, we would need it.

Bashing around in the restricted tumbling spaces I somehow got my arms onto [the dinghy] and clutched it, holding on even when any steering became doubtful and Kris, still hauling rightly or wrongly at the control column, began chanting again over and over, "Mayday, Mayday" ....

This isn't just a narrator, it's a character, too. While he's telling us what's going on, he's both experiencing the terror and engaging in action (grabbing the dinghy). If your first-person narrator would have an emotional or mental response to the scene you're creating, you have to show the response (or the conscious rejection of that response), or you'll lose reader identification. Again in *Second Wind*, Dick Francis does this delicately at the close of the hurricane scene, in this lonely line where the narrator shows himself blocking the emotion by switching from the personal "I" to the impersonal "one": "One could pass into delirium, and one could drown."

Establish your scene context, and then show the narrator reacting to it, even if deliberately refusing to react *is* the reaction.

WHEN FIRST PERSON IS NOT THE BEST (OR ONLY) PERSON

First person can limit the events you narrate directly, because you must show only what the narrator actually experiences. Sometimes that leads to clunky scenes. Conventional first person probably isn't the best approach for a story that involves several major characters in several settings.

If you have more than a couple major events happening outside the narrator's view, I'd suggest first that you rethink first-person viewpoint. First person is meant to give the reader one person's direct experience, filtered through her unique perspective. If a lot of action can't be narrated through that perspective, perhaps a third-person approach with several narrators would work better.

An alternative, but one I advise only with caution and consideration, is to use third-person narration for those scenes outside the narrator's view. Recent detective novels and thrillers have used this technique. Look at James Patterson's books and Robert Crais's Elvis Cole series for examples. Another approach is to write the overarching narrative in third person and only the villain's POV in first person. An example can be found in Julie Garwood's *The Bride*, which is mostly in third person, but uses first person to disguise the villain's identity:

> It hasn't been easy for me. I stand beside the priest, my expression as solemn as those of the other clan members. I also offer a prayer, though not for Helena's benefit. No, I give the Lord my thanks because the chore is finally finished.
>
> Helena took the longest time dying. Three whole days of agony and suspense I had to endure, and all the while praying she wouldn't open her eyes or speak the damning truth.

These variations on first-person POV can be confusing to the reader, because she ends up knowing much more about what's going on than the first-person narrator does. It helps to make a clear differentiation between the sections—a short third-person passage might be in italics, for example. (Long passages in italics can get annoying.) I've also seen the first-person passages in standard literary past tense ("I chose the first door, turned the knob, and yanked it open") while the third-person passages are in present tense ("The killer grabs the letter from the mailbox and rips it open"), or vice versa. Another approach is to mark transitions physically by giving them separate chapters. Here's an example from *Dead Line* by Brian McGrory:

> All of which explains how Hilary Kane and the mayor ended up at his apartment on the 28th floor of the Ritz-Carlton at 2:00 am, drunkenly and awkwardly pulling off each other's clothes. She wanted to be desired, to be able to look in the mirror the next morning and known that this man absolutely had to have her.

And in the next chapter:

> I don't want to be melodramatic and make this seem like I was meeting an unknown informant in an underground parking garage in the dark of an unfriendly night. That would be a lie. The garage was at street level.

McGrory makes the shift between third person and first person by clear demarcation of each section. The third-person passage is in the first chapter, and the character's name is mentioned. The language is formal and somewhat abstract, distancing her from the reader's identification even as she is victimized. Then the narration switches to the much different voice of the first-person narrator, a reporter who uses humor to ward off emotion.

In a book told mostly in third person, you might also have a long "as told to" passage in first person. An example is Odysseus's account of his travels in *The Odyssey*, where he must "sing for his supper," impressing his dinner hosts so they will give him transport home. In a case like this, it's a good idea to use first person, but you must signal the shift ahead of time so the reader understands the motivation to cause the long speech. Then demark the passage with white space or put it in a separate chapter, and use the first line to introduce the long quote, as my translation opens Odysseus's chapter with "And Ulysses answered:" then skips a few lines and begins the first-person monologue.

The point is that whatever method of demarcation you choose, just make sure you help the reader deal with the logical disconnect by setting the alternate viewpoint off in some way.

Multiple-First Person, or First Times Four

Another interesting but not-for-everyday variation is multiple-first person. Multiple-first provides what we now call the Rashomon effect, after the Japanese film that shows an assault four times, once from each of four perspectives.

This can be great fun, especially to show how the "reality" of an event varies depending on the perspective. But dangers are there, too. Unless the events are dramatic and the perspectives distinctive, the reader could be thinking "same-old, same-old" by the third go-round.

Sequential Narrative

More common than the repeating narrative (different perspectives on the same event) is the sequential narrative, where a number of narrators tell the story more or less chronologically, each taking a chapter or so. William Faulkner used this technique in *As I Lay Dying*, the story of the Bundren family trying to take the mother's body to town for burial during flood season. More than a dozen narrators (including the dead woman) combine to tell the story, each in short chapters, each advancing the story one more step. Each chapter reflects the perspective and the personality of the narrator, sometimes to the point of obscurity. The most famous chapter, and one I remember puzzling over in a course called Modern Novel 365, is narrated by Vardaman and simply consists of this: "My mother is a fish."

This method can also work in popular fiction, as long as the overall story is a strong one so that the reader is carried from one narration to another by the *narrative drive*—the propulsion of the plot through the story events toward some powerful conclusion. The plot itself has to provide the coherence and connectivity to link all those disparate viewpoints, so this probably isn't a good format for a quiet, contemplative story. I'd use it if I were writing about a group of characters linked by the plot, perhaps a dozen high-school football players who gradually realize that their coach is an alien, or a series of short-lived lieutenants commanding a platoon in-country in Vietnam, or maybe the six wives of Henry VIII.

And, of course, each perspective has to be distinctive yet cohesive. Twelve vastly different voices might be discordant and detract from the continuity of the story, yet twelve identical voices might as well be rendered in a neutral third person. (The fewer the first-person narrators, the more distinctive the voices can be without extreme discordance.) Faulkner's narrators are all southerners and mostly of the same rural lower-class background, so their voices have the same "accent," which brings together their varying perspectives.

Sequential Stories, Distinctive Arcs

Another use of multiple-third is to tell a story more or less sequentially through a smaller number of perspectives, each having its own story arc. Faulkner's *The Sound and the Fury* uses the sequential first-person narrations of three brothers, each brother's segment running seventy pages or so. (A fourth section was done in third person.) Each brother has an unusual perspective: Benjy is handicapped and unable to speak, Quentin is preparing to commit suicide, and Jason is something of a sociopath. In this case, they are linked by their family relationship and mental illnesses, but they're also thematically linked: Each, in a way, is describing the loss of their sister Caddy to vice and corruption. Each section has its own plotline, with a beginning, middle, and end, so that each brother's section not only advances the overall plot but also contains his own story: Benjy realizes his sister is gone forever, Quentin ends up committing suicide, and Jason is cheated of his money.

If you take on challenges like this, it's even more imperative to concentrate on what you want the reader to experience. If your purpose is to show the varied perspectives on reality (*Rashomon*), then you'll need to make those perspectives quite distinct. If you're using multiple narrators to tell one overall story (*As I Lay Dying*), then each narrator should probably be used to narrate only those things she experienced or witnessed. If multiple stories add up to one big story (*The Sound and the Fury*), you'll need to focus on the narrators-as-characters, giving each of them an individual journey, as well as a part in the overall story.

EXERCISE

TAKING ON THE CHALLENGES OF FIRST PERSON

1. If you're considering doing a story in first-person narration, free-write for a few moments on the advantages and disadvantages you'll face. Consider both structural problems (like action taking place simultaneously on two continents) and character problems (such as other characters having emotional journeys).

2. Which character will be the narrator? What unique perspective will she bring? What limitations will this perspective place on the narrative?

3. If you're going to try multiple-first person, what can you do to link the narrations for greater coherence? Will there be a single

overarching story that each contributes to, or separate stories, or separate versions of the same story, or something else?

4. Think over what you have of the plot. Is the narrator a character, too? That is, does the narrator measurably participate in the action of the story, reacting to events and causing things to happen?

IF I KNEW THEN ...: CONSIDERING TIME AND TENSE IN FIRST PERSON

When I first began experimenting with first person, I had a very hard time conveying a sense of immediacy for my narrator. I kept falling prey to a trap I call retrospective retelling. This is the tendency to relate the story in retrospect, as if it's all already happened. I found it much harder in first person to make every scene an actual *scene*, the real-time narration of an event. Instead, the narrator seemed to be relaying the story from some vantage point in the future. I found myself using phrases like "I didn't know then that ..." and "Later I understood that ...," which detracted from the sense of immediacy. This was especially difficult when I was describing an impression that would later turn out to be mistaken.

I decided I had to choose one or the other: Either the heroine was narrating the events as they happened (in the standard "literary past" tense), or she was retelling the experience from the future with all the knowledge of someone who had already lived through it (what I call "future retrospective"). Either choice has its advantages, but I didn't think I could adequately convey strong emotions like terror and curiosity in retrospect. And it's not easy to persuade a reader to fear for the narrator's life when she's making it clear that she's survived.

It can be done, however. Some authors have fun with this retrospective structure, playing with the anomaly of telling the past from the future as if it were the present. Elizabeth Peters's narrator directly addresses the issue early in *The Last Camel Died at Noon*, starting with a straightforward account of the day the last camel died, stranding her, her husband, and her son in the desert:

Let me turn back the pages of my journal and explain in proper sequence of time how we came to find ourselves in such an extraordinary predicament. I do not do this in the meretricious hope of prolonging your anxiety as to our survival, dear reader, for if you have the intelligence I expect my readers to possess, you will know I could not be writing this account if I were in the same state as the camels.

Marcel Proust's 3,400-page first-person epic *À la Recherche du Temps Perdu* (translated in English as *In Search of Lost Time* or *Remembrance of Things Past*) uses future retrospective as a way to foreshadow what is coming. It's a linking device that holds together a sprawling narrative spanning decades (and three volumes) and adds an extra dimension to the character of the young narrator. Here's a typical foreshadowing passage:

What the chauffeur wished was to avoid, if possible, the dead season. I have said—though I was unaware of this at the time, and the knowledge of it would have saved me much unhappiness—that he was on very friendly terms with Morel, although they showed no sign even of knowing each other in front of other people.

Proust's technique works because his story is very much a reminiscence from an older and wiser perspective. The title makes that retrospective approach clear. Notice how his foreshadowing creates conflict (always a good thing) by letting the reader know that the chauffeur and Morel are being deceptive. It also gives weight to what otherwise might seem like a trivial incident (a chauffeur taking his car and going back to Paris). Proust delineates the two time periods with his tenses: "I have said" is coming from that future perspective, while the simple past ("the chauffeur wished") denotes the time of the story.

If you're working in first person, the decision to have the narrator relay the story from some point in the future or more or less as they happen should be made early. Either method, or a combination of them, can work. What probably won't work, however, is telling each scene as some sort of historical record, as that will make the narration seem slow and detached. Try, as Peters does above, interjecting "future time" (for example, "I've been down that road since, and it's all changed.

Now it's the most generic of suburban highway strips. But back in 1982 ...") and then descending into the actual time of the story.

Harper Lee, in her masterpiece *To Kill a Mockingbird*, deals with the awkwardness of a child narrator by telling the story from the retrospective of the adult Scout. From the first page, she makes the approach clear:

> When he was nearly thirteen, my brother Jem got his arm badly broken at the elbow. ... When enough years had gone by to enable us to look back on them, we sometimes discussed the events leading to his accident. I maintain that the Ewells started it all, but Jem, who was four years my senior, said it started long before that. He said it began the summer Dill came to us, when Dill first gave us the idea of making Boo Radley come out.

While the voice is adult throughout the book, the action following this is narrated more or less in the time of the book. The reader gets a sense of the distance between the narrator's current life and the events of the book, but once the story actually begins, the scenes are told as they are happening.

Descending Into the Past

When you're doing this future-looking-back method, the clearer the time references, the better. Use future markers—like Lee's "When enough years had gone by ..." or "That summer I turned forty and lost my job ..."—to delineate the passages that have the narrator looking back. Then, when you descend into the past, try to narrate it directly as it happens. Here's another example from *To Kill a Mockingbird* that illustrates how Lee descends into the past and then picks up the story in straight time:

> That was the summer Dill came to us.
>
> Early one morning as we were beginning our day's play in the backyard, Jem and I heard something next door in Miss Rachel Haverford's collard patch. We went to the wire fence to see if there was a puppy—Miss Rachel's rat terrier was expecting—instead we found someone sitting looking at us. Sitting down,

he wasn't much higher than the collards. We stared at him until he spoke:

"Hey."

"Hey yourself," Jem said pleasantly.

"I'm Charles Baker Harris," he said. "I can read."

The "early one morning" and the specificity of detail (Miss Rachel's rat terrier, the collards) place us very definitely in a particular moment in the past, and the dialogue enhances the sense of immediacy. We're no longer in the future looking back; we're now watching the initial encounter with Dill play out as if it is happening in front of us.

To increase that immediacy, aim for the most active prose you can create without being obnoxious. Go for strong verbs, but they must be ones your narrator would use, nothing overwrought. "I shoved open the door" would be stronger than "I opened the door." Envision the setting and provide the sharp details and sensory aspects that will anchor the scene in the moment.

Immediate Action of the Present

One contemporary technique in first person is to narrate the story in present tense, as if the narrator is telling the story as it happens. This technique definitely increases the immediacy of the events, and eliminates the awkwardness of future retrospective. I also suspect it aids the author in keeping the first-person account sharp and active. It's hard to slip into "retrospective" when the action is unfolding right in front of you. It allows for a more stream-of-consciousness narration, including thought and feeling as it they happen.

Brad Meltzer crafts most of his thrillers in this fast-paced style. Here's an example from *The Millionaires*:

Now that lunch is over, most of the pews are empty ... but not all of them. A dozen or so worshippers are scattered throughout the rows, and even if they're praying, it only takes one random glance for one of them to be crimestopper of the week .... Three-quarters down the aisle, along the left-hand wall, a single, unmarked door. Trying not to be too quick and noticeable,

Charlie and I keep the pace nice and smooth. There's a large creak when the door opens. I cringe and give it a fast push to end the pain ....

The door slams shut, and Charlie is still silent. "Please don't do this to yourself," I tell him. "Take your own advice. What happened with Shep, it's not my fault, and it's not yours!"

Collapsing on a wooden bench in the corner, Charlie doesn't answer. His posture sinks. His neck bobs lifelessly. He's still in shock. Less than a half-hour ago, I saw a co-worker get shot.

The "There's a large creak ..." interruption gives this passage an immediacy. The present tense allows more of a running commentary of the event. This can be a lot of fun, or it can be tedious. Concentrate on making the narrator's experience and perceptions vivid and entertaining, with plenty of emotion and conflict. You're not cataloging events; you're telling a story. Every action should increase tension and further the plot.

In the example above, he's not just noting the worshippers in the church; he's thinking of them as potential adversaries, "crimestoppers of the week," who might turn him and his fugitive brother over to the police. He's not just walking down the aisle; he's trying to keep anyone from noticing that they're trying to hide from the police. He's not just trying to buck up his brother; he's begging him not to fall apart. Lots of conflict, lots of emotion—all presented in an urgent, immediate way.

EXERCISE

CONSTRUCTING NARRATOR VOICE AND ATTITUDE

1. When your book opens, what is the narrator's worldview? How does he perceive the world? Is there a dominant religious or political philosophy?

2. What's the narrator's self-image? How does this differ from the persona she presents to the world? How does this color how she presents the narration? (For example, someone who thinks of herself as persecuted will interpret an accident as something aimed at hurting her in particular.)

3. Is the narrator past-focused, present-focused, or future-focused? Is he optimistic or pessimistic? How will this affect the narration?

4. Choose one event from your plot. Jot down a few notes on the character's worldview, self-image, mood, and intention at this moment in the story.

5. Now write the narration of that event, using what you've learned about this character's POV. Try your best to let the character do the writing here. Once you're done, read it over and try to revise in a couple "asides" that reveal the internal thoughts, feelings, and interpretations.

THE ART OF MANIPULATION: THE TRICKS OF FIRST PERSON

Again, keep in mind that the narrator is a character, not just the mouthpiece. But first person adds the element of intentionality; that is, the narrator is able to manipulate the narrative to achieve some effect. So while in third person, intentional misleading would be cheating your readers, in first person, it's allowable.

Consider that we are seldom really honest about our own emotions, even to ourselves. We tell ourselves we're angry when we're really scared. We think that we're being helpful when we're really being controlling. That's why deception "feels" so right in first person, because we know we do it when we narrate our own lives. Narrator deception and self-deception will deepen the narrative and add *subtext*—what's going on, consciously or subconsciously, under the surface text. Think of a flirtation: When a man and woman discuss their favorite movie, underneath the surface banter, there's a whole secret conversation going on. This is a common type of subtext, but the sort that shows up in first-person narration lets the reader know something the narrator doesn't mean to express. The narrator in Robert Browning's "My Last Duchess" thinks he's doing a great job memorializing his late wife, while the reader is getting the suspicion the narrator loved her to death.

I the Lie: The Unreliable Narrator

Not every first-person "lie" has to be something serious (like how poor old Berenice got buried alive in Poe's story). It doesn't even have to be willfully deceptive. It can be an effort to "spin" reality to better suit the character's purposes or make him appear in a more favorable light. It can be the subconscious suppressing some important fact or the wishful-thinking interpretation of some event. The unreliable first-person narrator is at least as old as Laurence Sterne's classic *The Life and Opinions of Tristram Shandy, Gentleman*. This is something you might want to exploit as you craft your narrative; it's one option that really isn't available in third person. Readers expect that a third-person narrative will be more or less true when it describes the action of the scene. Gauge your own reaction to these examples:

> He inched forward and just tapped the car ahead of him. To his shock, the other car's bumper collapsed like a sheet of tin foil.

In this third-person, more objective-seeming account, the reader will generally assume that the narrative is correct and the character really did just tap the other car; its bumper must have been defective. But with first-person narration, there's room to be skeptical:

> I inched forward and just tapped the car ahead of me. To my shock, the other car's bumper collapsed like a sheet of tin foil.

Yeah, right, you think (if you're like me). Either he hit the car ahead of him way harder than he's letting on, or that's one seriously defective bumper. Now just to make it more fun, think about how the first-person narrator might embellish that to be more "persuasive":

> I inched forward and just tapped the car ahead of me. Really. Just a tap. I couldn't have been going more than 2 miles per hour. To my shock, the other car's bumper collapsed like a sheet of tin foil. But it was one of those foreign cars, and everyone knows they don't use the same materials we do here in the U.S. The cop asked if I'd been drinking, but those idiots define a single beer hours earlier as "drinking."

Now don't you just *know* the truth, that the narrator jammed on the accelerator and rammed right into the other car? And now that you know this narrator can't be trusted (at least when there's alcohol involved), how might that change your experience of whatever story he tells next?

Most people have built-in lie detectors, and that gives authors an advantage. We can be subtle and still guide readers to doubt our narrator's objectivity and honesty. They don't need many cues, but you do want to provide at least one. Here's where your real-life "reading" of other people comes in handy. How do you know that people are lying or fudging or exaggerating or spinning? Some of this will be body language and tone of voice, which won't be easy to replicate in first person, so concentrate on the language and sentence construction. What are the signals of deception, and how do they explain themselves and their actions?

Methinks he doth protest too much is one technique—emphasizing something just beyond the point of plausibility. Liars usually take things one step too far, and thus alert us to their deception. First-person narrators might be deceptive, or they might be self-deceptive, but when they deceive, they usually reveal it through an excess of sincerity.

Look again at the Rumpole passage about the hardness he has achieved with maturity:

> I suppose, when I was young, I used to suffer with my clients. I used to cringe when I heard their sentences and go down to the cells full of anger. Now I never watch their faces when the sentence is passed. I hardly listen to the years pronounced and I never look back at the dock.

Read it aloud and listen to your voice. Listen to what you instinctively emphasize, what rings hollow and unconvincing, and what sounds excessive.

I suppose: Hear the attempt at offhandedness, casualness?

I used to ... I used to: The repetition makes this almost sing-song.

Now I never ... I hardly ... I never look back ...: He sounds insistent, as if he's trying to persuade himself. He *never* looks back. He *hardly* listens. Clearly what he claims he doesn't notice is precisely what eats away at him—that he can't win them all, and when he loses, someone's life is ruined.

Another telltale sign is when the liar will provide just a bit too much information, especially information that's on the other side of relevance. He'll attempt to divert the blame ("It was a foreign car") or switch a bit too clumsily to a new subject ("Anyway, the Colts lost ...") or quibble about a term ("those idiots define a single beer as ..."). For more training in this essential art, watch those press conferences where a politician or a football coach tries to squirm out of some tough question.

They Can Lie, but You Can't

One word of caution: Readers like being teased but not outright tricked. The narrator can lie, but the author can't. If the narrator, for example, is the murderer, the author has to provide clues, however subtle, that this is the case. The narrator can lie about what has happened, but the attentive reader has to have enough evidence to suspect that something in the narrative is hidden or incorrect.

And the narrator can't completely leave out important events in order to keep the secret. Maybe the narrator can say, "And then I lost consciousness," when a straight narrative might go on to describe him beating the other guy to death. But the narrative can't skip the whole event and give no sign that it ever happened. Consider revising if you find in the end of the book your narrator saying, "I didn't tell you, but in between that trip to the grocery store and the drug store, I stopped at the hardware store and bought the hammer that was the blunt instrument that caused Tom's death." Instead, after your grocery store scene, try something like "I stopped off at the hardware store and picked up a few items for my toolbox." That's enough to keep from cheating the reader.

EXERCISE

LYING TO THEIR FACES

1. How is your narrator going to lie, shade the truth, or hide something from the reader? Why?

2. Have you given the reader a hint that there's some deception or concealment going on? How does this show up in the narrator's narration?

3. What are the consequences in the story for this deception? Is it ever clearly revealed as deception?

Interpreting and Misinterpreting in First Person

Something we all do, but never "hear" from anyone else, is the mental *translation* of conversation and action. You know what I mean—few of us take everything at face value. We're constantly assessing and interpreting—*What did she really mean by that? Whose ox is he trying to gore here? How stupid does she think I am? Doesn't he know how uncool he sounds?*

Well, one of the pleasures of first person is witnessing how another person interprets and misinterprets what is being said. First, this emphasizes the whole purpose of first person, to remind us that the interpretation of what happens is more interesting than a direct reflection of "reality," and maybe even that "reality" isn't a collection of facts but includes inner perception as part of a larger truth. First person also makes us aware that we are "the other" to someone else's "I"; getting into another's thoughts makes us realize that we don't necessarily think that way.

For example, in *Up Island* by Anne Rivers Siddons, Molly Redwine starts out in an upper-class Southern milieu where discreet deception rules. So she's learned to interpret everything as a metaphor or sign. The rash on her buttocks is a sign that her husband is being unfaithful. Swimming in the pool is a metaphor for a return to the womb. The fidelity of a pair of swans is a metaphor for a love her widowed father has lost and Molly will never experience. Her former friends' consolation means she's being fired from all their charity committees. Consider this example:

> From my committees and boards and panels: "Don't worry about a thing. We're coping splendidly. Why don't you just take the summer for yourself ... only if you think you might want to take longer, do let us know; we'll need to make some plans for the fall."
>
> Translation: "If you're going to be divorced by fall, maybe you'd better think about passing the torch. We love you, but you're not going to be who you were."

As long as Molly was part of that milieu, she could deal with the disconnect between what she knew to be the truth and what everyone around her presented as reality. But her husband's deceptions make her realize how much she has given up to maintain this facade of social civility. By the end of the book, Molly insists on challenging life directly, both her past (the loss of her mother) and her present (a lover's terminal illness), symbolized by her literal interpretation of a metaphor—she literally "throws her hat into the ring" as the first action of her new, honest life:

> "What the hell are you doing?" Dennis Ponder said.
>
> "Throwing my hat into the ring," I said back.
>
> I opened the door and walked to the edge of the porch and stopped.
>
> "It's not forever, Mama," I said aloud. "Just for right now. It was never really mine, anyway."
>
> And I gave the hat to the wind, which took it and whirled it away over the lashing trees, toward Gay Head, all the way up island.

Showing character change through the interpretation technique is a subtle way to show progression of the story's theme. Slowly, the character's interpretation gets more acute, moving perhaps from unthinking acceptance of literal meaning in the beginning of the book to a more subtle reading of people's motives later—or in Molly's case, vice versa, from constant suspicion to a decision to live honestly.

As you let your narrator interpret others' statements, allow for a bit of subtext. That is, since the narrator doesn't take a declaration at face value, the reader will probably interpret *how*, not just *what*, the narrator interprets. The style of the internalization is in itself a hint at the inner reality of this character. Look again at the phone exchange in McGrory's *The Incumbent*:

> "Jack, Agent Stevens."
>
> *Agent* Stevens. Isn't that precious beyond words? Perhaps I'd like to be identified herein as *Reporter* Flynn, or *Journalist* Flynn for all you National Public Radio types.

Jack wants us to know that he's not easily impressed, even by an FBI agent. In fact, he interprets the agent's innocuous introduction as snobbery, and that tells us something about what he values: It's definitely not professional titles. But the reader can, and will, glean even more from Jack's interpretation that he is a bit insecure and feels tougher if he can sneer at FBI agents and even NPR listeners.

Just as you imagine your character's speaking voice and narrative voice, listen for that internal voice; it might be cynical or snarky or sad, or it might reveal hidden antagonism or buried longing. The internal truth will come out in these interpretations, though not always directly. You might leave a bit of room for the reader to interpret, too, the slight difference between what the narrator interprets and what the reader has figured out—especially in the interpretation of self and relationships.

For instance, Dexter, the "good" serial murderer in Jeff Lindsay's *Darkly Dreaming Dexter*, has responded to early trauma by shutting down his emotions. He interprets his own behavior and the negative comments of others as a sign of his sociopathology, and he pretends to be proud of that. He doesn't even have dreams, he claims, because dreams are human, and he's not. He declares, "That is not self-pity but the coldest, clearest self-knowledge. I am unlovable.... Something in me is broken or missing."

But this statement leaves room for the reader to speculate, because Dexter's behavior throughout the novel is oddly loving: He ensures his foster sister's promotion by helping her solve her case, he protects his girlfriend, and he treats her children with respect and kindness. And so, by the end of the book, he is clearly loved, and therefore he must have been wrong when he said he is unlovable. The dynamic reverses in the end: The reality trumps his cold, clear, "true" interpretation.

This sort of juxtaposition of reality with interpretation is one of the hidden pleasures of reading and writing in first person. Much of this will probably come out subconsciously, and you'll read over your draft and find the narrator's little asides and translations strewn through dialogue passages. Take a moment and analyze your work for your own interpretation of the narrator's interpretive style. What does that style say about his attitude toward reality, toward others, and toward himself?

Then, see if the style does or should change as the events of the plot change the narrator. It doesn't have to be a radical change—a pessimist who interprets everything as a sign of impending doom is unlikely to become a sunny optimist in three hundred pages. But she can decide to allow another person to be optimistic, or she can hold herself back from scoffing at someone's naive pronouncement.

EXERCISE

TRANSLATING THE TRANSLATIONS

1. What sort of comment by another is sure to make your narrator react? Is it something naive? Something deceptive? Something manipulative? Something too honest? Consider why the narrator needs to interpret that sort of statement in particular.

2. What is the narrator's translating style? Does he just use his internal conversation with the reader to make fun of the other characters, or does he see himself as the only one who can sense a lie? What purpose do you want the narrator to have in translating others' dialogue?

3. What about the world the narrator lives or grew up in has made him believe that appearances are deceiving, that reality needs interpretation? Does he live in a world of deceit, where nothing is as it seems? Or did he grow up with a family of direct, non-subtle sorts, who always spoke what little was on their mind? How does his experience help mold his interpretive style?

4. Finally, what does the narrator's interpretive style reveal about him, and how will the events of the story change that?

WHY ARE YOU TELLING ME THIS? FIRST-PERSON FRAMED

Remember when I mentioned that existential problem of the purpose of first-person narrative? Why, after all, is the narrator telling the story? It can be fun to weave together narrative purpose and plot to deepen characterization and make the narration not just a *telling* of the story but part of the story itself. A famous example is Philip

Roth's *Portnoy's Complaint*. For 99 percent of the story, the reader can only assume that Portnoy is telling his story for no real reason. But then comes the last line:

PUNCH LINE

* * * * * * * *

So (said the doctor). Now vee may perhaps begin. Yes?

So all 270 pages are just a long prelude to an initial therapy session. It's a clever device that is consonantal with Portnoy's excessive personality, but it also shows that he has sought help for the problems he's so amply demonstrated during the story.

As I mentioned in chapter three, this technique of putting the main story inside another story is called framing, and it can help anchor the first-person narration within a context.

Constructing the First-Person Frame Story

Portnoy is unusual in that it saves the frame for the punch line. Usually, the frame is set up very early in the story, in the first couple pages. Here's an example from *Missing Pieces* by Joy Fielding, a thriller featuring a narrator whose sister married a serial murderer, then helped him escape from prison:

> It's quiet in the house in the morning, what with everyone gone. I have lots of time to tape my report. I call it a report, but really it isn't anything so clearly defined. It's more a series of reminiscences, although the police have asked me to be as specific and as orderly as I can, to be careful not leave anything out, no matter how insignificant something may seem. They will decide what's important, they tell me.

The reader can envision this narrator sitting at the kitchen table, the breakfast dishes stacked in the sink. She's taping her recollections of the events for the best of reasons, to provide evidence to the police. This frame affects the narration in several ways. For one thing, she says she's been urged by the police to be "specific and orderly," so the narration to follow shows her trying to organize her thoughts even as she records them. Her purpose evolves, however, as she gets into the story. At first, she's just doing her civic duty, helping the police out, but then she begins to value sorting through her memory and searching for meaning in the tragic events. She also is clearly speaking from a future beyond the main story, so she knows the "ending." It's a tragic ending, and her mood is somber even as she tells of the happier times before the serial murderer entered her sister's life.

The frame has an ending, too. After the main (serial murderer) plot resolves, the narrator makes her taped report to the police:

> I think that's everything. I'll probably edit out some of the more personal revelations before I hand this over to the police. I'm not sure that any of this is what they were expecting. But I've tried to provide substance, context, explanations. I've searched my memory and bared my soul. I'm sure there are still some pieces missing. But I've done my best. Hopefully, it will be of some use. At any rate, it's time to pick up the pieces. And go on.

If you're going to work with a frame story, determine if the frame itself needs some resolution. In *Missing Pieces*, the frame story allows the narrator to explain the consequences of her cooperation with the police. The narrator states, "And so the police can now indisputably link Colin Friendly to the disappearances of six more women. Six more cases closed."

Another frame is an old person dictating his memoirs to a secretary or a reporter, as in Anne Rice's *Interview with the Vampire* and Thomas Berger's *Little Big Man*. Sometimes, in this case, the frame is done from another person's POV—the reporter or secretary.

So if you're using a frame, you need a purpose for the narrator to be telling this story. You're bypassing that polite convention that allows first-person narration without any real purpose. Narrator purpose like "vindication" or "revealing the long-hidden secret" or "righting a wrong" or some other requirement for explanation would add force to the frame story.

EXERCISE

FRAMING THE FIRST PERSON

1. Look at your plot and your major character's journey. What frame might be appropriate for this story?

2. If you use a frame, how does it enclose the main narrative? How does the frame story resolve? (You don't necessarily need very much, but it does help have some closure.)

3. Who is the main character of the frame? If that's also the main character of the story within the story, what is the distinction between the two (such as one is in the past, experiencing the events of the story, and the other is in the future, looking back with greater wisdom or a different purpose)?

The Epistle According to ...

A common sort of frame for a first-person narration has the POV character introducing her journals or diary. The journal frame is an example of the epistolary novel, which is told through the use of documents (usually letters or a journal). This has always been one of the most popular ways to frame a story, as it gives the reader the illicit pleasure of reading someone else's mail or diary. A bookseller told me that she had customers convinced that the faux journal that made up Robert James Waller's *The Bridges of Madison County* is authentic. Of course, you can't expect that most experienced fiction readers will be so easily fooled. But the epistolary form is a good device for lulling readers into imagining, if only for a moment, that these people actually exist. Verisimilitude—the author's ability to make this journal or exchange of letters seem real—goes a long way toward aiding the suspension of disbelief that makes the reading experience such a pleasure.

But this suspension means that the book should seem to be meant for some audience other than the reader who bought the book. More than most novels, an epistolary novel requires a purpose, a reason why these words are being set down—to communicate with someone else, to explain or confess, even to remind a future self of some events.

If you're planning an epistolary novel, spend some quality time determining the purpose and audience. Ask the questions that we politely don't ask of most first-person narrators: Why are you writing this, and who is supposed to read it?

For example, if you asked Bridget Jones why she kept a diary, she might say, "To record my miserable attempts to diet," as she begins many days' entry with her current weight. If you asked, "Who is supposed to read this?" she'd probably exclaim, "No one! Just me! So I can see how much I've gained or lost, that's all!"

With that purpose (to record her weight) and audience (her future self), her diary entries seem appropriately dashed off. They are full of abbreviations that take some time to decipher, as well as observations about the many failings that Bridget, if she existed, definitely would not want us to read. In fact, to justify her binging and smoking lapses, she records all the miserable factors of her existence that make dieting so difficult. Here's a snippet from *Bridget Jones's Diary* by Helen Fielding:

Sun 26 Feb

8st 13, alcohol units 2 (excellent), cigarettes 7, calories 3,100 (poor).

2pm Oh why hasn't Daniel rung? Hideous, wasted weekend glaring psychopathically at the phone, and eating things. I cannot believe I convinced myself I was keeping the entire weekend free to work, when in fact I was on permanent date-with-Daniel standby.

The diary-like touches (the time and date on each entry), the punctuation errors, and the fragmented thoughts add to the sense that we're reading something not meant for our eyes. But as "dashed off" as the individual entries might feel to us, I can guarantee you the author spent a great deal of time creating that voice, and even more time shaping the entries into a romance plot.

That is, the epistolary format can be great fun, for the author as well as the reader, but you still must end up with a fully shaped story. Fielding is actually reinventing *Pride and Prejudice* using the same theme (you can't trust your first impressions), so some of her plotting work was done two centuries ago. However, her frame of the diary adds new life to the old story, and she never breaks away from it: Every event is told through diary entries in Bridget's unique voice.

The epistolary voice should depend on the character, the purpose, and the intended audience. Bridget writes in a half-literate code because she is the only intended audience. But many journals are actually meant "for posterity," that is, to be read by someone other than the supposed writer. The voice, then, should reflect the relationship of the fictional writer with the fictional audience and also be in agreement with the fictional purpose—what the writer is hoping to accomplish.

Bridget Jones's diary is going to be far more informal and distracted than the confession of a crime or a seduction letter. So, too, should your epistolary voice reflect the situation you're setting up. A recent example to look to is Marilynne Robinson's epistolary novel *Gilead*. In this, an elderly minister pens a long letter to his little child, and from the first line is the melancholy knowledge that this letter will be his only chance to pass on his hard-won wisdom:

> I told you last night that I might be gone sometime, and you said, Where, and I said, To be with the Good Lord, and you said, Why, and I said, Because I'm old, and you said, I don't think you are old....
>
> It seems ridiculous to suppose the dead miss anything. If you're a grown man when you read this—it is my intention for this letter that you will read it then—I'll have been a gone a long time. I'll know most of what there is to know about being dead, but I'll probably keep it to myself. That seems to be the way of things.

The minister's letter to his son isn't meant to be read for a long time, so in some ways it feels like an extended journal entry. But he never loses contact with his ultimate purpose of imparting some wisdom to his son, often referring to "you," both the little boy he knows and the young man he won't live to meet. As the author crafted this long epistle, she stayed true to her first-person narrator's purpose and intended audience.

In an epistolary novel, there's usually a defined audience—not the reader of the book, but the intended recipient of the letters. This gets even more complex when the epistolary frame is the exchange of letters between two people. This fascinating format actually creates two interlocking first-person narratives. Each has a separate personality and a separate agenda for writing each letter, and that informs both the voice and structure of the work. The interaction will also be affected; that is, if there is a "call" in one letter, there should be a "response" in the corresponding one. The epistolary exchange becomes then not just a narrative, but an *inter*narrative.

Fyodor Dostoyevsky's first novel, *Poor Folk*, was an epistolary exchange between two distant cousins who share a secret love. From the very first letter, the man shows his willingness to sacrifice when he spends his few pennies on a gift of flowers for her. She protests, thus setting up a novel-long conflict of mutual need and obligation:

April 8th

MY DEAREST BARBARA ALEXIEVNA,—How happy I was last night—how immeasurably, how impossibly happy! That was because for once in your life you had relented so far as to obey my wishes. ...

Well, good-bye, my darling. I have bought you two little pots of geraniums—quite cheap little pots, too—as a present. ... I kiss your hands, and remain ever your devoted slave, your faithful friend, MAKAR DIEVUSHKIN.

P.S.—One thing I beg of you above all things—and that is, that you will answer this letter as FULLY as possible.

April 8th

MY BELOVED MAKAR ALEXIEVITCH,—Do you know, I must quarrel with you. Yes, good Makar Alexievitch, I really cannot accept your presents, for I know what they must have cost you—I know to what privations and self-denial they must have led. How many times have I not told you that I stand in need of NOTHING, of absolutely NOTHING, as well as that I shall never be in a position to recompense you for all the kindly acts with which you have loaded me? Why, for instance, have you sent me geraniums? ...

Again good-bye.—Your friend, BARBARA DOBROSELOVA.

If you're interested in crafting a novel this way, let the form work for you. For example, see how Dostoyevsky dates the letters, letting us know how rapidly Barbara responds to Makar. The "P.S." adds an informal note but is actually the purpose of the letter—that is, begging for a reply. The author also uses the traditional greeting and closing (Makar's effusive avowal contrasted to Barbara's much more restrained "Your friend") to hint at an imbalance in their relationship.

Just don't let the discursive nature of correspondence distract you. This is still a novel, with a beginning, middle, and end. The letter exchange is how you narrate the events, but the events should still add up to a plot, where things happen that change the characters, their world, their relationship, and their tone. For example, the Dostoyevsky novel follows Makar's attempt to establish some financial security, even as he undercuts it by trying to help her out of poverty, and Barbara's responses grow increasingly frantic to escape this mutual-desperation partnership. The novel ends with a final exchange, as Barbara leaves the city forever with her rich new husband, and Makar writes one last time begging her to stay in contact, even as he admits she will never see the letter. Thus, the imbalance hinted at in the first letter comes to fruition in the end and is shown in his last imploring plea.

If you're planning such a format, I'd suggest figuring out the plot first, perhaps even drawing a timeline of events, and then imagining yourself as a character, confined to letters. If you do have the characters actually meeting, it might be better to have them discuss it later in their letters rather than actually showing the meeting. The final episode in correspondence should show some kind of closure: In *Gilead*, the minister scrawls a few last lines before he dies; in *Poor Folk*, Barbara cuts off contact.

Like all frame novels, the epistolary draws the reader in and creates the illusion of interactivity. But this oldest of novel forms seems paradoxically postmodern now, as it exemplifies Marshall McLuhan's edict, "The medium is the message." The medium—the epistolary in all its forms—becomes, at least in part, what is being explored. Consider how the actual medium you choose will shape the discourse. An e-mail correspondence, for example, is likely to be faster-paced than a snail-mail exchange, but considerably slower than an Instant Messenger chat. The medium chosen will also affect the voice—the level of formality, the word choice, even the punctuation. Most of us probably dispense with formal greetings and closings in our e-mails, and I know from painful experience that students dispense utterly with punctuation, even when e-mailing their teachers. Part of your task, should you decide to use a twenty-first century medium in the form of an epistolary novel, is to maintain the verisimilitude of the format without repudiating every rule of grammar.

If you're going the epistolary route, commit to it; discipline yourself to keep the action confined to the letters or a journal or a scrapbook. There's a peculiar logic to the epistolary frame, and it can be enormous fun for the reader—but as soon as you "break the frame" and go outside the epistolary structure, you lose the focus that is making the story such an intimate experience.

EXERCISE

TRYING OUT THE EPISTOLARY

1. Be tough on yourself: What will your story gain from being told in an epistolary format? What will it lose?

2. What frame can you use? Letters? Journals? Something else?

3. What do you see as the voice challenges of your story done in this format?

4. Sketch out your plot as you now conceive it. What problems will the epistolary format pose, and how can you fix them?

LAST WORD ON FIRST PERSON

First-person POV isn't as easy as it looks, and there are many elements to consider (though it's probably not as hard as I make it seem). The important thing to remember is you can't just fall back on what "feels right," because that will probably mean *your* voice predominates and the narration is, at best, retrospective and, at worst, self-indulgent. If you don't have to work at all at crafting the first-person narration—I'll be blunt—you're probably not doing it right.

- *Extracts from Adam's Diary* by Mark Twain. Twain's first-person Adam (literally the first person!) is poignant as he attempts to understand his new world and his growing love for Eve. Very strong voice.

- *The Sound and the Fury* by William Faulkner. One of the first and best multiple-first-person novels, a true *tour de force*, featuring the POVs of a handicapped man, his suicidal brother, and their sociopathic brother. A fourth POV section, in third person, gives the voice of reason to their former mammy.

- *Jane Eyre* by Charlotte Brontë. The great Gothic classic uses an unnervingly contemporary first-person voice to present a likeable heroine making her way in an eerie world.

- The Stephanie Plum series by Janet Evanovich. This series is a send-up of the postwar tough-guy private-eye novels, the not-so-tough bounty hunter heroine tempted from her work by her two irresistible boyfriends.

- *Devil in a Blue Dress* by Walter Mosley. Mosley's voice is sure and evocative as he explores postwar black Los Angeles through the first-person POV of a private detective.

- *Ultimate Prizes* by Susan Howatch. Howatch always does interesting things with first-person POV (her earlier books, *Cashelmara* and *Penmarric*, feature very effective multiple first person). This book displays the perspective of a vicar in denial about his own nature as he becomes obsessed with an inappropriate woman. It's a good example of how readers can be led to identify with even unlikable first-person narrators.

- *Zodiac* by Neal Stephenson. This cyberpunk (science fiction) novel exploits the comic first-person voice of a dangerously hip young eco-sleuth, the Green Party's answer to James Bond.

- *The Curious Incident of the Dog at Night-Time* by Mark Haddon. This is a lovely little book, a Sherlock Holmes-inspired detective story told entirely in the POV of an autistic boy.

- *An Instance of the Fingerpost* by Iain Pears. A *Rashomon*-like (multiple-first-person) exploration of the different perceptions of the same event.

- *Which Brings Me to You: A Novel in Confessions* by Steve Almond and Julianna Baggott. This is a contemporary example of an epistolary novel in which two young people, who started with an abortive tryst, choose to back up and restart their relationship in an exchange letters they call "an extended power-flirt."

SECOND PERSON

5

In second-person POV, *you* are the narrator. But it's not *you*, the author, telling the story. You likely will find that hard to understand, and, well, that's the reason second-person POV is rare. If, with first-person narration, the existential questions seem complex, they become just about unsolvable with second person.

Who, when you get right down to it, is this *you* who is narrating the action of the story? Is it the reader? (Most readers will quickly distinguish themselves from the narrator-you: "No way would I .... This isn't me.") Or is *you* humanity in general, the "universal you" so common in conversation? And who is speaking? An omniscient authorial persona instructing a fictional character? The narrator addressing his other self?

It's difficult for the writer to create a character around the second-person narrator and difficult for the reader to see that pronoun and not think it refers to himself. Some readers will instinctively react against being told that *you* are someone doing something that they are demonstrably not doing. Notice the third sentence in the first paragraph of this chapter, where I made the assumption that *you* will find "*you* the narrator" hard to understand. If, in fact, you had no problem understanding that equation, you might have protested inwardly, and perhaps even grown annoyed at my presumption. But if I would have written, "Many readers will find that hard to understand," you probably would have accepted that without a qualm. "Many readers" allows for you to be yourself, while *you* asserts a knowledge or control over you.

That's a small example of the problem that second-person authors face in every line. The second-person pronoun brings with it more context than *he/she* or *I*, and since our interaction with the narrator is initially through that pronoun, we can't help but be affected by its constant use. It might feel like an intrusion into our psychic space. It might feel like an accusation. Or it might feel like the highest form of commiseration. Regardless, the use of *you* as the primary POV is going to create a different story experience for the reader than the same story told in first-person or third-person POV. The question is: Is that the experience you want to create for your reader?

SECOND-PERSON BASICS

If you're considering writing second-person POV, here are some advantages:

- It is, in and of itself, narratively experimental, so second person can be a great foundation for a unique telling of either literary or commercial fiction.
- Second person will draw in the reader by obligating her to participate in the narrative.
- Second-person POV allows a direct exploration of the meaning of "self," a primary issue in Western literature.

Because of the experimental nature of this POV, it requires extra skill and delicacy in handling. Be aware of the many disadvantages:

- After a single paragraph, the reader's instinctive resistance to the "you" pronoun could mean a quick return to the bookstore shelf.
- Plotting might have to be sacrificed to the unusual narrative format.
- The paucity of second-person POV novels means you will have few models to follow. (This might also be seen as an advantage if you're striving for innovation.)
- Second person is less common in genre fiction, so if this is what you're writing, you may run into problems finding an editor and agent who think the project is marketable.

But if you're interested in creating experimental narratives, second-person POV might be your choice. It's particularly effective if you want to create a slightly vertiginous experience for the reader, to examine the definitions of self and other, or to explore the very nature of narrative.

IT TAKES MORE THAN YOU: BUILDING A STORY IN SECOND-PERSON POV

The term *you* has many uses in fiction, and most have nothing to do with POV. A character will tell another character: "You've had enough, old boy." That's just dialogue. Another character will use *you* in the universal sense, as the old song has it: "Nobody knows you when you're down and out."

"You," especially in American English, is often used to mean "I," or as the British would use "one." It's a distancing device when the topic might be emotionally threatening. This effect is important, and it plays a part in the experience of second person, which is sometimes disguised as "first-person distant," as in this Hemingway narrator's musings about the trauma of war in *A Farewell to Arms*:

> There were many words that you could not stand to hear and finally only the names of places had dignity. Certain numbers were the same way and certain dates and these with the name of the places were all you could say and have them mean anything.

But those uses of *you* don't make a passage second-person POV. In *The Bad Beginning*, Lemony Snicket writes, "I wish I could tell you that the Baudelaires' first impressions of Count Olaf and his house were incorrect." Here, he is writing in omniscient POV, with an omniscient narrator who is *apostrophizing*, or addressing the reader. The action is narrated by this all-knowing narrator, who just happens to want to make you, the reader, feel included.

Contrast that with an actual second-person POV passage from *Slackwire* by Dennis Schofield, where the *you* narrates the action:

> You almost answer. But bite your lip, hard enough to taste the bruise purpling. You are in the deeper shadow around the door or behind the wardrobe or have slipped beneath the bed, which creaked when he sat. The wind's coming up again, blustering and sucking at the bedroom window outside, rattling it, sucking the hu-

mid moisture from the brick walls. A finger of sparks creeps up Billy Thunder's spine into the back of his neck making his hair stand on gooseflesh. "Is there anybody there? Who's there?" So here it is: all along you hadn't known what you would do if he woke.

Here, the "narrativized you" makes *you* both the narrator and a participant in the action of the scene. (The term "narrativized you" comes from Schofield's doctoral dissertation on second person in fiction, a must-read if you're considering trying this out. See the reading recommendations on page 122 for more information.) The difficulties of writing and reading second-person POV mean that few novelists have ever succeeded, at least throughout an entire book. One who has is Jay McInerney, whose *Bright Lights, Big City* remains the most popular second-person POV novel. From the first line, "You are not the kind of guy who would be at a place like this at this time in the morning," to the last line, "You will have to learn everything all over again," the narrator is always *you*. It's a specific *you*, unnamed but not generalized, with specific characteristics: *You* are a Manhattanite, married to a model, working at a prestigious magazine. (Some critics pointed out that *you* shared a lot of history with the author in this instance.) We could do a search and replace and change "you" to "I," and we'd end up with a fairly conventional first-person narrative about how the big city corrupts, or, rather, how the young and shallow embrace that corruption. But replacing pronouns is not all it takes to create a successful second-person narrative.

Theme in Second Person: Radicalizing the Self

In his exploration of second person, Dennis Schofield points out that second-person POV in a passage serves "not only to radicalize notions of narrative 'person' and narrative discourse more generally, but also to radicalize the notion of 'self.'" When *you* are narrating the story, it forces the reader to participate in the making of the narrative, and when *you* are the main character, it forces the reader to participate at least mentally in the action.

It can be quite a trick—relying on the power of the pronoun *you* to create context, identification, and possibly even guilt. *You* often sounds like an accusation, but it can also create empathy. Some readers who resist the pronoun at first ("No, not *me!*") begin to recognize the universality in each story. "You have traveled [in the course of this night] from the meticulous to the slime," McInerney writes, and a tiny voice inside each of us says, *Well, we've all done that.* (You mean you haven't? Not even in college? Well, in the book, you have.)

This suspension of disbelief and cultivated empathy is the power of second person. As with all POV approaches, the crucial question is how it will improve the reader's experience. This is a good POV choice if the purpose of your novel is to explore notions of self, experiment with metafiction, or amplify some intriguing theme.

One theme that shows up constantly in second-person POV fiction is the inability of the narrator to truly inhabit the self—*Who is this?* Lorrie Moore's story "How to Be an Other Woman" asks this question. The narrator in *Almost You* by Daniel Gunn has to be reassured that he even exists: "Listen: You are somehow still alive, however hard this is for you to believe."

It's possible to explore that "lost" self with a first-person narration, but there's no doubt that the reader's instinctive push-pull reaction to the second-person narrative voice will create a corresponding sense of displacement, thereby making the medium the message and rendering the novel as part of the process of self-loss.

Framing the You

If you're interested in trying this out, consider that we often use "you" in narrative ways in our own casual conversation. If you frame your story to resemble one of those conventional uses of "you," the reader might find a resonance that will increase the meaning of the narration. This type of frame will probably be considerably removed from a standard plot-based narrative or character journey, but if you're considering second-person POV, you're probably interested in experimentation with form already.

The Courtroom-You

When, in our ordinary discourse, do we use *you* as a narrator/character? First, we admonish ourselves as *you*, actually dividing into two people: the authority figure doing the admonishing, and the miscreant being admonished ("You should know better!"). We rebuke ourselves ("What do you expect?").

This is what Schofield calls the courtroom-you, because it has accusatory power. In a novel, self-accusation could take the form of an actual indictment: "You are hereby required to present yourself to the court." Following that could be short chapters outlining the charges against *you*. Imagine rewriting Kafka's novel *The Trial*, in which a man is arrested on unclear charges and ends up accepting his inexplicable fate. A similar story with *you* as the defendant might give the meaningless destiny more meaning—or make it even more absurd.

The Travelogue-You

We use *you* when giving someone directions: "You go up Kingsley and turn left at Evanston. You will see a Shell station there." Schofield calls this "the travelogue-you," and it's probably the most common use of the second-person character. So consider how you would use this travelogue-mode in fiction. For example, a short story might be disguised as a travel article, as advice about what to see and do in Paris, when it's actually about a marriage failing and the couple's second-honeymoon effort to save it. Or, as in Giles Boutel's *Piece of Mind: An Interactive Short Story*, an ad for software might disguise an exploration of the growing dread of the future:

> Software for the future!
>
> Perhaps you feel it's time to consider your options for what lies ahead in an uncertain world. Perhaps you're just curious as to the options available to you. Whatever your reason—the best time to consider the future is now.
>
> Piece of Mind is a complete package—designed to illustrate the many and various avenues of financial opportunity which confront the modern person.

The Instructional-You

We also use *you* in how-to books and instructional pamphlets: "First, you must assemble the base of the bookcase. Then you assemble the tower." This opens up a number of possibilities for the story, from instruction manuals ("How to Commit the Perfect Murder") to self-help quizzes ("Are You a Good Lover?").

Moore's "How to Be an Other Woman" doesn't completely adhere to the instructional format promised in the title, but it instead uses the concept of the self-help book. In that story, *you* are a woman having an affair with a married man. While the story gives how-to advice ("Feel your face quiver and twice bolt out of Bergdorf's irrationally when you are sure it is her at the skirt sale rack choosing brown again, a Tylenol bottle peeking out from the corner of her purse"), it's actually about a woman realizing that she is borrowing another life because she's unable or unwilling to create her own:

> When you were six, you thought *mistress* meant to put your shoes on the wrong feet. Now you are older and know it can mean many things, but essentially it means to put your shoes on the wrong feet.
>
> You walk differently. In store windows, you don't recognize yourself; you are another woman, some crazy interior display lady in glasses stumbling frantic and preoccupied through the mannequins.

The complicity and empathy that come from the use of the instructional-you, which may be alienating at first, can gradually create deep character identification. This may be disorienting if the character is initially unsympathetic, like Moore's "other woman." But disorientation about identity is, of course, a desired result of the second-person POV.

The To-Do You

When Moore's "other woman" narrator learns that her lover's wife loves to make lists, she begins making lists of her own, lists of to-do items or regrets. Notice here that the narrator even begins to address herself in second-person:

> Clients to See:
>
> 1. Fallen in love (?). Out of control. Who is this? Who am I? And who is this wife with the skis and nostrils and Tylenol and does she have orgasms?

2. Reclaim yourself. Pieces have fluttered away.

3. Everything you do is a masochistic act. Why?

Another second-person "list" shows up in Italo Calvino's experimental novel *If on a Winter's Night a Traveler*—a list of books that all readers will understand:

Eluding these assaults, you come up beneath the towers of the fortress, where other troops are holding out:

the Books You've Been Planning To Read For Ages,

the Books You've Been Hunting For Years Without Success,

the Books Dealing With Something You're Working On At The Moment,

the Books You Want To Own So They'll Be Handy Just In Case,

the Books You Could Put Aside Maybe To Read This Summer,

the Books You Need To Go With Other Books On Your Shelves,

the Books That Fill You With Sudden, Inexplicable Curiosity, Not Easily Justified ...

These lists suggest a more extreme format: a story that uses the structure of a list, with each item made into a paragraph or a scene or a chapter.

The Disguised I

You is often a disguised way of saying *I*, especially when true self-awareness is too painful. (As mentioned earlier, the plot of *Bright Lights, Big City* could also be told in a first-person narration.) The use of *you* as a sort of ricochet adds to the sense that the narrator can't confront the inadequacy of himself.

Think about making use of the concept of *you* as a disguise, especially for *I*. If you're considering this unusual perspective, think about what disguise the *you* is wearing. In a disguised narration, *you* is really a first-person narrator distancing the events by pretending that the main character is someone else. *You* might be a way to increase reader identification with a character who might not be sympathetic. It might also be an attempt to universalize the experience, especially if it's not universal at all, to pretend that *you* and everyone else think and feel the same way.

If you write second person from any of these models—the accusation, the list, the instruction manual, the disguised first person—the reader is more likely to accept it because she does these things herself. There might be an initial jolt while she adjusts to that pronoun, but if you've captured the rhythm of this kind of discourse, it will quickly ring true.

Tense and Second Person

Most second-person POV stories are done in present or future tense, an attempt to make the *you* narration a bit more immediate and plausible to the reader. The time-specificity of past tense—the sense that this has already happened—increases the credibility of first-person POV and third-person POV by giving them the weight of settled history. But past tense will decrease the verisimilitude of second person. If, for example, you read, "In September 1999, you attended a U2 concert," you might have an instant "not a chance" reaction—because you know you didn't go to a U2 concert then. But you might not have such a strong reaction if you read, "You are attending a U2 concert," or "You will attend a U2 concert." The tense leaves the narrative just speculative enough to be acceptable.

Winter Birds by Jim Grimsley is an especially interesting example of second person because the frame is a grown man addressing his younger self, yet the narration still uses the present tense:

> You brush bits of powdered grass from your fingers. You dread going down to the river while your brothers are there, so you wait until you see them walking home on the road that divides the fields, three small figures swaggering through the dust. They handle the BB gun carelessly, trading it back and forth, each slinging the barrel over his shoulder like a hunter in some frontier television show.

The present tense of the *you* character is more plausible because it has the effect of making the reader feel like he is watching the action and experiencing it at the same time—not unlike a video role-playing game. (For anyone who doesn't have teenage kids, role-playing games [RPGs] are highly interactive games where the player creates his own character and chooses among various attributes and powers.)

Future tense also has a certain logic within second-person POV. Since the narrated events haven't yet happened, they seem more possible. Lorrie Moore experiments with this in her short story "How to Become a Writer":

> You will read somewhere that all writing has to do with one's genitals. Don't dwell on this. It will make you nervous.
>
> Your mother will come visit you. She will look at the circles under your eyes and hand you a brown book with a brown briefcase on the cover. It is entitled: "How to Become a Business Executive." She has also brought the "Names for Baby" encyclopedia you asked for; one of your characters, the aging clown-schoolteacher, needs a new name. Your mother will shake her head and say: "Francie, Francie, remember when you were going to be a child psychology major?"
>
> Say: "Mom, I like to write."
>
> She'll say: "Sure you like to write. Of course. Sure you like to write."

The experimental use of future tense spotlights the speculative nature of second-person fiction. After all, we can only speculate about what is going on in "your" head, and what's going to happen in "your" story. Future tense would go especially well, I think, with list-based stories—after all, what is a to-do list but a prediction of future action?

EXERCISE

FINDING THE YOU IN YOUR STORY

1. How could a second-person narration help your plot or characters explore an intriguing issue, such as the nature of the self?

2. What "you-oriented" frame might help organize this story?

3. Try writing a scene using *you* as the narrative pronoun. Don't cheat and use *I*—experiment here and see if you can maintain

the second-person narration. What problems did you encounter? What unexpected things happened?

READING RECOMMENDATIONS

- *Slackwire* by Dennis Schofield. This Australian novel is authored by an academic who wrote his thesis on second-person fiction. (The novel and thesis are available at http://members.westnet.com.au/emmas/2p/index2.htm.) His themes of betrayal and deception work well with the twisty nature of second person.

- *Deep in the Jungle of Doom* by R.L. Stine. This is a young-adult horror novel in the Goosebumps line, and follows the "Choose Your Own Adventure" format, making use of second-person POV's interactivity.

- *The Brain of Katherine Mansfield* by Bill Manhire. While this is set up as an adult version of a "Choose Your Own Adventure" novel, it is also an academic exploration of different forms of the "you" narration.

- *Winter Birds* by Jim Grimsley. This is a Southern Gothic, full of abusive alcoholic parents and pickup truck trysts, but made unique by the second-person narrator, a hemophiliac boy.

- *Bright Lights, Big City* by Jay McInerney. Don't bother with the film—it can't replicate the power of the second-person narration. This book shows how a trite plot can be given new meaning with an experimental narrative.

- *If on a Winter's Night a Traveler* by Italo Calvino. This is a fascinating exploration into the process of reading and writing fiction, alternating the first chapters of traditional novels with chapters in the second-person POV. The plot (which has to do with a conspiracy in the publishing world!) is developed in the second-person POV chapters.

- *Self-Help* by Lorrie Moore. Moore experiments with "instructional" second-person POV in several short stories, most notably "How to Be an Other Woman," "How to Talk to Your Mother (Notes)," and "How to Become a Writer."

- "Do You Want to Hear About It?" by Ruth Nestvold. This academic paper explores the use of second-person in hyperfiction and lists several second-person stories that make use of the interactive potential of Web-based fiction.

IMPERSONAL THIRD PERSON

6

Although third-person POV may seem like an oversimplified catch-all term for any viewpoint that isn't first person or second person, there are many possibilities for third-person narration: a narrator who is a stand-in for the author, a narrator who is a character in the book, several narrators, or no narrator at all. Therefore, there are many decisions you as the author must consider. The first distinction to make is whether the POV is *impersonal* or *personal.*

Impersonal third person means that no actual character narrates the passage. Impersonal POV forms include objective, classical omniscient, and contemporary omniscient. In the modern novel, these are seldom the only POV approach across an entire book; rather, they are used for specific purposes (like introducing the setting or situation) within a larger narrative done in a more personal POV. Comic novels, however, are often done primarily in impersonal POV because the distance adds to the ironic view and allows the reader to laugh at rather than sympathize with the characters. In third-person *personal*, on the other hand, the POV resides within a character. This chapter will cover impersonal narrators; in chapters seven and eight, I'll address the more common personal third-person narrators.

THIRD-PERSON OBJECTIVE

Objective is the most distant form of POV, the one with the least relation to characters. It's sometimes called "camera-eye POV" because it faithfully records what is seen and heard, but without any context or commentary that might suggest a human being is attached to the camera. Here's an example from *The Maltese Falcon* by Dashiell Hammett:

> She broke off with a startled hand to her mouth as the door opened.
>
> The man who had opened the door came in a step, said, "Oh, excuse me!" hastily took his brown hat from his head, and backed out.

"It's all right, Miles," Spade told him. "Come in. Miss Wonderly, this is Mr. Archer, my partner."

This camera-eye view makes readers not participants in the scene, but observers with only the information that comes from what we can see and hear. We don't know who the man opening the door is (though Spade certainly does), increasing the mystery and foreshadowing the coming murder. It is a cinematic device, replicating the feel of watching a film. This is effective in increasing suspense by keeping readers in the dark. But few books written after World War II maintain the objective POV beyond a few scenes or scene openings, as it deprives readers of the great advantage novels have over film—the ability to get inside characters.

Objective Basics

Objective POV is like no POV at all in that there's no feeling, thought, or personality in the narration. Both the pros and cons derive from the distance created. Here are some advantages:

- Objective is useful to quickly convey factual information.
- Descriptions done in objective will be considered "true" by the reader, unshadowed by the values and biases of a narrator.
- Objective adds a hard-bitten, gritty tone to adventure and detective novels.
- Because the information is so restricted, objective can show a character's actions without revealing any identifying detail.

Consider these disadvantages:

- Objective gives no interpretation of the facts presented and allows for no nuance.
- It ignores any internal reality, especially emotional reality.
- The clinical tone strips the narrative of color and depth.

Objective Purposes in Popular Fiction

Objective is counterproductive in character-oriented books as it disallows reader identification. So romances, women's fiction, coming-of-age novels, and family sagas—any story that is mostly about character journey and interaction—will feature very little of this distant POV.

However, objective is still often seen in thrillers and horror stories. It's especially useful in introducing villains, as it can show the villain doing something without revealing who he is or why he is doing it. Consider this example from *Time's Fool*, a book in The Tales of Jewelled Men series, by Patricia Veryan:

> The single candlelight threw a dim light on the window and the five men seated there. They were as so many statues; silent, waiting, all clad in a dark cloak and hood ... At last, one of them muttered irritably, "The squire is late." The man to his right shrugged. "And likely vexed." Across the table, a man drawled, "Tis all right." The smoke stirred, giving the only sign that the door had opened. A sixth man entered. Tall and clad exactly like the others, he moved soundlessly to the table.

In this instance, the POV is like that of a security camera left on all night and focused incorrectly. It records some of the action and all of the conversation but never once descends into the perspective of a character. The reader gets no details that might disclose the villain's identity—or at least no more than the author wants to reveal. The reader is not privy to any thoughts or emotions, or even the names of these men.

Objective is also useful in replicating a sociopath's POV, observing but not feeling, as in this example from *Hannibal* by Thomas Harris:

> Carlo brought a tape recorder from the house and a separate amplifier. He had a number of tapes, some of which he had made himself while cutting the ears off kidnap victims to mail to their relatives. Carlo always played the tapes for the animals while they ate. He would not need the tapes when he had an actual victim to provide the screams.

Notice that there are no descriptive words in that passage. The "straight" delivery of the events in the scene are not processed for the reader; this works not only to show the reader that Carlo operates without feeling but also to compel the reader's mind to fill in the horror that is not stated. Objective can also be useful in certain action sequences, particularly those that show a deliberate accomplishment of some task. Here's another example from *Hannibal*:

> Matteo laid out a worn pair of khaki trousers on the gurney and began to stuff them with a couple chickens and some meat and fruit. Then he took a pair of cotton gloves and filled them with ground beef and acorns, stuffing each finger carefully, and placed them at the ends of the trouser legs.

Here, the objective POV actually adds to the alienation of the activity, because we are given no reason for it, no motivation. As in the first example, if done correctly, this most distancing of the POV approaches has an inverse effect: The farther the camera pulls back from processing the action for the reader, the more the reader has to feel the dread and disgust that's left out of this description.

Still, when story and character are central, even one page entirely in objective might distance the reader too much. I recently read a book where the whole first scene was in "videocam" viewpoint—reporting only what could be heard and some actions of the participants. I felt perilously adrift. I didn't know how to evaluate anything because I didn't know whose eyes I was looking through (no one's!) or how anyone was speaking (angrily? sadly?). There was no emotion in the scene at all, no "interpretation," just the dialogue and a few actions. It was effective in a spooky way; I felt distanced, and maybe that was the point. But I didn't want to read the rest of the book because I felt like a distant observer of action I didn't quite understand.

Even though watching old detective or horror movies can be a fun way to research camera-eye perspective, remember that what works in film doesn't necessarily work on the page. Film has sound and light and color to create character and plot; fiction has only words. More than a page or two like this would drive a modern popular fiction reader nuts because the perspective is too restrictive and too uninformative. In pop fiction, readers usually want the context provided by the personal-POV scenes to know why this encounter is important. So use objective—sparingly and wisely—to convey limited information, to reveal a little but conceal a lot, to heighten tension by withholding emotion, and to highlight the dreadful and horrible by stripping it to the barest description.

Objective in Literary Fiction

The same attributes that make objective POV problematic in many story-oriented popular fiction genres can be effective in literary fiction. Because objective strips so much out of traditional narration, what's left takes on added importance, especially when the passage relates something that might seem trivial, like this breakfast scene in Cormac McCarthy's *The Crossing*: "He ate the last of the eggs and wiped the plate with the tortilla and ate the tortilla and drank the last of the coffee and wiped his mouth and looked up and thanked her."

B.R. Myers, in his famous 2001 *Atlantic Monthly* essay "A Reader's Manifesto," argues that the treatment of the trite and the majestic with the same flat prose is a negative hallmark of literary fiction. But if you consider that objective POV is meant to seem nonjudgmental and noninterpretive, that refusal to discriminate makes sense. Of course, it's only a *seeming* refusal; in fact, the author is making careful selections in all these passages.

One intriguing use of objective POV in literary fiction is the "list passage," which provides an obsessively detailed account of an event and leaves it up to the reader to figure out its meaning, as in this opening scene from Don DeLillo's *White Noise*:

> As cars slowed to a crawl and stopped, students sprang out and raced to the rear doors to begin removing the objects inside; the stereo sets, radios, personal computers; small refrigerators and table ranges; the cartons of phonograph records and cassettes; the hair dryers and styling irons; the tennis rackets, soccer balls, hockey and lacrosse sticks, bows and arrows; the controlled substances, the birth control pills and devices; the junk food still in shopping bags—onion-and-garlic chips, nacho thins, peanut creme patties, Waffelos and Kabooms, fruit chews and toffee popcorn; the Dum-Dum pops, the Mystic mints.

DeLillo's list of off-to-college supplies has the hypnotic effect of cataloging the aisles of a department store, creating a compulsive need to consume along with a horror of all these artificially flavored goods. While reading this modern list, a reader can't help but recall those lists of the names of patriarchs and heroes found in the Bible and classical literature. Those classical lists didn't require comment; perhaps DeLillo's camera-eye record of what's important to modern Americans provides its own commentary.

Objective POV, with its distance, detachment, and containment, can be used experimentally in literary narrative. It forces the reader to do the job of making meaning, while the author's job is simply to provide the material through selection and juxtaposition.

EXERCISE

OBJECTIVE POV: REVEAL AND CONCEAL

1. If you're considering using objective POV in a passage, what do you see as the purpose? Are you trying to distance the reader? Are you trying to conceal a villain's identity? Or letting a character keep a secret? What are you *hiding*?

2. What specific information or experience do you want to *reveal*? How does this relate to what you want to conceal? (For example, "I want to reveal the murderer's action but conceal his identity.") How can you accomplish both?

3. How can you best organize details without overt authorial interpretation? What details will provide the reader with the opportunity to make meaning?

4. Sketch out an objective-POV passage and read back over it. How do you need to revise to "reveal and conceal" in the right proportion? It helps to have a friend read the passage and give you the reader's perspective. You might inadvertently have slipped in too many clues about a murder, for example, or have one stray "feeling" line that detracts from the clinical tone.

THIRD-PERSON OMNISCIENT

A far more common impersonal POV is omniscient—or all-knowing—which goes beyond the simple objective facts to provide more information, such as interpretation, history, and context. There are two kinds of omniscient POV:

1. *Classical omniscient* has a narrator of sorts—a kind of authorial stand-in or godlike presence who knows everything about every character (thoughts, emotions, fears, motives). This narrator not only records the action of the scene but also provides whatever additional information or commentary he/she/it deems appropriate.

2. *Contemporary omniscient* provides the same comprehensive omniscient view of the world and the characters but without an obvious narrative persona acting as an intermediary between the reader and the story.

CLASSICAL OMNISCIENT

The classical-omniscient viewpoint traditionally features a narrator who, very much like the author, knows everything about everything in the book, including what's going to happen in the end. Until the twentieth century, most novels were written either in omniscient or first-person POV, and the omniscient novels featured a true narrative persona—some entity (not a character) who really did have an all-knowing understanding of the entire story. Classical-omniscient POV reflects an earlier age's greater discretion by placing a filter between the reader and the character. This filter, the omniscient narrator, is a constant reminder that this is a *book*, not a *real experience*.

Classical-Omniscient Basics

Most readers are familiar with classical-omniscient POV, having grown up reading Charles Dickens and Lewis Carroll. So the conventions of this sort of narration will not be new to you:

- Classical-omniscient POV can help connect large casts and several settings.
- Irony and humor are more accessible when characters are viewed from a distance.
- This POV lets you foreshadow coming events.
- Classical omniscient can serve as a bridge between character POVs.

- It can give outside "objective" commentary on the characters and a more detailed description of the setting than any one character could provide.
- It is helpful at scene introductions in setting mood and at scene exits in providing a cliffhanger to the next scene.

The disadvantages are the flip side of the coin:

- This approach can distance the reader from the characters.
- A classical-omniscient narrator can detract from the central role of the protagonist.
- It's sometimes hard to discern what any one character knows, which can be a real problem in crime novels.
- Because the author's voice usually dominates the narrative, classical omniscient can make you take the easy way out of plotting problems and lead to telling and not showing.
- Because the author's voice usually dominates, classical omniscient can eliminate the means of exploring the central characters through their individual voices.

Building Your Story in Classical Omniscient

Omniscient works best in "social" stories, which are more about the interactions of members of a group than about the personal journey of one character. You can find omniscient narration in many historical novels, fantasies, and science-fiction stories that explore a culture or milieu. It's also the POV of choice for many comic novels and is still popular in children's books because it allows the narrator to speak directly to the readers and poke fun at the characters. In some novels identified as literary fiction, yet not particularly experimental, the classical-omniscient narration emphasizes a more graceful exploration of the story theme.

In classical omniscient, the author's voice can dominate; that is, the narration doesn't have to reflect the voice of any character. Many elegant writers choose omniscient as a way to highlight their own strong prose style.

The Classical Narrator

In classical omniscient, there's a godlike persona in charge of what the reader learns. This is a definite narrative presence—not a character in the story, but a narrator who might or might not be the author's persona. Often the omniscient narrator knows more than all the characters put together, and even knows the future outcome. Here's an example from a classic British mystery, *Scales of Justice* by Ngaio Marsh:

> Alleyn liked cats. He stooped down and picked her up. She kneaded his chest and advanced her nose towards his. "Hoo, my good woman," Alleyn said, "You've been eating fish."
>
> Though he was unaware of it at the time, this was an immensely significant discovery.

Alleyn is "unaware," but the omniscient narrator is scouting ahead, warning the reader what is to come. "The fish smell is a clue!" the narrator explains portentously. You won't see this much anymore, at least in mystery fiction, because today's mystery readers are so highly trained (from reading older mysteries with helpful narrators like Marsh's) that they know without being told that the fish smell is a clue.

Omniscient narrators can also see through walls; they aren't confined to the narrow, physical perspective of the characters. In this excerpt from a newly discovered Louisa May Alcott story, *The Obsession*, the narrator can see two women in two different train compartments and knows they are both wives to the same bigamist:

> The carriage next to the one Rosamund [Tempest] selected held an equally heavy load of misery. Could she have known that the other Mrs. Tempest occupied the car directly in front of her own, it would have added a little sting to Rosamund's suffering. She was spared that knowledge, however, and thus it was that side by side, these two heavy-hearted women were borne away into the night. But not to safety.

With the benefit of the superior understanding of the narrator, the reader gets a more comprehensive experience of the story's action as a whole, unconfined by the limits of character knowledge. It's rather like taking a coach tour of Europe with the direction of an expert guide, who drives you to each church and castle, telling you all you need to know, plus perhaps a few scandals you shouldn't.

By offering comments on the characters and predictions about the future, the narrator is the author's assertion of ownership upon these people and this story. It's as if to say, "I know more about the characters than they do themselves; what's more, I am like a god in that I know the end of this story before it happens."

Anthony Trollope was an author who exploited the classical-omniscient narrator that anticipates the postmodern themes and techniques (designed to draw attention to the artificiality of the book form) of a century later. Trollope inserted himself as an arch, world-weary presence in his own novels, often, especially at the most dramatic moments, taking pains to remind the reader that he was making this all up and couldn't always be bothered to write that boring descriptive stuff. For example, here is a passage from *Barchester Towers* that every research-averse author envies:

> This narrative is supposed to commence immediately after the installa-
> tion of Dr. Proudie. I will not describe the ceremony, as I do not precise-
> ly understand its nature. I am ignorant whether a bishop be chaired
> like a member of parliament, or carried in a gilt coach like a lord mayor,
> or sworn in like a justice of the peace, or introduced like a peer to the
> upper house, or led between two brethren like a knight of the garter;
> but I do know that every thing was properly done, and that nothing fit or
> becoming to a young bishop was omitted on the occasion.

Is Trollope really the narrator here? No. He probably knew exactly how a bishop was installed. But he uses the faux-author/narrator to make a teasing interchange with the reader, hinting that he understands that the reader, too, really doesn't care about such details.

Irony and Perspective: The Purposes of Classical Omniscient

Omniscient narrators are often ironic, sometimes with a skeptical view of the characters' personalities and prospects. Jane Austen is famous for her omniscient narrative persona, which is ironic, detached, and amused by all these mere mortals. Here's an example from *Pride and Prejudice*:

> It is a truth universally acknowledged, that a single man in posses-
> sion of a good fortune must be in want of a wife. However little known

the feelings or views of such a man may be on his first entering a neighborhood, this truth is so well fixed in the minds of the surrounding families that he is considered the rightful property of some one or other of their daughters.

Austen is perhaps the most famous practitioner of the ironic omniscient narrator, used primarily in comedies of manners such as those later written by Georgette Heyer and Angela Thirkell. These books usually have several major characters pursuing difficult courses to love or success, with humorous results. This sort of narrator has a direct connection with the reader, one closer, in fact, than any of the characters have with the reader. It's almost as if the narrator and the reader are sharing a joke at the expense of the characters.

The ironic narrator allows the characters to be as earnest, eager, and foolish as necessary; the author doesn't have to fit the plot around one character knowing enough to perceive and report the foibles of the others in the story. Often, the narrator reveals an opinion that a character would not welcome, as Joseph Heller does in *Catch-22*:

> Major Major had been born too late and too mediocre. Some men are born mediocre, some men achieve mediocrity, and some men have mediocrity thrust upon them. With Major Major it had been all three. Even among men lacking all distinction he inevitably stood out as a man lacking more distinction than all the rest, and people who met him were always impressed by how unimpressive he was.

But keep in mind that the voice of an omniscient narrator doesn't have to be the author's actual voice. Your narrator can hold viewpoints and opinions that don't reflect your own personal view. Maybe you're not ironic and detached at all, but your narrative persona is. Consider this passage from *Heartbreak Hotel* by Anne Rivers Siddons:

> There had never been another birth announcement after Maggie's to come from the tall old house with the stone gateposts on Coleman Street. It was as though Maggie was stamped Sufficient at her birth, and any other child would have been extraneous, an afterthought. ... In the cities of the South—in Atlanta and Birmingham and Charlotte and Mobile and Charleston—there were perhaps a hundred Maggies

flowering in any given year, girls planted, tended, and grown like prize roses, to be cut and massed and shown at debutante balls and cotillions in their eighteenth year.

Do you sense the narrator's slightly arch tone there in the summing up of Maggie DeLoach's sufficient but conventional girlhood? Certainly, Maggie doesn't think of herself as one of a hundred identical Southern Flowers. And since the author is about to devote a whole book to her, I don't think the author sees her as quite so common. Indeed, the author is about to delineate what distinguishes Maggie from all the other Southern Flowers. So in a case like this, the narrator is not a character and not the author, either—but, instead, a complicated device that is probably meant to inspire more, not less, empathy with the central character. When Siddons makes the narrator a bit too excessively scornful, she gives the reader a chance not just to notice Maggie's faults, but to sympathize with her as human, unlike that damn narrator.

In addition to the fun you can have with tone, the godlike position of the narrator also allows for more playful and varied story possibilities by "dipping" into characters' minds as needed. After all, the narrator knows everything, even the thoughts and emotions of each character. And like a film director, the narrator can select which character to zoom in on at any given point.

To be clear, this is not "head-hopping"—the promiscuous shifting from one head to another—because the narrator controls it. Usually, the narrative will dip into one POV, come back up into the outside omniscient viewpoint, and then dip into another, so that there's no jump directly from one character to another.

Here's an example from a mystery story, "The Day of the Losers" by Dick Francis, with my comments in italics:

The four Stewards ... react[ed] with varying degrees of incredulity and uneasiness to the urgings of Chief Superintendent Crispin. ...

[*The "varying degrees" implies an omniscient narrator, because no character in the scene could be privy to each steward's thoughts.*]

Crispin held racing in as little esteem as crooked politicians and considered that catching the Birmingham mob was of far greater social importance than any horse finishing first. His inner outrage ... seeped unmistakably into his voice.

[Here, we have a dip into the mind of Chief Superintendent Crispin: We get his priorities (racing and politicians, unimportant; catching bad guys, important) and his mood (inner outrage). But notice the start of a return to the omniscient as his outrage "seeped unmistakably into his voice." While he can certainly hear his own voice, that observation can also be coming from above, from the narrator, and shows the inner-to-outer progress of the viewpoint in this paragraph.]

"The Birmingham robbers murdered nine people," he said forcefully.

Sir William Westerland listened to the arguments with his bland expression unimpaired.

[Here begins the switch to the next "head." We are in omniscient as we can "see" his expression, which Sir William himself can't see. But then comes the next line, descending into his mind.]

He had gone far in life by not declaring his views before everyone else had bared their breasts, their opinions, and their weaknesses.

[This could be omniscient or Sir William's own self-estimation, or both. But we're very much focused in his person here.]

This scene is in omniscient POV, but it allows us limited and controlled view into the perspective of the two characters. Notice that we go into a character's POV just as that character is preparing to take action. Once the character is *acting*, there's no real need to be in his head because we're going to see the action through the narration or dialogue. At that point, the perspective shifts back to omniscient so that we get a comprehensive view of the action. That's where the selection comes in—the narrator doesn't dip willy-nilly whenever, but only when a character has a unique perspective to offer. And to keep the POV shifts from being too jerky, there's a return to the omniscient narrator between each "dip" and then a gradual descent into the character's POV.

Despite the fact that contemporary readers now generally prefer a more "transparent" read—that is, we don't want to be told what to think, and we don't want to be told ahead of time what is going to happen—the classical-omniscient narrator survives, especially in books with large casts, because omniscient narration can aid in coordinating many characters in several places. Many authors use a dash of classical omniscient at the beginning or end of a scene to set the stage and the mood. Here's an example from *The Daughters of Cain,* a mystery novel by Colin Dexter:

> On Thursday, 8 September, as on the previous day, so many things were happening in close sequence it is difficult for the chronicler to decide upon the most comprehensible way in which to record events, events which were to some degree contemporaneous but which also overlapped and which in their full implications stretched both before and beyond their strict temporal occurrence.
>
> Let the account begin at Morse's flat in North Oxford.

That's almost deliberately old-fashioned, and yet it's very much in line with that postmodern insistence that "a book is just a book"—that this story isn't real, but a construct of some "chronicler" who struggles to make it comprehensible. The difference between this and the nineteenth-century Trollope excerpt is that after this passage, Dexter immediately descends into one character's POV and stays there for the rest of the scene-segment, without any more omniscient commentary. This accomplishes both the ironic gloss of the narrator and the deeper intimacy of personal POV, which is the most common use for classical omniscient now: to "pan" in on a scene at the beginning, before "zooming" into a character's POV.

Exiting in Omniscient

Omniscient can also be an efficient way to exit a scene and set up the next scene by "previewing" what is to come. This technique reverses the scene-opening process (omniscient pan to single-POV zoom), starting within a character's POV then spreading out to an omniscient view, as in this example from *Harry Potter and the Sorcerer's Stone* by J.K. Rowling:

> Harry had the best morning he'd had in a long time. He was careful to walk a little way apart from the Dursleys so that Dudley and Piers, who were starting to get bored with the animals by lunchtime, wouldn't fall back on their favorite hobby of hitting him. They ate in the zoo restaurant, and when Dudley had a

tantrum because his knickerbocker glory didn't have enough ice cream on top, Uncle Vernon bought him another one and Harry was allowed to finish the first.

    Harry felt, afterward, that he should have known it was all too good to last.

That last line segue is gracefully done—attributed to Harry, but a future Harry who knows what is going to happen next. This technique is often used in children's novels because it helps train the readers to anticipate something bad about to occur.

    This can be useful in adult fiction, too, as a way to end a scene on conflict. Scenes, especially in the middle of the book, should usually end on a moment of greater conflict. But sometimes the story must shift to a new scene (to change setting or to introduce a new important character) during a moment of lesser conflict. The omniscient exit can add tension to what might seem like a slack ending by providing a cliffhanger that hints that trouble is waiting just ahead.

Getting Creative with Omniscient

Now, after four hundred years of experimentation, omniscience has developed its own tradition and conventions, which modern writers can play with. The distance of omniscience can serve as an interactive tool by imposing the authorial persona as a not-entirely-trustworthy element that invites the reader to make choices.

    You'll still see classical omniscient a lot in children's books because the omniscient narrator helps teach children how to read fiction, how to interpret characters, and how to sense building suspense. Lemony Snicket's A Series of Unfortunate Events series uses an intrusive omniscient narrator who mixes nineteenth-century certainty with twenty-first century cynicism. The narrator is ostensibly the author, but is in fact almost another character—the author even dresses in costume as Lemony Snicket for book signings. This author-pretender starts the series by issuing a warning in *The Bad Beginning*:

> If you are interested in stories with happy endings, you would be better off reading some other book. In this book, not only is there no

happy ending, there is no happy beginning and very few happy things in the middle.

If you've ever used reverse psychology on a child, you will recognize this technique: The narrator's warning will draw in children to prove that they're tough enough. Snicket is making sophisticated use of the omniscient narrator, turning it into a tool to create a more interesting experience for the reader.

Plain old omniscient (and especially contemporary omniscient) will probably always be a dominant mode because it solves so many plot problems in stories with big casts and several settings. But as Snicket has so successfully shown, you're not bound to the old-fashioned omniscient. Think about the narrative persona as almost another character. What does this persona sound like? It might help to think about what sort of person this persona would be if it could take on human form. An older woman, ironic, obsessed with money, and secretly romantic, like the narrator of *Pride and Prejudice*? A favorite male teacher who hides a tender heart under tough techniques like the Lemony Snicket narrator?

And don't forget your audience. Omniscient, no matter what, is going to be viewed as a bit authoritarian in this individualistic age. So consider what sort of authority figure your audience would obey with pleasure. For a book aimed at preteens, a narrative voice that sounded like a cool older teenager would get a good response. For a mystery, maybe a slightly curmudgeonly but knowledgeable voice would draw in the reader.

Omniscient also gives you freedom in how you open scenes and impart information, as you don't have to filter it through any particular character. Jasper Fforde, like many comic novel writers, uses omniscient POV to maintain a detached, ironic voice and perspective. But this also allows him to insert passages from newspaper articles, biographies, and travelogues (all invented) into his narrative without having a character read them. In some books, in fact, most of his chapters begin with some excerpt, which might or might not relate to the scene to come, like this one from *The Big Over Easy*:

TITAN ESCAPES ROCK, ZEUS, CAUCASUS, EAGLE

A controversial punishment came to an end yesterday when Prometheus, immortal Titan, creator of mankind and fire-giver,

THE POWER OF POINT OF VIEW

escaped the shackles that bound him to his rock in the Caucasus. Details of the escape are uncertain, but Zeus's press secretary was quick to issue a statement declaring.... From the London Illustrated Mole, June 3, 1814

If you like the detachment and commentary of classical omniscient, and especially if you're writing a comedy, think about ways you can innovate within the POV. Your readers will be familiar with the conventions of omniscient and might appreciate creativity that plays off those conventions.

EXERCISE

CLASSICAL OMNISCIENT

1. Do you have any use for a narrative persona in this book? For example, in a comic novel, often an omniscient narrator can provide an ironic gloss to the situation and a jaundiced view of the characters.

2. If you want to go with an omniscient narrator in the classic sense, try this: Think of a film or TV star or news anchor that has just the right attitude for your narrator. Do you want your narrator to be wry and lofty like Alec Guinness? Or sharp and cutting like Joan Rivers? Or spooky and portentous like Vincent Price? Or sardonic and smart-alecky like Whoopie Goldberg? Or wise and reasonable like Walter Cronkite? Or generous and warm like Oprah Winfrey? What are the qualities you want in this narrator? Jot down two or three "markers" of this persona.

3. Now, keeping in mind that the omniscient narrator is often most effective in small doses, choose a passage, perhaps at the beginning or end of a scene, and slip in a bit of this narrator's voice and perspective. Imagine this persona surveying the scene or the characters and commenting on it. Do you want to sneak in a bit of foreshadowing ("little did they know ...") or is that too hokey for this story?

4. Classical-omniscient POV allows for, even encourages, creativity in providing a greater context, especially at the openings of scenes. Can you make use of this opportunity? (Most books will not, but if

you're interested, keep open the possibility.) For example, Jasper Fforde uses invented newspaper accounts, while Susanna Clarke, in *Jonathan Strange & Mr. Norrell*, uses footnotes referring to invented scholarly texts.

CONTEMPORARY OMNISCIENT

Generally, what you see in modern fiction is not classical omniscient, complete with attitude and persona, but a more restricted form I call *contemporary omniscient*. Contemporary omniscient is a more flexible version of omniscient that eliminates the narrative persona, though not the narrative control. How can you recognize contemporary omniscient? Consider who is in the scene. Is there knowledge, experience, description, or action that no single character in the scene can convey? If so, then you're in omniscient. Do you also have a narrative persona—not just floating knowledge, but a consistent human attitude (irony, disgust, gentle amusement) toward the events and characters? If so, you're in classical omniscient, not contemporary.

If you think of classical-omniscient narration like a film with an elegant voice-over by, say, Morgan Freeman, contemporary omniscient is more like those old movies where, in the introduction and during breaks in the action, a bit of text scrolls across the screen. (The Star Wars franchise does this at the beginning of each episode: "A long time ago, in a galaxy far, far away ...")

What contemporary omniscient lacks is Morgan Freeman—the narrative persona, that ironic, all-wise, witty voice commenting on events. What contemporary omniscient does have, however, is the comprehensive knowledge of everything in the story, including perhaps the background of the setting, the characters, and the history of the story. Yet, the whole of the knowledge presented in the narrative is greater than the sum of that possessed by all the characters. This approach allows for plenty of description and exposition of the kind that just doesn't work with a viewpoint centered on a single character ("Meanwhile, across town ...").

Contemporary-Omniscient Basics

Without the need to create a narrative persona, contemporary-omniscient POV is considerably more flexible than classical omniscient, yet it has most of the same advantages and disadvantages. Consider, first, the advantages:

- Contemporary omniscient is quite effective in books with large casts, several settings, and a comprehensive perspective.
- The contemporary-omniscient narrative can move efficiently from one character to another and one place to another, as suits the action.
- It helps make smooth transitions between several different simultaneous events ("Meanwhile, on an ocean liner in the middle of the Atlantic ...").
- You also have greater scope in presenting action and description within a scene because you are not confined to the perceptions of one or more characters.

Now, consider the disadvantages:

- Contemporary omniscient makes it easy to portray action, so it can lead to the sort of lazy plotting that has too much action taking place away from the main characters.
- Contemporary omniscient sometimes results in dry, factual narration, without the spirited voice of the classical-omniscient narrator.
- Without the overall control of a narrative persona, contemporary omniscient can become head-hopping.

Building Your Story with Contemporary-Omniscient POV

The background theme in contemporary-omniscient POV is the conflict between our need for society and our need for freedom—between community and individual. This also happens to be, I'd argue, the central theme of American fiction: the conflict between intimacy and identity. The omniscient POV gives a community perspective, but that can imply that an aggregate knowledge is better than individual understanding, leading to conformity, and hence a heightened tension for the protagonist. You don't need to force this theme into your story because it's already there if you've chosen this POV approach, especially when you combine it, as so many modern authors do, with a descent into an individual POV.

As you craft your story and scenes, consider how that overall theme connects with your own theme, and how you can use that connection to deepen your work. For example, the books in Ellis Peters's Brother Cadfael series explore the community-individual conflict in the setting of a twelfth-century monastery, a microcosm of the larger feudal society. Each book explores some aspect of "confinement"—for example, the security of monastic life compensates for the conformity forced on the monks. Brother Cadfael himself is an exploration of that conflict, as he has freely chosen a simple life after a career as a wanderer and warrior. So the stories are built around the ultimate violation of a society—the murder of someone in the community—and Cadfael's quiet assertion of his individuality by solving the mysteries.

Here is a scene from *Virgin in the Ice* that starts with Cadfael leaving the warmth and camaraderie of the monastery to pursue an individual quest. It begins in contemporary-omniscient POV with a glimpse of the community ("wise men") mind and follows Cadfael on his journey into the cold and dangerous world he is reentering. Notice how the narrative slips in Cadfael's name to show the narrowing of focus from his general to specific experience:

> Wise men stayed within their houses, clapped to shutter and door, and stopped the chinks between the boards, where thin white fingers reached through. The first snow and the first hard frost.
>
> All those four days since the first snow the weather had followed a fixed pattern .... But as Cadfael rode south the fields grew whiter, the ditches filled. The branches of trees sagged heavily towards the ground under their load, and by mid-afternoon the leaden sky was sagging no less heavily earthwards, in swags of blue-black cloud.

Peters uses many motifs of confinement to explore the attraction and resistance to community. In one book, a fugitive seeks sanctuary in the monastery. In another, a woman's body is found frozen in ice. In another, a monk is trapped in guilt, which only confession and forgiveness free him from. All these motifs are presented as an organic consequence of individuals trying to live in community and are subtly developed through the contemporary-omniscient approach. Here is a scene transition from *The Hermit of Eyton Forest*, where we move from Cadfael's POV back into contemporary omniscient, showing him rejoining the community after recovering a dead body:

> [He] made good speed from there along the road to Shrewsbury and rode in at the gatehouse after the end of High Mass, when the brothers were dispersing to their work until the hour of the midday meal. "The lord abbot has been asking after you," said the porter, coming out from his lodge.

Cadfael is active in his own POV (making good speed), but then enters the monastery and is immediately recalled into his community role by the lord abbot's command. Scene transitions like this are your opportunity to show the contrast between your individual character's POV and the view of the general society, just as Cadfael's personal excitement at a new mystery is shown as giving way to the community view (represented by Prior Robert) of murder as disruptive. Here is another example from *The Hermit of Eyton Forest*:

> [Prior Robert] looked down his nose with a marked suggestion of disapproval and withdrawal. The complexities of law and murder and manhunt had no business to intrude into the monastic domain, and he deplored the necessity of recognizing their existence and the very processes of dealing with them when they did force a breach in the wall.

Consider how you can use the transitional descent into a scene from contemporary omniscient to one character's single POV in order to show the transition from the more expansive viewpoint to a more specific experience. You might consider juxtaposing the "common wisdom" of the omniscient POV with a conflicting view from the POV character. This technique works particularly well in dramas and tragedies, where one person's action upsets the common order, and where neither the individual nor the community is all right or all wrong.

Setting the Scene

Contemporary omniscience still allows an overall narration of what is happening in the scene. Consider a scene taking place at the Battle of Waterloo. In contemporary omniscient, you quickly establish the date and place, pan the entire battleground, give a bird's-eye view of the movement of both armies, and compare the demeanors of the two commanders. You can even refer to it as the Battle of Waterloo, though it wasn't called that till the carnage was over. You can narrate it from above, showing everything that is happening in a way that even the commanders high above the fighting couldn't see, unless they had access to the Goodyear Blimp. You can "listen in" on simultaneous conversations down among the troops as well as up on the hill with the general, then fly across the battlefield to consult with Napoleon. You can even parenthetically define any terms that modern readers might not recognize.

Contemporary-omniscient POV allows this sort of comprehensive knowledge conveyance, though at the potential cost, it must be said, of character intimacy. All those young recruits at Waterloo are a single undifferentiated glory-seeking unit, and we learn very little about the great leader's inner thoughts. Omniscience can also be efficient in the beginning of a scene, as a "pan shot," a big overview perspective to describe the setting, for example, in a way that none of the characters would do, as in this passage from David Guterson's *Snow Falling on Cedars*:

> Amity Harbor, the island's only town, provided deep moorage for a fleet of purse seiners and one-man gill-netting boats. It was an eccentric, rainy, windbeaten sea-village, downtrodden and mildewed, the boards of the buildings bleached and weathered, their drainpipes rusted a dull orange.

This description comes not from any character, nor from an all-seeing god, but, rather, from the air, as a friendly background briefing, so to speak. This is often a good way to start a scene: establish a sense of the setting and introduce the characters before descending into a particular viewpoint. If your story has a particularly intriguing setting, you might start the first scene with a contemporary-omniscient description of the world. This is especially useful if the main POV character is quite familiar with the setting. It's hard to plausibly describe a setting through the POV of a character who knows it so well she doesn't even notice it anymore.

But omniscient doesn't mean dull. Descriptions from "above" shouldn't be just a list of geographical details. Rather, like Guterson's description of the "eccentric sea-village," such an opening should tell readers what's remarkable about the setting. Without the need to filter the description through the narrow perspective of a character, you can select details vivid enough so readers can imagine themselves there and draw conclusions that the characters wouldn't make.

Examining Character

To my mind, the greatest benefit of the contemporary-omniscient perspective isn't the room for author intrusion, but the ability to stand both outside and inside any character. This is especially important in popular fiction, where readers like to identify with the main characters and understand their motivations and conflicts.

With characterization, contemporary omniscient presents many of the same benefits and problems as classical omniscient. Without an actual omniscient narrator, however, the distancing of reader from character will be less acute. Think of the traditional omniscient narrator as a colored filter that changes your view of the people and events. Contemporary omniscient is more like a glass window; the distortion is minimal, but you are still separated from the characters.

And, again, with omniscience comes flexibility. Many modern authors use contemporary omniscient at the beginning of a scene to set the stage and give some background, then zoom into one character's POV. Here's a skillful example from *Harry Potter and the Sorcerer's Stone* by J.K. Rowling:

> Perhaps it had something to do with living in a dark cupboard, but Harry had always been small and skinny for his age. He looked even smaller and skinnier than he really was because all he had to wear were old clothes of Dudley's, and Dudley was about four times bigger than he was. Harry had a thin face, knobby knees, black hair, and bright green eyes. He wore round glasses held together with a lot of Scotch tape because of all the times Dudley had punched him on the nose. The only thing Harry liked about his own appearance was a very thin scar

on his forehead that was shaped like a bolt of lightning. He had had it as long as he could remember, and the first question he could ever remember asking his Aunt Petunia was how he had gotten it.

Here, an outside, omniscient view of Harry's appearance zooms into his own perception of what he likes about himself. Notice the change to the narrower personal perspective at the end of the paragraph: We know then only what Harry knows, and that doesn't include the truth about how he had gotten the scar.

Contemporary omniscient allows for not only physical observation but also psychoanalysis of a character, especially near the beginning of a scene. Here's an example from *Atonement* by Ian McEwan:

> She was one of those children possessed by a desire to have the world just so. Whereas her big sister's room was a stew of unclosed books, unfolded clothes, unmade bed, unemptied ashtrays, Briony's was a shrine to her controlling demon: the model farm spread across a deep window ledge consisted of the usual animals, but all facing one way—toward their owner—as if about to break into song, and even the farmyard hens were neatly corralled.

One of the decisions you must make as the author is whether you want the reader to know more about the characters than they know about themselves (for example, that Briony's "controlling demon" is her need to make order). Do you *need* to reveal this information that the character herself doesn't know? Do you *want* to? There's no right or wrong answer to these questions, but it's something to consider before you start inserting omniscient information about your characters. What is appropriate in a novel about a family interaction, say, might not be appropriate in a book tightly focused on the psychological growth or deterioration of the protagonist (in that case, the reader should probably arrive at the analysis herself, without being told ahead of time). Telling too much in omniscient POV might very well interfere with the reader's sense of suspense if your characters have secrets to reveal later or mysteries to solve. So don't assume the reader needs to know every detail of the backstory. Remember that you should show rather than tell the characters' personality quirks.

That said, contemporary omniscient can be an effective way around the awkwardness of having characters' mentally describe themselves (anything is better than the "she looked in the mirror at her lustrous blonde curls" technique), especially if you want to contrast reality with perception, as in Margaret Mitchell's famous opening to *Gone with the Wind*:

> Scarlett O'Hara was not beautiful, but men seldom realized it when caught by her charm as the Tarleton twins were. In her face were too sharply blended the delicate features of her mother, a Coast aristocrat of French descent, and the heavy ones of her florid Irish father. But it was an arresting face, pointed of chin, square of jaw.

No one in the scene could have the objectivity to characterize Scarlett as "not beautiful." Certainly Scarlett thought she was as fine as she could be, and the Tarleton twins agreed. That assessment is available only in this sort of omniscient opening. But notice how impersonal the assessment is. There's none of the attitude or irony of a Trollope or Austen narrator. This is the "just the facts, ma'am" approach of contemporary omniscient—cool, detached, and uninvolved.

Contemporary omniscient also provides an efficient way to compare and contrast a group of characters within a situation, without having to filter it through one person's POV, as Susan Elizabeth Phillips does here in *Hot Shot*:

> Despite the differences of age and sex, there was a sameness about the guests who sat in the carefully laid-out rows of lacy white wrought-iron chairs. They all looked prosperous and conservative, very much like people accustomed to giving orders instead of taking them—all except the beautiful young woman who sat toward the back. In a sea of Halston and Saint Laurent, Paige Faulconer, the bride's younger sister, was conspicuous in a maroon thrift-store dress from the thirties draped at the shoulders with a funky pink marabou boa.

Notice that both Mitchell's and Phillips's passages show the major character from an outside perspective, defining her in a few quick lines—in terms of how those around her define her and as something more than that.

Now think of expanding that omniscient awareness of the "consensus" opinion of the major character to include some actual specifics. This is a way to unobtrusively reveal the thoughts and feelings of secondary characters and groups without losing focus on the major characters. Contemporary omniscient can also give a sense of a collective mentality. Faulkner uses this technique in his story "A Rose for Emily," which I've mentioned is presented from the perspective of a small town. The collective is also evident in the opening of Guterson's *Snow Falling on Cedars*:

> The accused man, Kabuo Miyamoto, sat proudly upright with a rigid grace, his palms placed softly on the defendant's table—the posture of a man who has detached himself insofar as this is possible at his own trial. Some in the gallery would later say that his stillness suggested a disdain for the proceedings; others felt certain it veiled a fear of the verdict that was to come. Whichever it was, Kabuo showed nothing, not even a flicker of the eyes.

This is clearly not from the viewpoint of the accused man; the Japanese-American fisherman would not use a term like "insofar as" and would know what he felt, not have to speculate; furthermore, he would not be able to see himself "showing nothing." It's an outside, retrospective perspective, one capable of "polling" the witnesses to the scene after the event. It reflects not the opinion of a single person but the collective understanding that comes from cultural observation.

You might use this collective mentality when a major character is at odds with the wider society. The contemporary omniscient at the beginning or the end of the scene, shifting to or from the character's deeper POV, is a subtle way to let the reader experience the conflict between community and individual. Try this technique if you have a major character you think might come across as unsympathetic.

Just as in classical omniscient, you can start a scene in this viewpoint and narrow to a single character's perspective. Starting in contemporary omniscient doesn't mean you have to stay there. But don't get too flexible or the reader will lose that subconscious understanding of how to experience the book through the characters. Contemporary omniscient works best at the beginning and end of scenes, and perhaps in transitions from one character's viewpoint to another ("Meanwhile, across town, Johnny was even less informed on the details of the arrest.").

In fact, a book that remains resolutely in the omniscient perspective is likely to alienate many modern readers who are used to a tighter focus on major characters. If you decide to use contemporary omniscient, try to keep it limited to providing necessary outside information and perspective, and then descending into a character to narrate most of the actual action. (See "Smooth Shifting," beginning on page 204, for how to gracefully make this descent.)

Contemporary omniscient is often confused with multiple POV. But with contemporary omniscient, you are not confined to the perceptions of the characters. You can give an outside perspective and additional information, and that can ease the transition between characters' POVs.

Nowadays, omniscient is more likely to be a transitional tool, useful for setting up a scene or situation, providing exposition quickly and efficiently, showing a collective or crowd perspective, and making a transition between characters' POVs. So if you choose to use omniscient, you might still want to explore how single and multiple POV work (covered in chapters seven and eight), as omniscient is more often just a frame for those other approaches.

Imparting Information

The most common purpose of contemporary omniscient is to convey necessary information in a manner that reads effortlessly. While this is often done at the beginning of the scene, you might also find a need to insert information into the action. It might be awkward (and therefore implausible) that a first-person priestly protagonist would stop in the middle of a bus ride to explain how an obscure Vatican committee works; however, it is less cumbersome and more realistic simply to interrupt the narrative and insert a quick history lesson from some impersonal omniscient perspective.

Here's an example of such a passage from *The Genesis Code*, a thriller by John Case, with my comments in italics:

> Azetti's destination was a city-state nestled in the heart of Rome: the Vatican.
>> This isn't going to be easy, he thought, not easy at all.
>> [*Here, we're in Azetti's head, because we're "hearing" his thoughts.*

Now comes the transition from the personal POV to the impersonal. The author leaves Azetti as he's entering the Vatican City and breaks off to explain his specific destination. Now there's a line break—several blank lines alerting the reader to some change in scene or perspective.]

Like any independent state, the Vatican's affairs are managed by a bureaucracy—in this case, the Curia, whose mission is to guide the immense entity that is still known as the Holy Roman Empire.

[Notice the sudden impersonal tone and the present tense. Generally, narrative in fiction is presented in the literary past tense ("Azetti's destination WAS ..."), so any departure from that practice indicates some change. Here, it means that this information is true even outside the world of the book. Keep in mind that this is likely to remind the reader that the story's events (those in past tense) aren't true, as opposed to the "real" information in present tense; therefore, use this impersonal tone judiciously. It can cause the reader to give up the suspension of disbelief so important to enjoying most fiction. But in this story about "events ripped from the headlines," it has the intriguing effect of a CNN-like news background analysis, and as a result, might actually add to the verisimilitude of the story.]

.... In extraordinary cases, a part of the [CDF] congregation may be appointed to perform exorcisms, grapple with Satan, or take action in the case of attacks upon the faith.

[Still in present tense, still impersonal and authoritative in tone. Note that there is no attitude, no persona here; this is "just the facts" reporting with no personality attached, truly objective.]

It was in connection with these last responsibilities that Father Azetti had traveled to Rome.

[Here is the transition back into Azetti. Notice the link to the information just presented ("these last responsibilities" = "perform exorcisms, etc.") and the "exit" from the impersonal present tense to the personal past tense ("Azetti HAD traveled"). We are clearly back in Azetti, on his way to visit the CDF congregation offices. The author follows this transition with another line break and then picks up the narrative deep in Azetti's POV.]

When would you use this sort of omniscient exposition? It's best when the information has to be conveyed and the POV character wouldn't think or know it. But you have to make very clear that you're shifting into objective POV, or the reader might think, *Hey, wait a minute. If this is a time-traveler from the eighteenth century, there's no way she'd know that Neil Armstrong was the first person on the moon!*

But omniscient interruptions should be reserved for specific purposes. When you see long stretches of it without POV, it's usually because the author hasn't gotten to know the character enough to individualize the perspective. Here's a hypothetical example:

> John picked up his mitt and exited the dugout. As he passed first base, he looked up into the stands. There was the neighbor he'd had an affair with last year; she was sitting holding hands with her husband. Her belly was swelling with pregnancy under the jersey blouse. John crossed the infield and stepped up on the mound.
>
> His best pitch was the knuckleball, a particularly dangerous weapon that fooled batters but required a specially trained catcher. To make a knuckleball, a pitcher had to grip the ball at the seams...

Now, there's nothing inherently wrong with a mini-lecture on knuckleballs, but notice that the objectivity extends to John's former lover's expectant state and makes John seem almost pathological in his lack of response. The reader won't know if it's important or not that she's pregnant.

But because this sort of POV interruption can be disorienting and distancing, think the decision through before you drop in little impersonal bits of information. First, decide if you really need this information. I find there's a tendency to add in little expository lectures whenever I've done a lot of research. Once, in the middle of a scene in the heroine's POV, I dropped in a few paragraphs about how her home state of West Virginia broke off from Virginia over the issue of slavery. Why? Not because the reader needed that information to understand the scene, but because I'd recently visited the West Virginia capitol building and read a historical plaque about the secession. It was fascinating to me, but it clunked so much when I read it over, I knew it wasn't meant to be in the scene. So I filed the information, figuring I'd use it if I ever got a chance to write for *Jeopardy.*

If you decide the reader needs this information, does she need it right here, right now? Is there some other way of conveying this information? Can you filter it through one of the character's perspectives? I'd suggest this especially when the information is of importance to the character. A little mini-lecture on the process of getting political refugees asylum might work when the protagonist is an attorney working for a refugee organization and it's part of the job. But if your character is actually a refugee seeking asylum, her personal journey through the red tape would be more enlightening.

EXERCISE

CONTEMPORARY OMNISCIENT

1. How can a contemporary-omniscient POV help make your story work better for the reader? For example, a contemporary-omniscient narration can help link a large cast and several settings or provide a more detached view of the main characters. What would a contemporary-omniscient POV do for your story? With either kind of omniscient POV, you can still "descend into" a character at some point. Do you see one particular character whose POV will be central (like Brother Cadfael's in the Ellis Peters's mysteries), or several (like the townspeople in Stephen King's *Salem's Lot*)?

2. Think about what knowledge, unknown to the characters, you'd like to present to the reader—perhaps background about the setting or the family at the center of the story. Where would it be best to slip that in?

3. Now consider the ramifications of having the reader know more than the characters. If it's just background information, it might not make much difference how the reader learns it. But if it's something to do with a character's past or future, personality or relationships, consider letting the reader experience this through the character—learning, for example, the big secret of the character's family simultaneously with the character.

READING RECOMMENDATIONS

Objective POV

- *The Silence of the Lambs* by Thomas Harris. In some passages, Harris effectively uses a distant objective POV to convey the horror of the sociopath's crime scenes. This book provides good examples of how distancing can actually increase the reader's emotional reaction.

- *Accordion Crimes* by Annie Proulx. This novel has a literal "objective" focus, using the object of an accordion to unite sequential generations of American immigrants.

- *The Orchard Keeper* by Cormac McCarthy. McCarthy sometimes reads like the love child of Hemingway and Faulkner, his prose being alternately childishly terse and romantically florid. The objective POV comes through most in the terse passages.

- The Kay Scarpetta series by Patricia Cornwell. These forensic procedurals use objective POV to describe the pathologist protagonist's horrific autopsies.

- *Salem's Lot* by Stephen King. This book opens with a scene set in the future (that is, after most of the events of the book), showing the main characters from an objective perspective and posing a question ("What happened to them?") that the story will answer. Deftly done.

Omniscient POV

- *Master and Commander* by Patrick O'Brian. This first book in a brilliant adventure series uses contemporary omniscient to explore a young man's course toward leadership and another man's journey from alienation to community.

- *Atonement* by Ian McEwan. This novel set in World War II England proves that a skilled author can create in-depth characterization inside an omniscient narration.

- *The Windflower* by Laura London. This ultimate pirate romance uses contemporary-omniscient POV to control its large and boisterous cast.

- The Brother Cadfael series by Ellis Peters. These mysteries use a contemporary-omniscient narration to explore an unfamiliar world: a twelfth-century monastery.

- The Lymond Chronicles series by Dorothy Dunnett. The alternately distant and intimate narration of this six-book historical series keeps the hero intriguing and mysterious.

- *Psychlone* by Greg Bear. Contemporary-omniscient narration mingles with sharp dialogue in this near-future science-fiction story.

You might find yourself using the various forms of impersonal POV occasionally in your book, but I'll bet most of your narration is going to be told from a more personal perspective. That is, the characters, not some outside narrator, will be "telling" the story's events through their own unique perspectives. Most modern novels use either a single or a multiple third-person approach.

What's the difference between the two? Well, it's a matter of numbers. If your approach is to use only one character at a time as the narrator of the events of a scene, then you're using third-person single (also called "single-third," or just "single") POV. If you use two or more characters to narrate a scene's events, then you're using third-person multiple (also called "multiple-third," or just "multiple") POV. (Remember that we're still talking third person here, so the POV characters are "he" or "she," not "I.")

Single-third POV doesn't mean you're only allowed to use one character's POV throughout the entire book (though there are many books, especially those focused tightly on one character, that use one third-person POV exclusively). More often than not, however, POV is calibrated by scene. So when using single-third POV, you choose to use only one perspective in each scene, so a whole event-sequence is presented through one character. (You might have two or three POV characters in the book, but only one at a time "tells" the story.) In multiple-third POV, you might have more than one character narrating within a scene, so the event, or part of the event, is presented through more than one perspective.

Some writers jokingly refer to those dedicated to single-third as "purists" and those dedicated to multiple-third as "sluts," but both are acceptable if done well. Many editors prefer the single-third POV approach because it's so easily controlled, and it allows writers to develop their characters more deeply. Multiple-third seems deceptively easier to write because there are so many more choices available, both with the story as a whole and within each scene. But in some ways, the ubiquity of choices makes it harder to do well because you have to make the right choices at each point in the story. This doesn't mean single-third is always the best choice; if you use multiple-third, you have to do it so skillfully that all an editor notices is that the reading experience you're providing is exactly the right one for the story.

I've concluded that there are writers who are instinctual singles, and others who are instinctual multiples, and whichever approach feels natural is the one they find easiest to take. That doesn't mean that you shouldn't experiment and evaluate each choice, or that you can't grow beyond your natural inclination. However, it might be easier to learn to maximize whichever is most natural to you.

For those of you who are just beginning your POV education, I recommend starting with single-third POV as the default approach, sticking with one character's viewpoint until there's some reason to shift to another's. That way, you'll be forced to evaluate every time you shift. Soon you only shift when shifting has a purpose, and this is where POV control starts: knowing when one character's POV is needed, how to set up that change, and how to present it in the most effective way.

DELVING INTO SINGLE POV

Single POV puts one character's experience front and center in the scene, exploring an entire event only through that deep perspective. Often, the entire book can be done through the perspective of a single character (what I call third-person exclusive), but more commonly, each scene will be done through the POV of one character, sometimes shifting the next scene into the POV of another character, when appropriate. The reader doesn't leave the head and body of the POV character for the duration of the scene and, thus, gets to know that person's thoughts and feelings very well. The character's values, biases, emotions, background, and knowledge control how the events are narrated; so, for example, the narrative of a veteran baseball pitcher facing his former team will incorporate his knowledge of his former team's strengths and weaknesses, his resentment about being traded, his need to get revenge, and so on. It's his scene, and though it's in third person ("he"), his voice and perspective create the narration.

Think of tightly focused films that follow one character through an adventure and show only what he experiences. (Hitchcock did this in many of his greatest movies.) This limits the POV to one per scene, almost always that of a major character. The reader experiences only what the POV character experiences, but if you do it cleverly, you can leave room for the reader to interpret the events differently from the way the character does.

This POV approach decreases the distance between the reader and the character and, as a result, makes the reader more of a participant (identifying with the character) than an observer of all the characters. No matter what your eventual POV choice is, this one is worth mastering because it will train you to use POV to reveal the depth of characterization.

Single-third is also much more flexible than you'd think. Variations include starting a scene with an omniscient "pan shot" and narrowing to a single viewpoint after the stage is set; "entering" a scene on one viewpoint, then shifting halfway through to the other for the "exit"; and deep immersion, where you are so far into the POV character, the narration is done in that person's voice. Well-done multiple POV can be kind of a variation of single POV in that the writer goes deep into a character long enough to establish his perspective, prejudices, and values before switching to another character.

Single-Third Basics

The biggest advantage of single POV is that readers get a totality of experience in one character's POV—an entire event, from beginning to end. That accomplishes several objectives:

- The reader gets a coherent experience because it's filtered through only one perspective. For example, say a scene is taking place in a ballroom where one spy is going to surreptitiously transfer a purse full of money to an informant and get a vial of some vital ore in return. It will be much easier for the reader to keep track of the spy's movement through the swirling dancers, across the crowded ballroom, and into the antechamber if the POV never leaves the spy. The reader can participate intensely in the spy's nervousness and temptation just to keep walking out of the ballroom with the cash.

- It's also much easier for the reader and writer to keep track of "information control," or who knows what, when. This is very important in a mystery, where a villain might know he went to Princeton, but the sleuth should not know it until she learns it herself.

- You, as the author, can better develop a unique view of each event because you'll need to explore only one person's perspective. Once you establish that the spy is nervous, pessimistic, and primarily visual, you can concentrate on presenting the scene that way without worrying about how the calm, optimistic, and tactile informant would narrate.

- The reader can learn much more about the POV character through her thoughts, actions, and perceptions because there are no distracting viewpoints. Then, the next time the character is faced with a situation, the reader will be better able to anticipate her response, increasing both identification and participation. (Remember, the more the reader interacts with the story, the better.) For example, in the ballroom scene, once the reader has learned that the spy has come to hate her dangerous job and is tempted by thoughts of escape, she will tense up in a future scene when the spy is given a bag of diamonds to trade them for secret documents. How long, the reader wonders, can the spy resist temptation?

But single POV has disadvantages, too—the obverse of its advantages:

- The reader's confinement to one perspective means she's not getting a comprehensive view of the event. If you're in the ballroom with the spy, you can't simultaneously show the rival spy secretly watching her through a telescope, or get into the head of the informant to learn he has replaced the precious ore with talcum powder.

- Whatever biases, blindness, and mind-set the POV character possesses will distort the narration of the event, so it won't be immediately visible what the absolute truth is. If the spy is in love with the informant and trusts him implicitly, she won't be seeing him clearly and might not correctly interpret why he has talcum powder all over his tuxedo.

- While the reader is getting to know this one character, the others in the scene will remain somewhat unknown and less available for reader identification. This is especially a problem if the POV character isn't very interesting.

But there are always trade-offs, and the writer's purpose determines which choices will be most effective. Single POV is a good approach with protagonist-centered books when you want to increase reader identification. It's also a good approach for stories where characters are keeping secrets, because it's much easier to control who knows what with a tighter POV focus.

BUILDING YOUR STORY IN SINGLE POV

There's no doubt that single-third is limiting (and sometimes stressful to write), but you can use those limitations to your advantage to create the most intense reader experience by focusing the attention completely on one person's perspective. Third-person exclusive POV is very much like first-person POV in this way.

For example, if you want to chronicle a man's descent into madness, a protagonist-only POV will confuse what's real and what's hallucination. (If, however, you want to contrast sanity and madness, then you might want to add his therapist's POV to provide the reality check. Notice how your POV approach will vary depending on how expansive the story is.) You'll often see the third-person exclusive POV in books where the central character is experiencing some trauma: suspense novels where the protagonist is in great danger, psychological dramas where she uncovers some subconscious secret, or coming-of-age novels where she goes through some major life-change.

If you're doing this, think of the limited perspective as liberation. Without the distraction of another POV, you can put the reader squarely and entirely in the protagonist's perspective. The rewards might be surprising. Here, for example, is John Updike fulfilling many writers' secret fantasy—while on the subway platform, his protagonist Bech, from *Bech at Bay*, recognizes the critic who gave him a bad review: .

> Bech was three bodies back in the crush, tightly immersed in the odors, clothes, accents, breaths, and balked wills of others. Two broad-backed bodies, padded with junk food and fermented malt, intervened between himself and Featherwaite, while others importunately pushed at his own back. As if suddenly shoved from behind, he lowered his shoulder and rammed into the body ahead of his; like dominoes, it and the next tipped the third, the stiff-backed Englishman, off the platform. In the next moment the train with the force of a flash flood poured into the station, drowning all other noise under a shrieking gush of tortured metal. Featherwaite's hand in the last second of his life had shot up and his head jerked back as if in sudden recognition of an old acquaintance. Then he had vanished.

Featherwaite, the victim of this not-so-random act of violence, might have an interesting perspective, too. But adding that would just detract from Bech's version of the murder, which included premeditation, his coolness, and his vivid details. We would not have the unsettling experience of being up close and personal with a murderer—being *one* with a murderer—if we had to also be the victim.

As in life, you can't do it all or have it all, so the questions you as an author must always ask are: What do you most want the reader to experience, and how can you make that happen? Indeed, once you give up the notion that you can accomplish everything in a novel, you find that you'll achieve a good deal of it through the POV approach you choose. As long as you keep in mind who the reader's vehicle is through the scene, and make that experience as intense and intriguing as possible, no one will mind the lack of other perspectives.

This approach requires more focus initially, while you get to know the protagonist, but once you fit into his clothes, writing from his POV will become second nature to you, and you'll find a way to work around any limitation.

The Dilemma of Dual Protagonists

Some types of books have more than one central character—for instance, a romance with a hero and heroine; a suspense thriller with a detective and a villain; or a women's fiction book about three sisters. These types of novels probably shouldn't be done in third-person exclusive (one POV for the whole story) but are the perfect candidates for single-third, as it will let you provide a deep insight into each major character for one or more scenes.

Many romances, for example, use the hero's POV for some scenes and the heroine's POV for others, the proportion varying usually by who is truly the main protagonist. (I define the "main protagonist" as the one who has the longest or most complex journey in the plot.) Thrillers might have most scenes in the protagonist's POV, with a few scenes revealing the villain's twisted thought processes. This POV approach is one of the most common in modern fiction. It provides a tight focus on one character's experience of an event, while allowing some flexibility in showing other events from other POVs.

Obviously, even this flexible approach creates limitations. But writers need to start thinking of limitations as liberations, in some sense. That is, by limiting the number of minds you explore, you liberate yourself from having to explore too many minds. You can do a better job with POV when you focus on only one or two characters deeply enough to express their perceptions, thoughts, and feelings.

In this approach, you don't switch back and forth between the two main characters within a scene. You choose one to narrate the scene, and then stick with it. In a story primarily about a relationship (hero-heroine, detective-villain), we learn much from how one character views the other and interprets the other's actions, creating a doubling effect. Here's an example from *Dangerous Deceptions* by Lynn Kerstan:

> [Kate] turned, graceful as the dancer she was, in a gentle circle. Her hair, sleeked back from her face, was caught in a thick braid that fell to just below her waist. When she came around again to face the audience, her chin went up the barest notch. *Here I am*, she appeared to be saying. *What am I worth to you?*
>
> More than I will ever have, Jarrett thought with a shot of regret.

This excerpt gives the reader an understanding of one character's perception of what's happening and allows for all sorts of playful stuff: You can tell when the POV character is misinterpreting reality, what his prejudices are, and how his mind works. For example, though Jarrett never mentions his poverty, we see that it bothers him that he can't afford a lady like Kate. We also know that he is visual, interpreting her personality through the expression on her face.

But notice that you can also create suspense by withholding the other character's thoughts from the reader. By avoiding Kate's POV above, the author prompts questions such as, "What is Kate really thinking? Does she notice him as he notices her?" The reader will experience, along with Jarrett, that bit of anticipation that comes from knowing something is going to happen, but not what, when, or how. Anytime you guide the reader to ask questions, you increase the reader's identification with the character, and, thus, the interactivity between the two of them.

Whom to Choose?

As mentioned in previous sections, if you have more than one POV character in the book, you'll have to decide who will narrate each scene. Again, your choice of narrator will depend a lot on what your purpose is. If you want to give the reader the most thrilling experience, you might choose the character who is in danger in that scene. For the most emotional experience, you might choose the character who is going to suffer the most intense emotion. If you're like me and you like to surprise the reader, you might choose the character who has a secret (especially if the reader doesn't know the secret) or, conversely, the character who doesn't know there's a secret (especially if the reader does know).

Here are some possible reasons to go with one or another viewpoint. Choose which of these seems to provide the most illuminating perspective. This will differ given your unique circumstances, so you have a lot of flexibility in choosing what you want to emphasize:

1. *Who has the goal in the scene?* The character with the goal usually drives the action of the scene. He's the one who decides what he wants and takes steps to get it. John, the POV character in *Desolation Angel* by Robert Crais, really wants to make the FBI Top Ten Most Wanted list by setting off a bomb:

John settled back again, stretched his arms along the backrest to enjoy the sun and the sounds of the children playing. It was a beautiful day, and would grow even more beautiful when a second sun had risen.

After awhile, he got up and walked away to check the Most Wanted List. Last week he wasn't on it.

This week he hoped to be.

No one else has as much stake in this scene as John, and no one else knows he's planted a bomb but him. This makes his goal in the above scene the most important. Remember, we don't have to approve of the goal in order for it to be important to the story.

2. *Who is present during the action?* It's usually better to go with the eyewitness than the one who just hears about it later (the sports reporter at the baseball game rather than the anchorman back in the studio). In this excerpt from *New England White* by Stephen Carter, Julia, a college dean, and her husband are driving when he hits something in the road:

> About to climb into the warmth of the car, she spotted by moonlight a ragged bundle in the ditch a few yards away. She took half a step toward it, and a pair of feral creatures with glowing eyes jerked furry heads up from their meal and scurried into the trees. A deer, she decided, the dark mound mostly covered with snow, probably struck by a car and thrown into the ditch, transformed into dinner for whatever animals refused to hibernate. Shivering, she buttoned her coat, then turned back toward the Escalade. She did not need a close look at some bloodstained animal with the most succulent pieces missing. Only once she had her hand on the door handle did she stop.
>
> Deer, she reminded herself, rarely wear shoes.

In this case, Julia is not the one driving but, rather, the one who discovers the disaster. Her POV provides the surprise in the scene and is individualized by her unique way of perceiving; she notices the shoes and realizes, along with the reader, what that means.

3. *Who has the most at stake externally?* This is the character who is in the greatest external danger in the scene. Usually, the danger is physical, and the POV character's life, health, or freedom is at risk. This heightens

the tension of the scene, and the reader's identification with the character. Here, Tom Ripley, from Patricia Highsmith's *The Talented Mr. Ripley*, is on the run, afraid that he will go to jail if he gets caught:

> Tom glanced behind him and saw a man coming out of the green cage, heading his way. There was no doubt the man was after him. Tom had noticed him five minutes ago, eying him carefully from a table, as if he weren't *quite* sure, but almost. He had looked sure enough for Tom to down his drink in a hurry, pay, and get out.

4. *Who has the most at stake internally?* For the most emotionally wrenching experience, you might go into the POV of the character whose internal risk is the greatest. In *The Secret Diaries of Miss Miranda Cheever* by Julia Quinn, a young husband buries his unfaithful wife, trying his hardest to hate her, yet knowing that hating her will destroy what remains of his innocence:

> Then there was the loss of his innocence. It was difficult to recall now, but he had once given mankind the benefit of the doubt. He had, on the whole, believed the best of people—that if he treated others with honor and respect, they would do the same unto him.
> And then there was the loss of his soul.
> Because as he stepped back, clasping his hands stiffly behind him as he listened to the priest commit Leticia's body to the ground, he could not escape the fact that he had wished for this. He had wanted to be rid of her.
> And he would not—he *did* not mourn her.

The young man's life is not at stake here, but his psyche might be. Through his POV, the reader can feel not only the grief that any funeral-goer might experience, but the very specific conflict of a man who sees no good options: if he mourns, he risks his heart; if he doesn't mourn, he risks his soul.

5. *Who has the most intriguing perspective, or who will narrate the event in the most entertaining way?* This might be the fish-out-of-water perspective, such as in the case of *The Amazing Adventures of Kavalier and Clay* by Michael Chabon, which features a Brooklyn boy with a great imagination:

> Sammy ... dreamed with fierce contrivance, transmuting himself into a major American novelist, or a famous smart person, like Clifton Fadiman, or perhaps into a heroic doctor; or developing, through practice and sheer force of will, the mental powers that would give him a preternatural control over the hearts and minds of men. In his desk drawer lay—and had lain for some time—the first eleven pages of a massive autobiographical novel to be entitled either (in the Perelmanian mode) *Through Abe Glass, Darkly* or (in the Dreiserian) *American Disillusionment* (a subject of which he was still by and large ignorant). He had devoted an embarrassing number of hours of mute concentration—brow furrowed, breath held—to the development of his brain's latent powers of telepathy and mind control.

Sammy has a particularly intriguing perspective: both innocent and extravagant. This lets the reader anticipate that future scenes in his POV will be narrated with similar imagination.

6. *Who's got a secret, and do you want the reader to know?* Sometimes you just want the reader to know there is a secret, not necessarily what it is. In *Mallory's Oracle* by Carol O'Connell, we don't know why this pawnbroker is afraid of the young man pawning the watch, and don't learn until later that the watch was stolen during a murder. Without betraying the secret, the pawnbroker's POV is taut—notice the words *fear, pain,* and *bleed*—and creates the feeling of violence without violent action:

> Safely locked behind wire and glass, the old man in the cage only feared the pain in his mind might bleed from his eyes, and so he kept them cast down as he examined again what the boy had brought him.

A scene with a POV character withholding a secret can build suspense, leading the reader to guess what's being hidden. Whenever you get the reader guessing, you increase the interactivity of the scene and her investment in the story.

7. *Who is not revealing his true personality through dialogue and action?* Honest, open, up-front, what-you-see-is-what-you-get types of people generally don't make great POV characters because we don't need to be in their heads. They'll blurt out anything on their minds. It's characters

who think subversively, smile when they're angry, and create that disconnect between internal and external who add an extra dimension to POV. Here's an example from *Cold as Ice* by Anne Stuart:

> [Van Dorn] was clearly a physical man, one who liked to touch when he talked to people. It was part and parcel of his charm.
>
> Unfortunately Genevieve didn't like to be touched.
>
> But she'd done worse things for Roper, Hyde, Camui and Fredericks, so she simply upped the wattage of her smile and let him pull her over to the white leather banquette.

The reader can get to know the real, "untouchable" Genevieve only through her own POV because she is showing another persona to the outside world. But even the real Genevieve withholds a bit; she intimates that she has had to perform more nefarious acts for her employer, but doesn't specify, as if she'd really rather not remember. This technique will help deepen characterization by forcing the reader to consider not only what the character is hiding, but how she would hide it—what "mask" she would put on to deceive the world.

These are just a few of the many ways to choose which character would be the best narrator. Each elicits a different potential narrator, so there will never be a consensus choice; the answer depends on what question you ask. That's why ten different writers can take the same set of characters and the same situation and write ten different scenes. You individualize the scene by what you choose to highlight and whose perspective you present.

You can see that this is not a checklist; any one of these is sufficient to make a choice, and some are obviously mutually exclusive. But you can also see how many different ways there are to analyze your choice, and it all boils down to one question: What effect do you want to have on the reader at this moment?

I always thought it was obvious who would be best to narrate a scene, until I tried an exercise with my POV class. I asked them to take a scene they'd already written, analyze why they'd chosen a particular POV character, and then deliberately imagine it from the POV of another major character. I was amazed when most of them decided, upon analysis, that they liked that second choice better because it gave a more intriguing perspective. So going with the instinctive first choice isn't always best. I know that when I'm displeased with a scene, I experiment with giving the POV to another character. Often, that's all it takes to make the scene come alive.

The Scarlet Pimpernel: An Exercise in Dualing Perspectives

In a recent workshop, I gave my students a POV problem from a famous novel: Baroness Orczy created a character with a devastating secret—Percy is far from the useless fop he pretends to be; in fact, he is the notorious and dashing British spy, the Scarlet Pimpernel. His wife Marguerite's brother is imprisoned in Revolutionary France and will be imperiled if it becomes known that he is connected to the Pimpernel. So, if she finds out Percy's secret, she will feel betrayed. Now imagine that we are designing a scene around the day that she discovers the secret.

Imagine a pivotal plot section in two scenes: one at 7 P.M. in their manor house, and the second an hour later as they are dancing at a society ball. Let's say in scene one of two, the unwitting Marguerite gathers all her courage and tells Percy she loves him. He is, of course, inwardly squirming because she trusts him and he's lying to her. At the end of the scene, she overhears him talking to someone else and realizes that far from being harmless, he's the infamous Pimpernel. She's now the one hiding something: she knows his true identity. In scene two, at the ball, she is feeling betrayed but keeping quiet about what she's learned so as to trap him or discover more about his motivation. Percy doesn't know she knows, and now he's trying to find a way to tell her the truth because he wants to be honest with her since she has trusted him enough to offer up her love.

To simplify: Percy has a secret in scene one, and Marguerite has a secret in scene two.

So who should be the POV character in the confession/discovery scene? Who is the best POV character for this scene, and why? The first thing to keep in mind is there is no wrong answer, so don't try to figure out what I'd tell you to do. Figure out which serves your purpose best.

I have found that about half of those presented with this variation on Pimpernel would do the first scene in Marguerite's POV and the second scene in Percy's POV; the other half would do the opposite.

What's really funny is nearly everyone has a different explanation for why. One person said she'd provide Marguerite's POV first because she's the one with the agenda of confessing her love, and, therefore, it is her goal that was driving the scene. Then she'd switch in the second scene to Percy's POV because now *he's* got the new goal of somehow telling her the truth. So for that writer, the question "Who has the goal?" controls the POV choice.

Another said she'd also start with Marguerite but because Marguerite has the greatest emotional stake in the first scene (as she is risking so much telling Percy she loves him). Then in the second scene, Percy is the one with the greatest emotional stake because he is trying to find the courage to confess the truth. Another said, "Oh, no, Percy has the most at stake in the first scene because he's the one consumed with guilt, and in the second, Marguerite has more at stake because of her great sense of betrayal." Both the above students were then asked, "Which will provide the more intense emotional experience?" Yet again, they came up with different answers—because they were considering different emotions.

Yet another student said, "Use the POV of the one with the secret— Percy first, Marguerite second—because then the thought processes will be most intriguing as each considers the consequences of concealing and revealing the secret."

I surprised myself by agreeing to ask myself that question, "Who has the secret?" But I also had a different reason from my students. I thought I'd rather be in the POV of the person who *doesn't* know the secret. That is, Marguerite doesn't know that Percy is lying about his identity, and Percy doesn't know she's discovered he's lying. Given that the most powerful person is the one who knows the most, the one who has the secret has the power. I, instead, wanted to be in the POV of the *less* powerful one. Why? I see the great fun in the dual perspective of the reader knowing the secret and knowing the POV character *doesn't* know the secret. Thus, the reader can participate in that cluelessness and powerlessness while retaining the "power position" of knowing the secret.

I realized what I like to do is promote the dual perspective for the reader whenever possible, when the reader is in the POV of the character whose experience and understanding is *different* from the reader's. The reader retains her own understanding while getting to participate in the other, too.

I also realized then that any of these choices would be a great reason to choose a particular POV character in a particular scene, and that each one would create a different effect, even if the scene's events remained the same. The writer who chose Marguerite because she was feeling the most intensely is going to craft the scene differently, and relate Marguerite differently, than I would when I was emphasizing her cluelessness.

The point is that there is no "right" way to write a scene. If a scene isn't working, if it's boring or generic, try examining what effect each perspective will cause in the reader. And experiment. Even if a scene is already written, try rewriting it from another character's POV. It's always a good idea to look beyond the obvious choice when you're choosing a POV character for a scene. The obvious might be the right choice, or it might be just another cliché.

EXERCISE

CHOOSING THE POV CHARACTER

1. Choose one event from your book that could be narrated by at least two different characters. You don't have to have written this scene, as long as you know more or less what's going to happen. (If you only have one POV in your book, this might not be relevant, but maybe you can explore what effect that POV will have on the reader.)

2. First impression: Who would you have narrate this event? Quick now, just your initial impression! Why? Try to explore why your instincts led you to this character.

3. Read over all those questions about different ways to choose a POV character (who has the goal, who has the most at stake, etc.). Which of those questions seems most crucial for this particular scene?

4. Now, in your head, change your POV choice for this scene. (Again, you don't have to write the scene—just think of it from

this perspective.) If you did this scene from the hero's POV, the one trying to keep the secret, conceive of it from the heroine's POV, the one who doesn't know the secret but is gradually coming to realize that he's hiding something. You might have some initial resistance to this, but push past it. Remember, you can always change your mind again.

5. Think of how this change would affect how you handle the scene. For example, if I chose "Whose goal drives the scene?" as the POV question, then I have to rethink the goal because the heroine's goal is different from hero's. I might focus the scene on the steps she takes to achieve her goals and end with the achievement or failure of the them—and its consequences. In this character's POV, the goal-setting and goal-getting will be paramount, so this is what she will be focusing on, and it will shape the scene differently depending on whose goal it is. Make some notes about how differently you'd handle this scene from the other POV.

6. Finally, jot down how the reader's experience of this scene would change with the new POV. You might decide that you like your original choice best, but this is just a way to explore the options available and learn how to exploit the POV choices available.

Setting the Scene

Without a doubt, using an omniscient narrator is the most efficient way to describe a setting. However, it's not always the best way. How the POV character describes a setting tells us not only about his surroundings but also about how he perceives, what he perceives, and how he feels about it.

Put yourself into the body of the POV character and imagine how this person would perceive the setting. You don't need to write an *Architectural Digest* article on the place, just what strikes this character as important and interesting.

Here's one boater's description of fifteenth-century Bruges, from *Niccolo Rising* by Dorothy Dunnett:

> ... passing three miles of ankles and a handful of knees, if you were lucky. Accessible ankles, what's more. You didn't find grand ladies with steeple headdresses and shaved brows and pearls on their slippers among the quays and sheds and warehouses and pens and tie-posts of the two ports of Bruges. You got pertly laundered white caps and slyly hitched work-gowns, enough of them to please even Claes, Julius thought. The liveliest girls called down to one youth or the other.

You probably figured out that this pretty-girl-focused narrator is a young man. But notice how the author slipped in other details, too, like the buildings that crowded along the canal. And Julius's technique of defining in the negative ("You didn't find grand ladies") gives a glimpse into other aspects of the culture.

Consider also what a character's current situation is, and see how that would color his perception of the setting. That house might seem warm and cozy to you, but if it's the headquarters of the villain, the heroine is likely to view it as dangerous and forbidding, wondering if that warm glow in the fireplace comes from someone's burning corpse. A spy on the run wouldn't notice the texture of the wallpaper but would make a quick assessment of the most available escape routes and accessible weapons.

Emotion, motivation, experience—these will color the POV character's description of the setting. In this scene from *Bee Season* by Myla Goldberg, Eliza is a grade-school student who has been dropped into the remedial class and resents it. Notice that she also describes the things around her in the negative:

> Eliza only half-listens as Bergermeyer works her way down the row of seats. In smarter classrooms, chair backs are free from petrified Bubble Yum. Smooth desktops are unmarred by pencil tips, compass points, and scissor blades. Eliza suspects that the school's disfigured chairs and desk are shunted into classrooms like hers at the end of every quarter.

Because Eliza tells us about her new "disfigured" classroom by comparing it to "smarter" ones, we get a very clear idea of her feelings about her environment and the low status that goes along with it—and how they make her feel about herself.

It can also be fun to sneak something the POV character notices—but won't be revealed as important until later—into the description, as Colin Dexter does here in *The Daughters of Cain*:

> Morse now accepted a second cigarette; and as Mrs. Rodway read through the letter Lewis turned his head away from the exhalation of smoke. He was not overmuch concerned about the health risks supposedly linked with passive smoking, but it must have some effect; had already had its effect on the room here, where a thin patina of nicotine could be seen on the emulsioned walls. In fact, the whole room could surely do with a good wash-down and redecoration. The corners of the high ceiling were deeply stained, and just above the radiator an oblong of pristinely bright magnolia served to emphasize a slight neglect of household renovation.

Lewis is a policeman, trained to notice his setting. But he's also nonsmoker surrounded by two smokers, and the effects of smoke are very much on his mind as he looks around the room. He notices first the smoke-stained walls, and then, in passing, a single unstained oblong. Later in the book, that unstained piece of wall turns out to be a clue to the murder.

The Art (and Craft) of Keeping Secrets

Here's one major difference between first-person and third-person narration: In first person, the narrator is almost in conversation with the reader, so we expect some lying or deliberate misinformation; but in third person, we are in someone's head, so what we "hear" is what the narrator actually thinks, not what he's "telling" us. It's true that some third-person narrators might be mistaken or delusional, but they really can't "lie" inside their heads. If you write, "Everyone thought he committed the murder, but he didn't," then the reader has every reason to believe that the POV character is telling (thinking) the truth, at least as far as he knows the truth. The reader will feel that she was cheated if she later finds you tricked her and the POV character really *is* the murderer.

If the POV character actually is innocent but you don't want the reader to know that yet, he shouldn't make such a definitive statement of his innocence. Again, the reader will "know" that as the truth, so the suspense will be gone. So how do you handle keeping a secret while in his head? Set up his internal monologue to avoid the subject until you want the reader to know the truth. If the POV character is planning to murder the heroine, it wouldn't be plausible for him not to think about the plan, because people have to *think* in order to *plan*. But those who are murderers, those wrongly accused of a murder, or those who think they might be guilty of something related to the murder are likely to try to avoid thinking about the murder altogether. It's that old devil denial that keeps us functioning even when we're consumed with dread or guilt.

Consider how your POV character might believably block the subject in order to avoid pain or guilt. He must mentally approach the subject and then back away. Otherwise, the reader will assume that the character *doesn't* think about it, not that he's *avoiding* thinking about it. You want the reader to notice that there's this big white elephant in the living room of his mind, and he's refusing to look at it.

How do you do that? Maybe the POV character starts to think about the subject, and then forcibly cuts it off. We won't know if that's pain or if that's guilt; we just know this is a very sore subject with him. Here's a scene from Allegra Goodman's *Kaaterskill Falls*, where a young husband, an Orthodox Jew, can't stop thinking about his wife's insistence on starting a new business—something that could scandalize their small community. At Shabbat services, he has to force himself to concentrate on something, anything else:

> Isaac is annoyed at himself for being troubled by it. He walks into the sanctuary; and, as the service begins, he tries to put the talk out of his mind. He stares intently at the pages in front of him, although he knows the prayers by heart. He closes his eyes as he sings and tries to concentrate on the words. Lechah dodi likras kallah, pinei Shabbas nikabelah. Come, my friend, to meet the bride; let us welcome the Sabbath. And he turns with the other men toward the door of the synagogue. All of them bow

to the door expectantly, as if, like a bride in white, the Sabbath were coming to walk down the aisle between them. They sing as if to make it so.

In this passage, the cutting off of the thoughts, the recitation of the old prayer, and even the eye-closing show his need to escape this dilemma. There's just enough of the involuntary thought before he cuts it off to give the reader a notion of what the secret is.

Punctuation helps here. A dash (—) signifies a broken-off or interrupted thought. An ellipsis (...) indicates a trailing off or fading out of one thought into another. The reader will be hearing the difference in her mind as she reads.

Once you're deep in a character's POV, you can cue the reader to notice something without revealing it entirely. You do this by using the character perspective as a diversion: He notices just enough to narrate but no more than that. Give him a reason to not take note of some object, person, or scrap of conversation than the reader will notice by distracting the POV character at that moment. Later, you can exploit this loose thread by revealing that what he didn't take much note of was a major clue. You're playing fair with the reader because you do show that clue, but you're plausibly concealing the importance of it.

For example, put yourself back in the Scarlet Pimpernel scenario, and in Percy's POV. He doesn't know that Marguerite has found out his secret identity as the Pimpernel, and now at the ball, she jots something down on a piece of paper and hands it to him; he puts it in his pocket. If this act is shown at the center of his perspective, that is, if he is paying attention to her movements and her actions, it wouldn't be plausible that he would take the note but not look at it. But imagine that his attention is focused on his enemy Chauvelin. He only peripherally notices that his wife has handed him a note, and so it's plausible that he would automatically jam it into his pocket without reading it. You can even state that straight out: "Without reading it, he jammed the note into his pocket, and turned back to gaze at Chauvelin." The reader will know that the note is important and will likely show up later, maybe when Percy goes home and gets out of his formal clothes.

THE POWER OF POINT OF VIEW

If you want to produce a clue for the reader without forcing the character to react, give him a plausible reason for denying the importance of the clue or paying it no mind.

Creating the Supporting Cast

You might wonder, if you are in one POV, how you can describe what other characters are thinking and feeling. Well, when you're conversing, how do you know what your listener is thinking and feeling? You don't. You intuit it through your conscious and subconscious analysis of her speech, her body language, her vocal tone, and her facial expression. Using all these indirect tools, you can (usually) tell when someone is mad at you or even when someone is lying to you.

Remember that few, if any, of your readers can read minds, so when they're deep in the POV of a character, they're not going to expect to be privy to another character's thoughts. In fact, "mind-blindness" has made most of us quite adept at interpreting other people's involuntary indicators. In this way, single POV replicates real life. We don't ever precisely know what someone else is thinking or feeling. We are confined to our own perceptions and to what we can interpret from the other person's behavior, tone of voice, expression, and word choice. (In fact, whenever we start thinking we know someone entirely, we're setting ourselves up for disappointment.)

Single POV gives the reader the familiar experience of a character also confined to her own perceptions of the world, her own thoughts of the events, and her own understanding of this interaction. The author's job is to delve deep enough into the POV character's perspective to narrate the action through that filter, while also including the physical details that clue the reader in and allow for interpretation of the other characters' thoughts and feelings.

That's how single POV works best—letting the POV character perceive and narrate the interaction in enough detail that the reader can also interpret the other characters' thoughts and feelings. Here's an example from *Master and Commander* by Patrick O'Brian, in which the POV character perceives the other character's attitude but doesn't quite understand it; the reader, however, might be able to interpret the situation. Jack is the new captain of the ship, and James is his first lieutenant.

Jack's ordinarily a bold fellow, but his new leadership responsibilities have made him more cautious about risking the ship and his sailors:

> [James said] "... I hope all was well with you, sir?"
>
> "Yes, yes, —no one killed, no serious wounds. [The other ship] ran away from us too fast to do much damage: sailed four miles to our three, even without her royals. A most prodigious fine sailer."
>
> Jack had a notion that some fleeting reserve passed across James Dillon's face, or perhaps showed in his voice; but in the hurry of things to be done, prizes to survey, prisoners to deal with, he could not tell why it affected him so unpleasantly until some two or three hours later, when the impression was reinforced and at least half-defined.

All the reader needs is the signal ("had a notion") and the clue ("some fleeting reserve")—and, of course, the knowledge of the situation accumulated from reading the previous chapters—to suspect that James is questioning Jack's courage, a suspicion confirmed in Jack's mind a little later:

> "... the other settee has a cargo of quicksilver hidden in sacks of flour, so we must handle *her* with great care."
>
> "Oh, of course," said James Dillon. Jack looked at him sharply, then down at the charts and at Stephen's drawing .... "Could the fellow possibly think I am shy?" he thought. "That I left off chasing because I did not choose to get hurt and hurried back for a prize?"

Jack's realization of what James is thinking doesn't just affect his mood; it influences his actions. A moment later, he decides that rather than send the first lieutenant to command the hazardous shore attack, he's going to do it himself. This decision wouldn't seem pivotal if the reader hadn't been able to share Jack's suspicion.

Sometimes the POV character is wrong. Sometimes he's misinterpreting what another character is thinking. That's the most fun of all! Remember that doubling effect I mentioned earlier—that the savvy reader can identify with the POV character, *be* the POV character, while simultaneously maintaining her own identity, knowledge, and understanding? This is the effect that makes reading fiction such a profound cognitive and emotional experience—and what makes carefully constructed POV so instrumental in a successful novel. So don't look at the inability to "read minds" as a limitation. In fact, forcing yourself to stay in the POV character's perspective can help you create better scenes with more physical detail, character interaction, and motivation.

Navigating Love Scenes

A single-POV love scene can be evocative and unique because we can dive deep into the one character and really experience the totality of being in such a vulnerable, intimate situation. The tension and conflict will be greater when we don't know how the other partner feels or what he thinks, and we can participate in the insecurity of questions like "Is this love or just sex? What's my lover thinking about? Does my lover think I'm attractive?" You can add a lot of humor and sensitivity with such interior monologue and reveal much about character. Perhaps our heroine has thus far been stifled— she was in a marriage that lacked intimacy or she's been told by a previous lover that she's not adventurous enough, and she's now thinking, "Maybe I should moan louder?" But then she second-guesses herself. And then there's the big question: Even if the sex is great, will he love her if he knows the truth—that she's deceiving him about her actual identity?

If we decided to juxtapose their perspectives by using third-person multiple POV, this might be the time to go into the lover's POV to reveal that he thinks she's just fine. (She's beyond fine; she's incredible. And anyway, he's already figured out that she's not who she pretends to be, that she's an undercover cop, and, boy, does he think that's sexy.) But that's a way of *resolving* conflict. Maybe it's too early in our book for that; maybe we still want to *intensify* conflict. Our purpose in this scene isn't to reassure the reader that the lover is properly appreciative but to give more of the experience of being nervous and feeling vulnerable. Then, through the heroine's actions and those of her lover (like the sweet things he's murmuring in her ear), the reader can participate in her overcoming that nervousness and insecurity and joyfully embracing her own passion. Throughout the adventure, the reader remains on the same path that the POV character is on, so the resulting payoff (the unconditional love and a terrific relationship) is greater when the reader has to wait, along with the heroine, for the reassurance.

What's even more powerful about this technique, however, is that by focusing the purpose of the scene on the POV character's values, background, goals, and conflicts, we can make a much stronger and sexier scene. For example, what does she *value*, both physically and emotionally, in lovemaking? Maybe she likes a slower, more tender touch, physically, and a teasing, lighthearted approach, emotionally. Maybe due to her background (her secret identity), she doesn't want the emotions to get too intense because she's afraid that if she falls in love with him, she'll have to tell him the truth. Her goal, then, might be just having a good time without getting too intense—and yet, her inner self must be calling out for some recognition, some signal that the lover subconsciously knows her soul, even if he doesn't know her real name. That's the conflict in the scene, and that gives us a hint about how the scene should end—when, in a moment of passion, he says her true name.

There's no way a scene focused like this is going to be one of those "generic love scenes" that writers and readers lament. Certainly, you can do that in multiple POV, too, but then you'd be weaving together two sets of thoughts, needs, and conflicts, and it could get complicated. The single-third path here is much more clear. Here's an example from *Lessons of Desire* by Madeline Hunter. The POV character, Phaedra, is an early feminist and thinks of love as a way for men to control women and seduction as surrender—even as she can't help but respond to a man's lovemaking:

> He intended to stay here all that night. She never permitted that with her friends, but she could hardly wake him up and demand he go back down to the blanket on the stones in the chamber below. Still ...
>
> She stared at the dim lights playing cross the stones above her. His gaze had been warm and touching during that last long look, but it had also demanded that she acknowledge the power of their joining. It had contained the deep intimacy still binding them, and refused to permit her to disentangle from its hold.
>
> But there had been something else, something she had never seen in a man's eyes before, at last not when a man regarded her.
>
> She had just gazed into the eyes of a conqueror.
>
> She wondered what it was that he mistakenly thought he had won.

The shock of her realization that he thinks he conquered her will be intensi-fied if we've stayed in her perspective the entire time, so that we not only have felt her need to protect herself, but also her desire to surrender.

In fact, love scenes often benefit from the "deep immersion" technique of descending so entirely into the character that the narrative takes on the "sound" of her thoughts.

Describing the *Me* in POV

Learning how to describe the POV character is a tough task because we re-ally don't think of what we look like all that often (unless we're very vain). One cliché is to have the POV character looking in the mirror and describing what she sees, but that's become something of a joke now. You can also wait until the next chapter in someone else's POV and let that person do the de-scribing. But that's not always feasible, and it demands that the reader stick with a character for a whole chapter without having a clear picture of her in mind. Here are a few alternative solutions.

If your overall POV approach allows limited omniscience in spots—that is, you're not doing the entire book from deep, in-character POV—you might start a passage or a scene from an outside perspective. Describe the character, and then narrow into her POV, as Eileen Dreyer does here in *With a Vengeance*:

> Maggie O'Brien was still securing her medic vest when she opened the door to the command center at the corner of Ohio and Wyoming. A normally unprepossessing 120 pounds over a five-foot-five frame, Maggie looked instead like an extra from a Chuck Norris movie. Her thick umber hair was tucked up under a blue kerchief, and her rather normal figure was rigged out in a blue-dyed urban cammo .... SWAT-babe ... was on duty. ...
>
> She hoped nobody noticed that her hands were shaking.

Notice that the description is made more interesting because it's noting a contrast between her normal "unprepossessing" looks and her "SWATbabe" persona. This helps prevent the reader from skimming that descriptive pas-sage because what's described isn't just her looks but a sense of alienation from herself. It also provides a bridge back into her own POV, because it's not just about her looks but also her self-image.

This contemporary-omniscient scene opening is so common in fiction that readers generally won't feel dislocated when you then zoom into the character's POV, as long as you do it gently—using the character's name or pronoun and some "head word" (a verb that denotes internal processing, like "she thought" or "she hoped") that clearly indicates we're back in her mind. It also helps if the transition into the character's POV contains some specific anchor in time and place so that it's clear we're now out of the generalized "timelessness" of the contemporary-omniscient ("whenever") and into an actual moment in the story ("this hot afternoon").

Another descriptive technique involves contrast between the POV character and another character. This is a bit trickier because the character himself has to be currently assessing the other character, and that has to fit into the story. Peter F. Hamilton accomplishes this contrast well in *Judas Unchained*: "Renne found herself having to look up slightly; Isabella was several centimeters taller than she, almost Tarlo's height." This is not the place to describe the difference in their hair and eye color, because that doesn't matter to Renne at this point. The reader is going to learn only that Renne isn't overly tall. But if you continue to scatter a few of these details throughout the narrative, the reader will piece together a picture of the character.

You can also use action to convey physical details:

It took only one shove of his shoulder to break open the door.

She dug frantically in the dirt, ruining her $65 manicure. But what did she care now? She'd already destroyed her $90 hairstyle.

She yanked away, leaving several long strands of her dark hair in the tree branch.

In his hand, the baseball looked like a golf ball.

When you scatter details through the narrative, you have to trust that the reader will put it all together (along with other POV characters' descriptions) to form a coherent picture. If the character's physical appearance is really important—for example, if he's the spitting image of some movie star and an agency wants to hire him as an impersonator—then it's better to go with the concise contemporary-omniscient description than twist the character into knots trying to describe himself. As long as it's at the start of a scene or passage, a more distant POV probably won't bother the reader at all.

The Cumulative Effect

One happy circumstance of writing in single-third is that once the hard work of establishing a character's perspective and way of thinking is done early in the book, the reader takes over and applies that knowledge to later scenes. With every passage you write in a character's POV, you're training the reader to think and perceive like that character.

For example, let's say, in an early scene, you show the heroine coming up with a complicated solution to every problem. The next time, you can be in the hero's POV, and he'll notice the heroine preoccupied, contemplative, jotting down notes. He might not know what's going on, but the reader does, because the reader had that earlier experience of elaborate planning in the heroine's POV. The reader can *imagine* what's going on in her head, while the hero thinks she's just being inattentive.

Here's an example from a comic novel, *Nobody's Baby But Mine* by Susan Elizabeth Phillips. The reader and the POV character, Cal, don't know it, but the heroine has planned all night for a complicated prank:

> The Lucky Charms clattered into his bowl. "When I want your—" He broke off in mid-sentence, unable to believe what he was seeing.
>
> "What's wrong?"
>
> "Will you look at this?"
>
> "My goodness."
>
> He stared incredulously into a mound of dry cereal. All the marshmallows were missing! He saw lots of beige-colored frosted oat cereal, but not a single marshmallow. No multicolored rainbows or green shamrocks, no blue moons or purple horseshoes, not a single yellow whatchamacallit. Not one solitary marshmallow.
>
> "Maybe someone tampered with the box," she offered in that cool scientist's voice.
>
> "Nobody could have tampered with it! It was sealed up tighter than a drum when I opened it. Something must have gone wrong at the factory." He sprang up from his stool and headed back into the pantry for another box. He emptied his old cereal into the trash, ripped open the

new box, and poured it in the bowl, but all he saw was frosted oat cereal. No marshmallows.

"I don't believe this! I'm going to write the president of General Mills! Don't they have any quality control?"

"Would you like me to fix you a nice wheat bran bagel with a little honey on it? And maybe a glass of skimmed milk to go along."

He was furious. Wasn't there anything in life he could count on these days? … He yanked his keys from his pocket and stalked out to the garage. He wouldn't just write the president, he decided. He was going to sue the whole damn company. By damn, he'd teach General Mills not to ship out inferior cereal. He jerked open the door of his Jeep, and that was when he saw them.

Marshmallows. Hundreds of tiny marshmallows … across the dashboard, on the front seat, and all over the backseat.

This is why head-hopping tends to ruin the fun—going back and forth between them would diminish the pleasure of noticing, even if Cal doesn't, that something is up if the caustic Jane responds so meekly ("My goodness") to his angry consternation.

Remember, readers today want a more interactive experience. They need enough cues to know how to participate, but they don't necessarily want to be told everything. Leave room for them to have some fun.

While single POV isn't for every author or every book, it's helpful to learn the techniques of focusing on one person's perspective. Even in multiple POV, you'll be parked in one character's mind at any given moment, and you'll want to exploit that perspective to narrate that section of the scene.

EXERCISE

TRYING OUT SINGLE-THIRD

1. If you're considering single-third POV, the protagonist will probably be your major narrator. Who is that? Do you have more than one protagonist (as in a romance) or a protagonist and a major antagonist? (Antagonist/villain POV is never required, so don't assume because you have one that you need to go into that POV.)

2. Next to the names of the protagonist and any other potential major POV character, jot down four or five words that give a sense of this person's perspective during the book. This can include mood, situation, background, temperament, and any other quality that seems relevant.

   For example:

   Hamlet: angry, grief-stricken, well-educated, indecisive

   Gertrude: excited, widowed, queenly, guilty

   Claudius: in love, murderer, usurper, guilty

3. Look over a scene you've already written, or sketch out a scene. Who seems, at first thought, to be the best POV character for this scene? Look at the traits you identified in the second part of this exercise, and revise the first couple paragraphs of your scene to reflect one or more of those traits. Add in the character's thoughts and feelings if necessary.

4. If that isn't working, try closing your eyes for a minute and putting yourself in this character's mind. Then open your eyes and start to write. Respond to this prompt:

   What's happening now, [character name]?

   Answer in the first-person voice of the character. Don't worry if it doesn't come too easily, and don't stop to edit. Just write in the *I* mode until the character (or your subconscious) takes over. Then go back and see what of that first-person voice you can translate into third person.

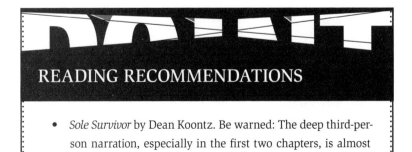

READING RECOMMENDATIONS

- *Sole Survivor* by Dean Koontz. Be warned: The deep third-person narration, especially in the first two chapters, is almost unbearable in its evocation of the grief felt by man who has lost his entire family. When Koontz is on target, no one does pain better, and this novel is especially resonant after 9/11.

- *Bee Season* by Myla Goldberg. This is a gentle but incisive novel narrated in third-person present tense by a grade-school student who discovers she has an uncanny ability to win spelling bees.

- *Mrs. Dalloway* by Virginia Woolf. This is a good example of a modernist novel that explores a character's thoughts with clarity and depth.

- *The Golden Leopard* by Lynn Kerstan. Here's a hero with some serious secrets, and a POV that intends to keep them. Great weaving in of backstory and revelation.

- *For My Lady's Heart* by Laura Kinsale. Kinsale is one of the premier modern romance writers, always trying something new with POV. This medieval novel is written in the voices of its characters—in early modern English, that is.

- *Darwin's Radio* by Greg Bear. This novel combines aspects of science fiction and thriller, following scientists who discover a virus that causes a fetus to move to an advanced stage of evolution. The narrative voice of each character reflects a careful, scientific approach, gradually deepening into controlled panic.

- *The Metamorphosis* by Franz Kafka. This novella, about a man who wakes up as a giant insect, provides a great lesson in focusing tightly on the reactions of one character to the situation of the plot. Kafka also does an impressive job of narrating the physical "feel" of an unfamiliar body.

- *The Corrections* by Jonathan Franzen. A tight focus on the major character POVs in this novel shows that big family dramas don't need to be done in omniscient.

PERSONAL THIRD PERSON: MULTIPLE

8

Every writer's creative process is different, and the way writers imagine and construct their stories can have a lot to do with the POV they choose. Whereas single-third POV writers tend to "receive" the story from inside a character—seeing an event through a character's perspective from the very beginning, exclusive of what other characters might be thinking—writers of multiple-third POV (which uses at least two viewpoint characters within a scene) "receive" the story in a more comprehensive way, almost cinematically. They can visualize a scene playing out, seeing the characters and hearing their reactions. The perspective is more complete and global, even as the story is just beginning to take shape.

Thinking about it even more deeply, and getting a little existential here, I'd assert that those attracted to multiple POV often believe that reality can only be apprehended through a composite of perceptions—that the reader will figure out what the truth is only by hearing several people's versions of the event and putting them together. Single-third POV advocates seem more interested in what a subjective view of reality teaches about people—learning more about a single character by hearing how she perceives an event. Again, neither approach is wrong. It's almost a difference in worldview, and both create unique experiences for the reader.

The reason why third-person multiple has earned a bad reputation is because it's easy to do it badly, and that's a real problem, especially for newer writers. Multiple POV can quickly devolve into head-hopping, indiscriminate switching between character POVs, and head-hopping is intensely annoying to many readers (and editors). Such POV promiscuity makes it difficult for writers to create a sustained plot narrative or identifiable characters. But that is neither the desired nor the inevitable result of conceiving a story in multiple POV.

Many accomplished multiple-POV writers are actually using a variation of single-third POV—allowing two or three characters to narrate an event, but creating each POV passage as detailed as possible and concluding one character's "part" before the scene viewpoint switches to another character. These scenes present more than one version of reality, but the reader finishes the scene with an understanding of not only how each character's perspective is unique but also how it contributes meaningfully to move the overall story forward.

MULTIPLE-THIRD BASICS

Third-person multiple became common as the popularity of omniscient narration faded in the twentieth century. The omniscient narrative can also sample several characters' perspectives, but the difference is that a multiple viewpoint has no narrator or authorial perspective. In true multiple viewpoint, you are never outside the perceptions of some character or another. You tell only what the characters know. So in that way, it's more restrictive than contemporary omniscient but also more personal. Here are a few other pros to consider:

- With a large cast, multiple POV allows the reader to experience the event from different perspectives, and that's especially fun to give a *Rashomon* effect, where every participant has a distinct version.

- Multiple POV can give a second character's version of an event without having to replay it in the next scene from the new POV character. (That's a real problem with single POV—making two scenes out of one event to show his-and-her versions.) Instead, at a judiciously chosen moment, you can shift from one POV to the other so both perspectives are explained.

- In a dual-character scene, multiple can show how much in accord or discord the characters are. This also allows the reader to become intimate with more than one character at a time. This can be helpful in a romance or other books with two major characters.

- Multiple also allows you to cut from one place to another, one person to another, without ending the scene. It's much easier to convey a variety of information this way.

- In a densely populated scene, it can scan the crowd to show differing reactions. This is most enjoyable in comic novels, which use juxtaposition to create irony.

On the other hand:

- Multiple POV can be dangerous, especially for newer writers, because the greater freedom can easily lead to head-hopping. (You can avoid this by staying as long as possible in one POV, and then shifting only for a good reason.)

- Multiple can decrease reader identification with any one character if there's not enough time in that POV.

- The multiple-POV approach can sometimes reduce reader involvement by telling rather than showing. That's because it's often easier just to switch POVs to have a character explain what's going on in the scene. However, this will decrease suspense by telling too much too quickly, without giving the reader time to guess what's unfolding.

- Multiple can also lead to redundancy if every line of dialogue or action is followed by the other character's interpretation of it. In fact, multiple works most effectively with longer passages given to only two or three characters in a scene. Of course, it depends on your preferences and the actual story. But the smaller the "cast," the more controllable the approach is, and the less likely you are to devolve into head-hopping. With only two or three POV characters, the reader can get to know each of them intimately, as long as you spend sufficient time in each person's perspective.

BUILDING YOUR STORY IN MULTIPLE POV

Multiple POV works best with books that aren't tightly focused on one protagonist. It can definitely enhance books with several settings and major characters, especially when you need to convey information or "experience" from several perspectives more or less at the same time. Think of disaster films like *Airport* or *Jurassic Park* that follow the activities of many characters through the same basic set of events. With multiple POV, you can show the pilot in the cockpit and the air-traffic controller down on the ground, all without contorting the narrative.

Multiple POV also works well in romances, using the POVs of both the hero and the heroine in the same scene. It's also a popular choice for "team stories," in which a group of characters are working toward the same goal, even if for different reasons and with different methods. Family dramas often use multiple POV to create the sense of conflicting perspectives of the same event. But multiple POV is so common, you'll find it in most types of books that aren't strictly first person. Even mysteries, which have conventionally used only single-POV scenes, are more flexible these days.

Considering Story Scope: How Many POVs and Why?

As you build your story, think about why multiple POV seems right for this story and what you hope to accomplish with it. First, consider whether this is a *personal* novel or a *social* novel. Do you see the story as personal (the journey of one or two characters)? If so, think about what other POVs you're thinking of introducing, and whether they'll add enough to make up for the change in focus from the major characters. Aim for as few nonmajor POVs as possible in a personal novel. As you plan or revise the novel, see if you can change the passages in a minor-character POV to be in the POV of one of the major characters. This helps keep the reader's attention on the main character's journey through the plot.

If this is more a social novel (exploring the actions and interactions of a group, however large or small), you might be working with only a few major characters who are present together in many scenes. Conversely, you might have several settings and a lot of characters, but a tightly compressed time frame, so that events are happening at the same time to different characters in different places.

Either way, it might help to outline the plot and note which characters are available to narrate that event and what perspective each character could bring to the narration. For example, Terry Pratchett's comic science-fiction novel *Guards! Guards!* uses a collage of characters who are instrumental in causing or repelling a dragon attack, including:

- The sleeping dragon
- The police captain, drunk and disappointed with life
- The wizard librarian of the Unseen University (an ape, by the way)
- Brother Fingers, the messenger who can't remember the series of passwords to the secret meeting
- Brother Doorkeeper, the one who knows the many passwords
- The Supreme Grand Master, who wants to resurrect the dragon and set it loose in the kingdom
- A thunder god, who thinks maybe he'll interfere with the lives of men again
- The innocent farm boy-turned-cop, Carrot

The varying perspectives, agendas, and voices of these many narrators contribute to a comically suspenseful chapter. Each advances the story a bit or describes a slice of the exotic setting.

Once you have all the major events outlined (or all you can envision at this point), go through and find the minor characters who play no real role in the plot, even though they might be involved in one or more scenes. Most novels have what in film are called "the spear-carriers," the walk-on characters who come and go, serving coffee, delivering packages, and driving cabs, but have no essential and individual effect on the plot. Usually, they appear in just one scene. These characters are seldom worth wasting a POV on. (The exception is the minor character in a mystery who discovers the dead body. It's conventional to have this character's POV in the first scene—for the body's discovery—and never again.)

Brother Doorkeeper in the scenario above might have a lofty title and a very important job, and I'm sure he thinks of himself as the hero of his own story; however, he has virtually nothing to do in this scene but demand more and more passwords for admittance. A good guideline is that any character whose journey you're not going to pursue probably shouldn't have a POV—and one novel only has room usually for about three to five journeys. So out goes Brother Doorkeeper as a POV character, though he can still be an antagonist for Brother Fingers; we'll just never get into his head.

Which of the other characters you give POV to in this scene depends first on what they have to add to the narration and what perspective they bring. For example, while the Supreme Grand Master will provide a Machiavellian savvy, Carrot can describe his new surrounding with charming naiveté. The drunk police captain can regard every event as further cause for despair, and the librarian can compare the current situation to those chronicled in his many books. The trick is to make all those perspectives sufficiently distinctive for the reader. POV is story currency. The reader will assume that every POV character has some value in the plot and trust that he is in POV at that moment because that perspective is particularly enlightening or entertaining. Don't waste this trust by going in and out of characters' minds haphazardly.

Another consideration for choosing POV in scenes is how involved this character is. Think of a continuum of involvement starting with "hardly involved" and ending with "highly involved." The opening of the Pratchett novel features the assembled city fathers in a secret meeting to decide on the solution to the kingdom's doldrums. This is a populous scene, and the cast includes:

- Brother Doorkeeper, who keeps asking dumb questions
- The Supreme Grand Master, who is manipulating the rest of the council
- Brother Watchtower, who longs for a new king
- Brother Plasterer, who is the only dissenter about the dragon
- Brother Fingers, who thinks bringing in a dragon will intimidate the snooty wizards

The more involved characters are usually the best POV characters, and are the ones, like Brother Fingers, who bring their own agendas to the scene.

How POV Affects Scene Structure and Action

One of the benefits of multiple POV is that it reminds writers to keep major characters involved and acting toward their goals. This should be evident in scene structure, which is driven in part by the initial POV character's goal at the beginning of the scene—what she wants, what obstacles she encounters, whether she achieves the goal. When you shift to another POV character, that person's goal becomes primary because we're seeing the world through his eyes, and, of course, to him, it's what he wants that counts most. POV characters shouldn't just be witnesses to someone else's actions and achievements; they should be involved themselves in the scene action.

Recognizing (and Avoiding) Head-Hopping

If you're using the multiple-POV approach, you're going to shift from one character's POV to another's because it accomplishes something. You'll also be controlling the depth of penetration into the persona of each character, the type of information revealed, and the amount of time spent in each POV. (For example, you might want to reveal the secret romantic dreams of the heroine, but only the events witnessed by the minor character of the maid.)

As readers become more critical and intolerant of sloppy writing, head-hopping—or the indiscriminate shifting from one character's POV to another's—has become a cardinal sin in the publishing industry. Head-hopping, like bed-hopping, is promiscuous: it's too much intimacy with too many people. It's the refusal to make choices and to take responsibility for the consequences. It lacks the control of other viewpoint approaches, and its shifting from one POV to another without any discernible reason makes the narrative chaotic, even schizophrenic. For a reader, it's like being trapped in a car with a driver who keeps changing lanes every ten seconds. Head-hopping trivializes the significance of being privy to the thoughts of the important characters, and it confuses the reader, who expects that knowing the history and inner secrets of a character signifies that person's essentiality to the plot. Head-hopping is multiple POV run amok without any plan, purpose, or regard for the effect on the reader. In other words, it's not what you're going to do!

To identify head-hopping, print out a scene and, using a marker, highlight each shift in viewpoint. If you can't state a purpose for a shift, change back to the previous POV. If you're not sure what constitutes a shift, choose the character you want as the major viewpoint character. Change that person's name and pronoun (*he* or *she*) to *I*, as if it were a first-person narrative, and then read it out loud. For example, you might have a passage like this:

> Paula (POV character) sat confused in her Grandma Kate's living room. She couldn't understand why her elder sister Linda always got depressed on Paula's birthday. Silently, Kate wished she could explain that Linda was actually Paula's mother, but she knew that her niece would never believe it.

Shift the POV character pronoun to *I*, and you get something impossible like this:

> I sat confused in my Grandma Kate's living room. I couldn't understand why my elder sister Linda always got depressed on my birthday. Silently, Kate wished she could explain that Linda was actually my mother, but she knew that I would never believe it.

Paula can't know what Kate is silently thinking, so it's clear there's been a shift in POV in the middle of that paragraph.

"Stray" viewpoints like Kate's are what will alert an editor that you're not handling POV in a skillful, deliberate way. It shows a lack of control. In the case above, the reader is learning something that Paula doesn't know, and that cheats the reader of the experience of participating in Paula's figuring it out.

This is especially a hazard when you stray into the POV of minor characters. (Do we really need to know that the maid thinks it might rain?) Only use the POV of a minor character when she has some essential information or perspective and there's no other way to impart it. And don't just insert it in the middle of a paragraph that is otherwise in the major character's POV.

EXERCISE

RECOGNIZING HEAD-HOPPING

The exchange below is an example of head-hopping. Read it and think about what problems you see. Can you tell whose head you're in, and when shifts takes place?

The maid crept in, afraid to do more than just set the tray down in front of Lady Bolton. Golden-maned Jane Bolton dismissed her with a weary hand and gratefully drank the coffee down. "So we are ruined, then?"

The blue-eyed Charles was glad that she was taking it so calmly. "I fear so," he said with an inward wince. Jane saw him pale as he mentally counted up their combined gambling losses—20,000 pounds.

Truesdell, the butler, marched in. He took note of his depressed employers and decided to take matters into his own well-manicured hands. "20,000 pounds? We shall sell the Rembrandt, sir."

Charles shook his head, not believing what he heard. "But we haven't got a Rembrandt."

Truesdell allowed himself a small smile. "Then we'll just have to steal one, won't we, sir?"

Now that you've identified what's wrong, here's the same example, but this time I've italicized everything that indicates a POV, however fleeting, and added comments in brackets.

The maid crept in, *afraid* to do more than just set the tray down in front of Lady Bolton. ["Afraid" is the maid's emotion.] *Golden-maned* Jane Bolton dismissed her with a weary hand and *gratefully* drank the coffee down. ["Golden-maned" indicates that someone outside is seeing her hair, but "gratefully" is Jane's emotion.] "So we are ruined, then?"

The *blue-eyed* Charles *was glad* that she was taking it so calmly. "I fear so," he said, with an *inward wince*. ["Blue-eyed" is another outside reference, but "glad" and "inward wince" are from inside Charles.] Jane *saw* him pale as he *mentally counted up* their combined gambling losses—20,000 pounds. ["Saw" is from Jane's perspective, but "mentally counted up" is from Charles's.]

Truesdell, the butler, marched in. He *took note* of his depressed employers and *decided* to take matters into his own well-manicured hands. "*20,000 pounds?* We shall sell the Rembrandt, sir." ["Took note" and "decided" are in Truesdell's head, but though he cannot read Charles's mind and "hear" him mentally counting up the gambling losses, he somehow knows the sum is £20,000. That's an information slip.]

Charles shook his head, *not believing* what he heard. "But we haven't got a Rembrandt." ["Not believing" is in Charles's POV.]

Truesdell *allowed himself* a small smile. ["Allowed himself" means we're back in Truesdell's POV.] "Then we'll just have to steal one, won't we, sir?"

Now rewrite the scene so that it's in Jane's POV for several paragraphs, and then Charles's POV for the rest of the passage. What did you change?

Purposes and Perspective

In general, writers use multiple POV to show contrast between characters' knowledge, perceptions, goals, and interpretations—juxtaposing their differences. But you might also use it to show secret agreement or a movement toward accord. Letting the reader know all the available information is one purpose for multiple POV. For example, in a three-person scene, perhaps each person has a piece of information, and you want the reader to know each piece. That's a good place to use multiple POV, as long as you make it clear which character knows what.

In this excerpt from *Getting Hers* by Donna Hill, see how the POV is "passed" from one character to another and each has a little bit of new information to contribute:

Kim's alabaster complexion was dutifully shielded behind the black veil that dipped down dramatically from her wide-brimmed black hat. She brought a white handkerchief beneath the veil and dabbed at her dry eyes. Bastard, she muttered.

The reverend droned on about what a wonderful man Troy was while an endless stream of grievers marched up to the grave to toss a rose or utter words of sorrow and condolence to Kim. ...

On the far side of the proceedings, Tess McDonald desperately wanted a cigarette. Funerals, cops, pre-dawn phone calls, hot sex and situations out of her control always elevated her craving. Casually she looked the crowd over. Nothing particularly unusual, except that someone in attendance murdered Troy Benning.

From the opposite side of the hole, beneath the shadow of a spanning oak, Nicole Perez murmured Amen, along with the mourners. And good riddance, she added under her breath. ... No one could ever find out what really happened—or didn't. She swallowed hard and tugged in a deep breath. This would all be over soon and the three of them could move on with their lives— whatever that may be.

Kim knows Troy was not as nice as the eulogy describes, Tess knows that he was murdered, and Nicole knows how it was done and maybe who did it. In this way, the reader gets the information that would be gained from an omniscient narrator but in a much smoother and more intimate way.

You could also use multiple POV to show different understandings of what's going on. In this passage from *Sea Swept* by Nora Roberts, two brothers start a scene with very different attitudes toward their present situation. Note the head words here that signify we're in a new POV (I've italicized them):

Hell, the kid had even been doing his homework—most of the time. He had turned in the much-despised essay and was halfway through his probation without incident.

Cam figured his luck had been running hot and strong for the past couple of weeks.

As far as Phillip was concerned, it had been the worst two weeks of his life. He had barely spent any time in his apartment, had lost his favorite pair of Magli loafers to the gnawing puppy teeth of Foolish, hadn't seen the inside of a single four-star restaurant, and hadn't so much as sniffed a woman.

Or, you might want to show discord between two characters without having it erupt into dialogue, as Susan Elizabeth Phillips does here in *Hot Shot*:

Paige imagined Susannah [during the consummation of her marriage to Elliott] picking up her reading glasses along with the latest issue of *Town and Country* from the bedside table and speaking in that quiet, carefully modulated voice of hers: "But of course, dear. Just tap me on the shoulder when you're finished."

Across the table Susannah spotted the cynical smile on her sister's face but decided to ignore it.

You might also want to show how differently two characters perceive what is happening. In this example from Patricia Veryan's *Shadow's Bliss*, the woman is just trying to be helpful, while the man is falling in love:

> She guided him to her own chair, then wet her handkerchief from the water pitcher and set to work. The cut was jagged and had bled profusely, but she was accustomed to tending the hurts of her father and her three brothers, and was not squeamish.
>
> Her hands were very gentle. Enveloped in a sweet fragrance, Jonathan could not resist watching her from under his lashes.... A wave of longing swept him. She was so close; so tender and delicate and beloved.

Or, as LaVyrle Spencer does here in *The Gamble,* you might want to show characters actually moving toward accord:

> He supposed many a day she opened the shop tired and grouchy, while he and the gang slept soundly on the other side of the wall [in the saloon]. "Listen, I'm sorry about the noise."
>
> She hadn't expected him to say such a thing. Neither had she expected to hear herself answer as she did. "And I'm sorry about Evelyn Sowers."
>
> It struck them both at once—they were smiling at each other.

You can use multiple POV to explore your purpose, whether it's to show discord and accord, to sample the feelings and thoughts of a group of people, or to connect the action or reaction of two characters.

Multiple POV means exactly the opposite of "anything goes." In fact, multiple POV might better be known as "multiple-single," as in any moment, the narrative still reflects the perspective of one character or another. This is another good reason for limiting multiple POV to a small group of important characters that the reader can get to know well. After you determine your purpose, the next task is to choose which characters are going to carry the POV in any scene, and assemble them in the order that will best suit the purpose.

POV Order: The Right Head at the Right Time

Take some time as you write to experiment with POV order. In single-third POV, you have to decide who narrates what scene. Multiple-third does not make this decision for you (everybody narrates every scene!); instead, you have to decide not only who presents us each scene, but also who narrates what *part* of the scene. (With which POV will you enter the scene? Which POV exits?)

Again, who your POV character is depends on your purpose. Go back and look at "Who to Choose?" beginning on page 163, and think about what effect you would like to have on the reader. If you want heightened emotion, you'll come up with a different order than if you want greater suspense, and if you want comedy, it will likely be yet another order.

With multiple POV, however, there are more than just a couple options because there are so many different permutations available: how many POV characters you'll use in the scene, how often you shift, when you shift, and, above all, why you shift. However, shifting loses its effectiveness if you do it too often. Save it for a time when we really need the new POV to give us a new understanding of the situation, to conceal or reveal a secret, or to maintain or create suspense. And then, do it just at the right moment. You'll get extra drama if you shift right at a cliffhanger moment, such as when a disaster is about to happen or when a character discovers a secret. Shifting at these moments creates suspense because the reader has to then imagine the first POV character's response to the disaster or revelation, while experiencing the new perspective of the second POV character.

The longer you can stay in one POV, the more powerful the shift to another will be. A long passage in one POV means you get to know your character's experience of reality, and so does your reader. This gives the POV shift more importance because the reader will know something has happened to cause the change.

In his Chronicles of Narnia books, C.S. Lewis usually opens and closes scenes with an omniscient narrator. But once inside the scene, he craftily uses the POVs of the characters who drive the action—the ones who have nefarious plans or are concealing some secret. In this example from *The Last Battle*, two talking animals discover the pelt of a dead lion in a waterfall, and each has a different agenda. Puzzle, the foolish donkey, just wants to please his friend, the ape, Shift, so, he risks his life to retrieve the pelt. Shift, however, is thinking ahead. The consummate con artist, he plans to—well, you'll see. First, we get Puzzle's perspective:

> But at last, when he was almost tired to death, and bruised all over and numb with cold, [Puzzle] succeeded in gripping the thing with his teeth. And out he came carrying it in front of him and getting his front hoofs tangled up in it, for it was as big as a large hearthrug, and it was very heavy and cold and slimy.
>
> He flung it down in front of Shift and stood dripping and shivering and trying to get his breath back. But the ape never looked at him or asked him how he felt. The ape was too busy going round and round the thing and spreading it out and patting it and smelling it. Then a wicked gleam came into his eye and he said: "It is a lion's skin."

In Puzzle's POV, we're given a glimpse of his motivation when he flings the pelt down, expecting praise or sympathy and getting nothing friendly in response. He recognizes that Shift's interest has changed and notices that "wicked gleam."

We don't yet know what Shift has planned or how it involves Puzzle and the lion skin. We know only what Puzzle knows ... or perhaps we know a tiny bit more, because, well, we know he's a character in a novel, and he doesn't! We know that Shift *must* have a secret plan for this lion's skin. But we don't know what the secret is. We just know he's taking advantage of Puzzle's need for approval and that he's not that friendly fellow he's presenting himself to be. For this moment, we're enjoying the experience of gradually coming to suspect Shift.

A new writer might use multiple POV to switch immediately to Shift and have him detail his nefarious plans. But then we'd know we'd know Shift's motives way too soon, before we could experience that gradual dawning of suspicion. We wouldn't get the full "Puzzle" treatment, and we wouldn't be able to identify with his cluelessness. Fortunately, Lewis knew how to draw out the suspense—and suspense is all about postponing. This isn't easy to do when you're inside the head of the character with the secret, so Lewis takes his time, staying inside Puzzle until he's sent away to the market.

One way to gracefully switch POV is what I call the entry-exit technique: having entered an event from one POV, we exit from another. For instance, as Puzzle leaves, the perspective changes to Shift. Now he's the one with the goal: to make some reprehensible use of the lion pelt. But notice how the POV still conceals his actual intent by focusing on Shift's actions (finding the needle and thread) and emotions (smugness at being so clever) but not his thoughts:

> As soon as he was alone, Shift went shambling along, sometimes on two paws and sometimes on four, till he reached his own tree. Then he swung himself up from branch to branch, chattering and grinning all the time, and went into his little house. He found needle and thread and a big pair of scissors there; for he was a clever ape and the Dwarfs had taught him how to sew. He put the ball of thread (it was very thick stuff, more like cord than thread) into his mouth so that his cheek bulged out as if he were sucking a big bit of toffee. He held the needle between his lips and took the scissors in his left paw. Then he came down the tree and shambled across to the lion-skin. He squatted down and got to work.

This is great fun. Shift can still conceal exactly what his scheme is, and as long as he doesn't consciously formulate a thought like "He meant to use the lion skin as a disguise," we'll still be in the dark on the details. But now that we're in Shift's head, we can scout for clues to his plans. Additionally, we can get that illicit doubling effect of participating in his actions while suspecting his motives.

Note that this doubling can be achieved most effectively if we stay in one POV for long enough to actually experience the event through that one character. Once you've established the character's perspective and knowledge, the reader can take over and imagine (even when not in his POV) what he's thinking and feeling. In this case, whenever we see Shift after this scene, we don't have to be in his POV to know that he's scheming and conning. This is real identification, and it's what we're aiming for; yet, it does require adroit handling of the POV shift.

Keep in mind that whatever POV we're in, that's the character whose immediate goals and conflicts are important to the reader. By controlling the order of the POVs, you control the effect each POV has on the scene. Take advantage of that power.

You should also choose your shifting moment wisely. Make the shift itself a signal that something has changed or something new is going to happen, such as shifting just before or after a character reveals a secret.

Choosing the Shifting Point

Now that you know your options for shifting and how to shift smoothly, let's talk about appropriate times to shift POV. Look for the places in the scene that will make for more graceful shifts while calling subtle attention to some hidden clue, conflict, or theme. In fact, you might look at your own scene's unique structure and see what the scene segments are. (I define a segment as any unit of a scene, any discernible piece of action.) Stay in one POV through one unit of the scene and switch only when that segment is done.

There are some basic structural markers that are natural spots for a POV shift. For example, scenes can often be easily broken in half, with the change occurring at some pivotal moment in the middle. This is the entry-exit technique; you start the scene in his POV, and halfway through switch to hers. Or you might divide the scene in thirds, with an introduction, the major event in the middle, and the aftermath of the event in the end. The physical entrance or exit of a character in the scene is also a potential shifting point, as the scene personnel has changed.

Here are some other opportunities for shifting. Let's look again at Hemingway's famous short story "The Short Happy Life of Francis Macomber," which we first examined in chapter one. Recall that there are three major characters on this safari in Africa: Francis Macomber, a middle-aged American with a younger wife; Mrs. Macomber, the wife; and Robert Wilson, the macho hunter leading the safari. In the opening scene, they come back to camp with a dead lion, and Macomber lets everyone think that he fired the killing shot. In fact, as his wife knows, Wilson did the killing. Mrs. Macomber doesn't try to conceal her scorn for her husband, "the coward." In fact, she slips away that night for a fling with the much more virile Wilson, and she doesn't even try to keep it a secret.

The final scene of the story has them going out on another shoot. This time, Macomber restores his lost manhood by shooting a buffalo, earning the respect of Wilson. But his wife doesn't fall back into his arms. In fact, when the wounded buffalo attacks him, she shoots Macomber. Here is the big moment:

> Wilson had ducked to one side to get in a shoulder shot. Macomber had stood solid and shot for the nose, shooting a touch high each time and hitting the heavy horns, splintering and chipping them like hitting a slate roof, and Mrs. Macomber, in the car, had shot at the buffalo with the 6.5 Mannlicher as it seemed about to gore Macomber and had hit her husband about two inches up and a little to one side of the base of his skull. Francis Macomber lay now, face down, not two yards from where the buffalo lay on his side and his wife knelt over him with Wilson beside her.

Three characters all play an important role in this dramatic scene. If you were given the assignment of rewriting the scene, going into each POV once, how would you order it and when would you shift? (Macomber is dead for the last couple pages, so he might not be the best narrator at that point!) Here are some considerations:

Information control. Here's where you shift to control what information the reader gets. Readers have debated for decades whether Mrs. Macomber really meant to kill her husband (Wilson certainly thinks so). If you wanted to control the timing of the revelation of her motive, you might start the scene—as they go out on the hunt—in Macomber's POV, furious with his wife for sleeping with Wilson. His POV then provides her motive. As an experienced hunter, Wilson can effectively narrate the middle section where they shoot the buffalo, and he can also give his expert eyewitness testimony about how Mrs. Macomber took the fatal shot. He can also pose the question of whether she intended the death. Finally, to answer that question, you could end the story in her POV, as she's the only one who truly knows her own mind.

Attention focus. You might choose to shift when some change in the events means the POV character's thoughts are no longer relevant, so you shift the reader's attention to someone else. For example, Macomber's attention in that pivotal moment is all on the buffalo, so you could shift then to Wilson's POV, as he's a bit farther away and can see Mrs. Macomber take aim.

Power shift. Start in the POV of one character during some power struggle, and when something happens and the power shifts, switch to the other. In this approach, you might start with Mrs. Macomber's POV, because in the beginning, she has sexual power over both men. But then, when Macomber kills the first buffalo, the power shifts to him, as he has now conquered his sense of cowardice and no longer needs his wife's approval. Finally, in the end, Wilson has the power because he knows (or suspects) that Mrs. Macomber has committed murder. Or, for variety, you can shift to the character who has just *lost* the power struggle.

Perspective juxtaposition. Sometimes it's fun to shift to show how differently the characters view a situation. Show the event from one person's perspective, then "review" it from the other's. For example, we learn Macomber regards his killing the buffalo as a great triumph, and a shift then to Mrs. Macomber's POV would show that she sees the event as a threat—now she can no longer manipulate him with her contempt.

Emotion overload. Paradoxically, it's sometimes best to shift away from the POV of a character who is undergoing some heavy emotional upheaval. Set up the situation in that POV, and just when the emotion gets too excruciating, shift to a more detached POV to keep the emotion from becoming too melodramatic. So you might be in Macomber's POV as he psyches himself up for the last chance to prove his manhood. Then, just when he's about to shoot, switch to Mrs. Macomber's POV, who watches the hunt even as resentment consumes her. After she realizes what she's done, shift to Wilson's POV for the aftermath of the shot.

Smooth Shifting

There's a real art to shifting without jolting the reader. You want to shift smoothly, without a bump, but also clearly and decisively so that the reader knows she's in a new POV now. Give her a way to get oriented immediately in the new mind. Here are four basic techniques:

1. Use the new POV character's name right away.
2. Quickly use a head word (like *thought*, *felt*, *mused*, *wondered*, *ached*, or *tasted*) to convey thought, feeling, or perception from the new perspective.
3. Use some action for transference of perspective.
4. Use some object, like a prop, for transference of perspective.

Sometimes authors add an extra line break to signify a change of POV. But if you shift more than a couple times in a scene, you'll annoy the reader by putting in line breaks each time. If you shift POVs every page and use extra lines each time, it's just a waste of paper! Better to go with smooth but clear transitions.

Furthermore, you should almost always start a new paragraph when you start a new POV. If you're doing a quick pan of the group, you might keep that all in one paragraph, but even then, you should start a new paragraph as soon as you establish the primary POV for the next passage.

It's not a rule that you can only shift to each POV once in a scene (although it's often more effective). If you want to shift back to a POV— for example, Macomber to Wilson to Mrs. Macomber to Wilson—the same basic guideline applies: know why you're shifting and what experience this "returning POV" will give to the reader. Then, do it gracefully. Just keep in mind that ordinarily, the longer the passage in each POV, the more textured the experience will be. In fact, by using a longer passage, you get most of the benefits from single POV (deeper reader identification, more character development) without the hassle (blinkered perspective, character "shut out").

You probably figured out that multiple is, in some ways, more complicated to work with than single. It certainly has more choices involved, which is both a benefit and a challenge. But if you consider what your purpose is, you'll find the choices are easier to make.

What's in a Name?

One minor note: Multiple POV can complicate what you call your other characters, and it might mean that they are called one name in their own POV sections and something else in another's POV—not just in dialogue, but in the narrative itself.

For example, Macomber's wife, Margaret, thinks of herself, as most of us do, by either our given name or what our intimate friends call us, so in the scenes where her POV controls, you would identify her as "Margaret" or "Margot." (*"Conversation is going to be so difficult," Margaret said. Margot said pleasantly, "If you make a scene, Francis, I'll leave you."*) But Macomber thinks of her mostly in relation to himself (this could be why she wants to leave him!), so in his POV, she would be identified mostly as "his wife." (*He realized that his wife was not in the other cot in the tent.*) Wilson is a punctilious sort of fellow. He might sleep with another man's wife, but he wouldn't be so forward as to call her by her first name. (*Mrs. Macomber, in the car, had shot at the buffalo with the 6.5 ....*)

Will this confuse the reader? Not if you identify first name and surname early on. (This should probably be on first reference: Margaret, [Macomber's] wife, looked away from him and back to Wilson.) Then use the "self" term exclusively in her POV to establish her identity in her own mind. This will likely be her name or nickname. It's fine if it's different from what others call her, as long as you establish it's what she calls herself. "Margot" might be "Margaret" to her mother, "Mrs. Macomber" to her servants, and "Dear" to her husband. One way to help the reader keep this straight is to have each character use the same name for her in dialogue that they do when they are the POV character. So Margot is always Mrs. Macomber to Wilson, whether we're hearing him speak or think; it would be too confusing for readers if, when in his POV, he "thought" of her as Margot.

Of course, there are complexities within complexities here, as with most POV opportunities. What do you do when a character is undercover, using a false name? Presumably, in his POV, you might use his real name (or nickname), however he thinks of himself. Consider this example:

Trent wrapped his brass shield in a sock and hid it away, then closed the drawer and walked back into the living room where Lil Barfy waited.

"Hey, Jonesy," Barfy said, holding up a beer. "You want one a these before we go bust that safe?"

Trent shook his head, too nervous to speak, certain that Barfy would hear "cop" in his voice.

Just be sure you never slip up and have Barfy think of him as "Trent"; that name exists only in Trent's POV database, not Barfy's.

In Part Three, we'll explore some techniques to help you develop the POV characters and their ways of narrating. We'll start with individualizing their perspectives, then explore the different levels of penetration within each POV passage, finishing up with some tips and tricks and troubleshooting.

EXERCISE

PRACTICING SHIFTING

1. For one of your scenes, list the names of all potential major POV characters. Then jot down terms that give a sense of each person's perspective during the scene. This should include goal or conflict. For example:

    Macomber: revealed as a coward, determined to prove himself
    Margot: regretting her marriage, determined to escape
    Wilson: feels contempt for this couple, but unwillingly drawn to each of them

2. Look over a scene you've already written, or sketch out a scene. Who seems, at first thought, to provide the best opening POV character for this scene? Look at the goals and conflicts you identified in question one, and revise the first couple paragraphs to reflect those. Add in the character's thoughts and feelings if necessary.

3. Find a good shifting point in your scene. Why does this seem an effective place to change POV? What effect will that have on the reader's experience?

4. In one or two sentences, make a transition from the first POV character to the second. Be sure and use the new POV character's name and some kind of head word to indicate the shift.

READING RECOMMENDATIONS

- The Harry Potter series by J.K. Rowling. An entire world is created here, with a multiple POV approach so sure and character voices so well-defined, it's got to be magic.

- The Aubrey/Maturin series by Patrick O'Brian. These Napoleonic-era books chart a friendship between a ship's captain and a surgeon, replicating the voice of each of the dual protagonists with such authenticity that one critic insisted they must have been written by "Jane Austen's admiral brother."

- The Chronicles of Narnia series by C.S. Lewis. It wasn't till I was grown and rereading these books aloud to my own children that I realized how profoundly early exposure to these books had influenced my own voice. Playful, intense, emotional—no one does child POV as well as Lewis.

- *Ain't She Sweet* by Susan Elizabeth Phillips. Phillips is a master at juxtaposing multiple POV and character dialogue, and she somehow manages to make even the snobbish homecoming queen sympathetic.

- *Martian Time-Slip* Philip K. Dick. The invariably interesting Dick uses multiple POV to explore schizophrenia and its connections to "normal" thought.

- *Big Trouble* by Dave Barry. Humor columnist Barry often uses multiple POV to juxtapose male POV with female POV for comic effect. This novel also uses multiple POV to show the chaos of modern Florida.

- *A Tale of Two Cities* by Charles Dickens. This famous novel uses a combination of multiple and single POV to show the doubling of two cities, two nations, and two men in love with the same woman. The late scene where Sidney Carton goes to the guillotine is intensely tragic due to the tight POV.

part three

the master
CLASS

Now that I've explained the "macro" aspects of POV, it's time to get micro: actually getting into your characters' perceptions and their individual ways of describing the world and events. Just as characters have individual voices in dialogue, they have individual viewpoints, too. The unspoken thoughts of the character narrating the scene—the POV character—should reflect his or her distinctive personality, voice, and worldview. Creating convincing and engaging viewpoints involves understanding how the elements of POV and character interact, how POV reflects the unique character, and how this is developed within the scene. You can also use a character's POV to set up that character's journey in the story, her self-image, or what she needs to overcome.

The first step in individualizing POV is getting to know your characters. Once you've chosen a primary POV character, get to know him or her from the *inside* out. Keep in mind that readers these days want an experience, not just a view. They want to see through the POV character's eyes, think his thoughts, feel his feelings, and hear what he's hearing. In order to create an authentic narrative voice, ask some key questions about your POV character: How does this person perceive the world? How does she come to understand her environment? What does she choose to notice and to ignore, and why? What does she want to do with what she learns?

In addition to understanding your character's emotional and intellectual dimensions, POV reflects *perceptual* ability, which varies depending on a person's sensory and cognitive skills—the way we take in information and the way we make use of it.

THE FIVE SENSES

Most of us have one or two dominant senses. For example, I'm an auditory, not visual person. I can see you every workday, and I can't describe you.

But after a couple phone conversations, I can recognize a voice. So as a POV character, I would not note my future love interest's looks, beyond a vague realization that he's gorgeous. But his sardonic tone, the catch in his voice as he greets me, the deliberate pace of his speech—these I would remark on silently.

As an illustration, think about your own perceptual strengths and weaknesses. Which of the five basic senses is strongest for you? Can you actually taste the difference between Pepsi and Coke? Can you distinguish the perfumes of every lady in the room? Can you tell just by the tone of a friend's voice how she's feeling? Do you love to touch different fabrics? Are you very sensitive to color and can't work in a yellow room?

Now apply the same sort of questions to a character, and you'll start to individualize her POV. Identify her dominant sense, and then think about how that will affect how she narrates a scene. A visual person will focus more on what she sees (*She was so intent on that garbage truck backing up that she missed what Judy said*). A tactile person will always be touching things and reporting on the texture (*Betty grabbed the doorknob. The brass was cool and smooth under her hand, and it wouldn't turn*). A little of this goes a long way, but even a couple focused sensory references can give the sense of how this character takes in the world around her.

OTHER MODES OF PERCEPTION

Sensual perceptivity is not the only way to "absorb" the world. There's also temperament (optimist/pessimist, emotional/rational) and personality style (problem-solver, logician, competitor, and so on). Learning style also affects perception. You'll notice that schools these days tend to offer different methods of instruction because they recognize that children have different learning preferences. For example, a teacher will provide an assignment sheet but also read it aloud in class, so that both the visual and auditory learners will understand the assignment. Hands-on activities are also encouraged to facilitate tactile and kinesthetic learning.

Visual people learn more through their eyes; they have good visual memory, are intrigued by color and motion, and will watch a video to learn how to build a bookcase. Kinesthetic learners need to participate in the lesson. They learn geometry by using a t-square to build that bookcase or learn algebra by measuring out quantities of flour and sugar for a cake. My son's physical science class, for example, built a roller coaster of plastic piping to learn about centripetal force—a tactile way of reinforcing the concept. It would also be tactile but more action-oriented if they went to the amusement park on a field trip and got on an actual roller coaster and experience g-force against their own little bodies.

Think about how your character learned (or didn't learn) in school. Also consider the character's profession, for we usually choose to do what we are naturally attuned to. Artists tend to perceive the world through their most developed sense, which will probably be the one they use in their art. An engineer will try to understand the logic, the structure, of what he's perceiving. A lawyer is a negotiator and a talker, and she'll acquire knowledge most through questioning and listening.

There's also a less obvious perceptive mode—a sixth sense—we call intuition. It's probably a combination of superior emotional intelligence and hypersensitivity to external stimuli, but what it means is that you can sense the emotion, intent, and fears of others. You can figure out if they're telling the truth or lying, if they're trustworthy or not. This is a wonderful "extra" sense to bestow upon certain types of characters, like cops and journalists, who have to make quick judgments. To display this sense in POV, imagine how it feels to know something instinctively, and show it that way. For example, a character's stomach might knot up or the nerves in his arms might go on alert when someone intends harm.

Thinking About Perception: A Party Game

Now consider how these ways of perceiving will be exhibited in the narrative. Imagine a group of characters with lots of different perceptual abilities arriving at a raucous party and having to make sense of the chaos.

A painter will blink, and the chaos will settle into form, color, and composition, with fluid beauty in the ladies' dresses and the balloons and candlelight. Meanwhile, the musician hears a symphony of raised voices, music, ice clinking in glasses, and muted sobbing, and knows that the party is at its height. An architect will enter and consider how knocking out a couple walls will make for better traffic flow. A writer might walk into the same party and see the girl crying in the corner and construct a scenario to explain her sorrow. Reality is only grist for the story mill.

A problem-solver sees the world as a set of problems to be solved. She will walk into a party and notice what's wrong—the music is too loud, the ice has run out, and a girl is sitting ignored in the corner crying. But though the problem-solver focuses on problems, she is no pessimist; rather, she's busy devising solutions—turning down the stereo, sending her boyfriend into the kitchen for more ice, and comforting the weeper.

A competitor sees life as a game. When he enters the party, he will choose a side—that weeping girl has already been cut from his team—and scout the opposition and ascertain the prize. He likes to know the rules ahead of time, and he expects a fair outcome: The swift ought to win the race, and he ought to go home with the most beautiful woman.

A materialist will scan the crowd and see diamonds and Rolex watches, calculating the approximate net worth of the party and never noticing the human tragedy in the corner.

These are examples of only a few perception types. You'll probably come up with more on your own. Just remember, less is more. Few people are both visually and auditorily superior, and logical besides. So, instead of using all five senses in a scene, consider that the more evocative viewpoint will have one perception dominant. A musical hero would close his eyes to better hear the music of his lover's sighs—and never even see the fire in her eyes.

Perception, like temperament, is not a single character trait but, rather, an inborn or developed way of interacting with the world. This will be exhibited in consistent, if not predictable, ways as it locks into place with other aspects of the personality. So perception and temperament need not always "match"—an artist may be contemplative or exuberant, a problem-solver may be cheerful or lugubrious. POV is your chance to show how the character's

THE POWER OF POINT OF VIEW

perceptivity affects his understanding of the world and, therefore, his response to it.

UNDERSTANDING PERCEPTION

Here are some "character" lines. Imagine what sort of perceiver the viewpoint character would be (some suggested answers are below if you'd like a little help):

1. It was too dark to see his expression, but she heard the injury in his low voice.

2. He glanced around as he entered, locating the windows and doors and plotting the best escape route.

3. "Someone else could probably help you more," she said, but already she was strategizing alternate actions.

4. He pondered her motives for calling him. Was she out to hook him again?

5. David was sitting, arms crossed, leaning away from his brother. Janie realized she had interrupted an argument.

6. The mountains below were spread with the scarlet and gold Persian carpet of autumn.

7. She rubbed her cheek against his chest, feeling his warmth through the threadbare fabric, wishing she had enough money to buy him a decent shirt.

8. Only half-listening, he arranged the forks and knives and salt-cellars into battalion formation, then leaned over and recruited another squadron from the adjacent table.

(1. Auditory, intuitive. 2. Visual, spatially oriented. 3. A problem-solver, rational. 4. Suspicious, pessimistic, contemplative. 5. Intuitive, aware of body language, visual. 6. Visual, artistic. 7. Tactile, empathic. 8. Strategic-minded, not auditory, tactile.)

INDIVIDUALIZING YOUR CHARACTER'S POV

Look at your own POV character—the readers' "eyes and ears" in the story—and answer whichever of these questions intrigue you. (When I use *you* below, I'm talking to the character.) Freewrite the answers in the character's own first-person voice: "I learn best by ..."

1. How do you learn best? Observation? Participation? Trial and error? Rumination and cogitation? Consulting experts? Writing?

2. How open are you to new ideas and information? Do you change your mind frequently, based on what people have told you? Are you a traditionalist, deciding on the basis of "what's always been"?

3. When you walk into a party, what do you notice first? The mood? The people? The decorations? The things that need to be fixed? The background music? The food on the buffet table? Whether or not you fit in?

4. Is one sense more highly developed than another? For instance, do you tend to take in the world primarily through vision? ("I'll believe that when I see it!") Or are you more auditory? Do you determine if a person is lying by the tone of voice? Do you love to talk on the phone? What about the sixth sense—intuition? How often do you rely on your "gut" and then have your feelings confirmed?

5. Do you usually notice problems around you? What is your response? Do you write an angry letter to the editor? Shrug and move on? Analyze what's wrong and how to fix it? Take it as evidence that the world is falling apart? What about problems within yourself?

6. Would you say you were an optimist or a pessimist? Would your friends agree?

7. Are you more interested in the past or the future, or do you live in the now? Are you one to keep holiday traditions? If you had to move tomorrow, how long would it take you to make new friends?

8. How do you decide if you can trust someone? By experience with this person? First impressions? Intuition? Do you test the person somehow? Or are you just generally disposed to trust or not to trust?

9. Are you a deliberate, careful speaker, or do you talk without thinking first? Do you use slang, or do you use diction your old English teacher would approve?

Now read over what you just wrote, and list five to ten "hallmarks" of your character's POV, such as: visual, problem-solver, pessimist, dark view of humanity, expects the worst, looks for trouble, wary and curious, always on the lookout, oddly sentimental about some things, speaks slowly and distinctly, as if talking to children.

How Perception Changes Scene

Use your knowledge of the POV character's perspective modes to make his narration of every event unique to him. This not only contributes to the authenticity of the scene and strengthens a reader's investment in the story, but taking time to consider the different perceptive modes and creating a distinct POV is also an excellent way to reveal character. Here are some examples of how perception might affect a POV character's experience of the scene and what details you choose to reveal about him.

A *deliberate, judicious* character will think before speaking, so show that thinking:

> Thomas waited until they were alone. He chose his words carefully, knowing the wrong word could mean beheading. "I would not want to offend Your Grace, but his wife—it is said in the kitchens, mere rumor, perhaps, that she is spending more time with the stable boy than perhaps most ladies of her station would do."
>
> He waited for the duke's response, and when there was none except for that cold stare, Thomas realized it was not time for further revelation.

An *impulsive* person's thoughts will be chaotic and action-oriented—often the action will come first and the thought after:

Thomas took the duke's arm and pulled him toward the window. "Come and see this. You'll want to see it." Well, he reflected, His Grace might not actually want to see it, but a cuckolded man deserved to know the truth.

He didn't see it coming, but he felt it—the duke's glove. Fist enclosed. As he went down, he thought, kill the messenger, why don't you? And then he didn't think anymore.

A *pessimistic* person's thoughts will prophesize doom:

Thomas watched the hard-faced duke enter and cross to the back window. Oh, woe. The duke would see his wife and the stable boy, right out there in the stable yard. There was no avoiding it. He didn't even bother to try to divert the duke's attention—what good what it do? No matter what, he would get blamed for it. It was his job around here. Whipping boy.

An *optimistic* person's POV will always show an expectation of the best:

Thomas watched the duke enter and cross to the window. That could be trouble. Then again, maybe it was for the best. Maybe the duke would see how unhappy his wife was, take pains to win her back, and give her the child she wanted so badly. Then the old castle would ring with the joyous sound of laughter and childish voices!

Same situation, same role—but a different type of character in each POV. It's not just the action that changes with the change in character, but the very narration of that action—the word choice, the attitude, the sentence construction, the perception, the value system (the first Thomas values his position; the next values the truth; the next values his martyrdom; the final values babies and marital harmony), the analysis of what's going on, and the level of connection to reality.

OTHER FACTORS THAT INFLUENCE ACTION

Several other factors contribute to a deeper understanding of the character's POV. The character's knowledge, values, background, biases, and emotions also affect how the events are narrated.

Here's an example from Mark Twain's *The Adventures of Huckleberry Finn*, when Huck turns against the two con men—the duke and the king—he's been traveling with:

> So, thinks I, I'll go and search them rooms. Upstairs the hall was dark, but I found the duke's room, and started to paw around it with my hands; but I recollected it wouldn't be much like the king to let anybody else take care of that money but his own self; so then I went to his room and begun to paw around there. But I see I couldn't do nothing without a candle, and I dasn't light one, of course. So I judged I'd go do the other thing—lay for them and eavesdrop. About that time I hears their footsteps coming, and was going to skip under the bed; I reached for it, but it wasn't where I thought it would be, but I touched the curtain that hid Mary Jane's frocks, so I jumped in behind that and snuggled in amongst the gowns, and stood there perfectly still.

First, Huck's narration will reveal his base of *knowledge* about the two men he knows to be thieves. He has traveled with them and has figured out that they are con men trying to steal a legacy from the rightful heirs. So that knowledge shows up both in his thoughts and his actions—he knows the money must be in their room. He also knows that the king wouldn't let the duke have the money. And he knows what it means when he hears them approaching—that he's in danger if he lets them know he's turned against them. All this unique information is running through his head as he enters their room.

His *values* will also be affecting his perspective and how he narrates this scene. His decision to return the money is cemented when the kind Mary Jane sticks up for him, chastising her maid for accusing him of lying (he is, of course, "telling a stretcher," so her kindness is even more appreciated):

> "I don't care whether 'twas little or whether 'twas big; he's here in our house and a stranger, and it wasn't good of you to say it. If you was in his place it would make you feel ashamed; and so you oughtn't to say a thing to another person that will make *them* feel ashamed."
>
> "Why, Maim, he said—"

"It don't make no difference what he *said*—that ain't the thing. The thing is for you to treat him *kind,* and not be saying things to make him remember he ain't in his own country and amongst his own folks."

I says to myself, *this* is a girl that I'm letting that old reptile rob her of her money!

Huck doesn't have a lot of values—he's the original American rogue—but he does value the sort of kindness he's seldom received. So his POV makes his motivation clear in selecting this incident and showing in his internal voice that he's violating his own meager moral code by letting the con men steal from her.

Another hallmark of his POV will be his *background.* Huck's rural background comes through in every syllable of his narration. But his experience as an abused child is shown in his quick assessment of the situation and his immediate solution as the con men leave the room—this is a boy who knows how to sneak around:

> But I knowed better. I had [the sack of stolen money] out of there before they was half-way down stairs. I groped along up to my cubby, and hid it there till I could get a chance to do better. I judged I better hide it outside of the house somewheres, because if they missed it they would give the house a good ransacking: I knowed that very well. Then I turned in, with my clothes all on; but I couldn't a gone to sleep if I'd a wanted to, I was in such a sweat to get through with the business. By and by I heard the king and the duke come up; so I rolled off my pallet and laid with my chin at the top of my ladder, and waited to see if anything was going to happen. But nothing did.
>
> So I held on till all the late sounds had quit and the early ones hadn't begun yet; and then I slipped down the ladder.

The POV character's *biases* will also affect the narration. A bias is simply an assumption or preference, one based not on evidence or rationality but on taste or temperament. (One person's bias, after all, is another person's value; biases tend to be more trivial, though often just as intense.) Huck has a bias against doctors, and this comes through his narration as he debates whether to tell an adult about the theft:

THE POWER OF POINT OF VIEW

> When I got by myself I went to thinking the thing over. I says to myself, shall I go to that doctor, private, and blow on these frauds? No—that won't do. He might tell who told him; then the king and the duke would make it warm for me.

Maybe it's not justified, but Huck doesn't trust the doctor, or most authority figures, for that matter. In this passage, we learn not just about Huck's actions, but what goes into his decision to take action.

And don't forget the *emotion*. If you've put this character in a situation that will challenge him emotionally, show how he responds, but make his response unique to him. This requires some real delving into who this guy is. Try the interview technique. For example, "Huck, how did you feel when you realized you've been traveling with two con men?" Or "Don't you feel guilty for helping them steal from that nice girl?"

Just try freewriting the answers in the character's first-person voice. Ask about those POV components: knowledge, values, background, biases, and emotion. Then see what you can use at the pivotal moments when the character is challenged, as in the above passage where Huck chooses, perhaps for the first time, to do the right thing.

Remember, if it's important to him, it's important to the reader—as long as we're in his perspective. That doesn't mean you have to dwell on any aspect of his perspective, or tell the whole history of why he is so good at stealing; just give the reader enough so that the character's experience is textured and deep.

This doesn't have to happen in slow-paced introspective passages. Instead, read over what the character told you about himself and think about what you want to pass on to the reader. Try inserting snippets of this in the narrative of a scene, as Twain did in the scene where Huck steals back the stolen money. POV isn't revealed just in introspection. We also use action to reveal who we are and how we're feeling.

CHARACTER SELF-TALK

Because of modern readers' demand for constant action, pages and pages of introspection—also called internal monologue—are less desirable in the modern novel. Now novels are more likely to show character through action and behavior than through "self-talk" or narrative description. But introspection is a real phenomenon. Think of when you talk to yourself—when you're reminding yourself how to do something, when you're trying to buck yourself up, or when you're trying to convince yourself to make a decision. Characters can do that, too. Some characters are more contemplative, more given to self-talk, than others. But even the least introspective character might have flashes of thought amidst the action, and how he thinks is going to reveal as much as the thought itself.

So select wisely. Most of us have a lot of junk in our brains—song refrains, shopping lists, momentary observations of the passing scene. Edit those out. Even in the most stream-of-consciousness narrative, you don't want to faithfully report all the junk. Rather, use internal monologue to reveal hidden bits of insight. The reader will accumulate all the information: when the characters think, what they think, what they deliberately don't think, what lies and half-truths they tell themselves, and how they phrase their thoughts to build a collage of character. The trick is making the meaningful appear meaningless, just a stray thought or a random memory. But the well-trained reader knows to regard them as hints to the character's inner life.

This can help shape your plot as well as your character. Consider what your character is hiding. Remember: What you conceal is what you reveal. So show the character hiding. Here's an example from *Never Let Me Go* by Kazuo Ishiguro, where the narrator is a young Englishwoman who cares for patients recovering from surgery:

> There have been times over the years when I've tried to leave Hailsham behind, when I've told myself I shouldn't look back so much. But then there came a point when I just stopped resisting. It had to do with this particular donor I had once, in my third year as a carer; it was his reaction when I mentioned I was from Hailsham. He'd just come through his third donation, it hadn't gone well, and he must have known he wasn't going to make it. He could hardly breathe, but he looked towards me and said: "Hailsham. I bet that was a beautiful place." ...
>
> So over the next five or six days, I told him whatever he wanted to know .... He'd ask me about the big things and the little things. About our guardians, about how we each had our own collection chests un-

der our beds, the football, the rounders, the little path that took you all round the outside of the main house, round all its nooks and crannies, the duck pond, the food, the view from the Art Room over the fields on a foggy morning. Sometimes he'd make me say things over and over; things I'd told him only the day before .... At first I thought this was just the drugs, but then I realized his mind was clear enough. What he wanted was not just to hear about Hailsham, but to remember Hailsham, just like it had been his own childhood. ... [W]ith the drugs and the pain and the exhaustion, the line would blur between what were my memories and what were his. That was when I first understood, really understood, just how lucky we'd been—Tommy, Ruth, me, all the rest of us.

What the narrator is revealing is her nostalgia for her youth at an idyllic boarding school. What she is concealing is what the boarding school trained the students to become. That doesn't become clear until much later in the book, when the reader has gradually come to understand not just what she's hiding, but why she has to hide it.

Think about what you want to reveal in the beginning, middle, and end of the story, and craft events within scenes to lead organically to revelations of the secret. What else is happening in the story? Look for opportunities to set up scenes to allow the thoughts to creep through.

You can also use introspective bits (it doesn't have to be a long passage) to set up where the character is at any point in his journey. Such revelation can be far more interesting if it's not too obvious and self-conscious, if it shows something that isn't quite true but that the character wishes were true. After all, one of the purposes of self-talk is to remind us of what we want to be, of who we want to be—and that internal wish or declaration is a clue to the internal conflict.

Establishing that conflict alerts the reader to this character's "need to change." For instance, when the sophisticated executive Portia, in *Match Me If You Can* by Susan Elizabeth Phillips, finds a client attractive, she quickly backtracks and reminds herself of one of her cardinal rules: "A fling with Champion would be exciting, but she never let her personal life interfere with business." The astute reader is going to read that declaration and know that sometime before the end of the book,

Portia's personal life is going to interfere with her business because the author has selected, from many cardinal rules, the one which has to be violated for Portia to grow.

Phillips uses Portia's internal POV passages to chart the change in her, from the pleasure-denying perfectionism at the start of the book through temptation and partial resistance—not to Champion (that would be too obvious), but to his chauffeur: "Bodie inhabited a secret compartment in her life, a sordid, perverted chamber she could never let anyone peer into." And finally, near the end of the book, Portia has a movement toward surrender and understanding:

> As she gazed at [the candy], she knew Bodie had been right about her. All her life, she'd been driven by fear, so frightened of falling short that she'd forgotten how to live.

Similarly, you can use your character's POV to show what she is thinking at any point in the story, and those thoughts can lead your reader to see what needs changing, how the change happens, and what the results are.

CHARACTER CHANGE THROUGH PARALLEL SCENES: METAPHORS AND MOTIFS

Your characters, particularly the protagonists, are on a journey through the story, and they change in response to the plot events. Their POV will also change, both the way they interact with reality and the way they express it. One way to show this change is to use parallel scenes, ones that center on a similar event but evolve in different ways because they occur at different points in the character's journey.

In Don DeLillo's story "Still-Life," New Yorker Keith staggers to his ex-wife's house just after the World Trade Center collapses around him, and she takes him to the emergency room for an MRI on his broken wrist. He is a man described as "dangerously alive," hurtling through life without reflection or regard for the consequences. As a result, his initial response to the 9/11 disaster is to put it behind him and move on. He is so alienated from the actual experience that he can't even recall seeing the towers fall. When he's asked about that, he tells, instead, the account he heard from the plumber who picked him up as he walked away from the destruction. Notice the similar emphasis on "hearing" in the passage below. In his POV, seeing is believing, so he doesn't let himself "see," but hearing is safer for him—it's somehow once-removed from reality. He retreats into his senses, and as soon as the memory of death intrudes, he forces himself back into passive hearing:

> The noise [in the MRI tube] was unbearable .... He listened to the music and thought of what the radiologist said, that once it's over ... you forget instantly the whole experience, so how bad can it be ... he thought this sounded like a description of dying. But that was another matter, wasn't it .... He listened to the music. He tried hard to hear the flutes and to distinguish them from the clarinets ....

Notice how he uses self-talk (*but that was another matter, wasn't it*) to push away the perilous thoughts of death, which might lead back to the memory he's been suppressing.

Like DeLillo, you can use this sort of doubled motif as a way to show growth (positive or negative) in a character, to demonstrate a gradual and understandable change in how he perceives and reacts to events. That means using two parallel scenes with some similar action (such as treatment for the injury), with the change in the POV attitude showing the change in the character. So the 9/11 survivor here tries but fails to take refuge in the senses. Then later, Keith's own need to recover teaches him to "sink into life" instead of just "sliding" across the surface, and in doing so, he finally remembers the chaos of that clear morning:

> He raised the hand without lifting his forearm and kept it in the air for five seconds. He did this ten times .... It wasn't the torn cartilage that was the subject of the effort. It was the chaos, the levitation of ceilings and floors, the voices choking in smoke. He sat in deep concentration, working on the hand shapes, the bend of the wrist to the floor ....

The character is still the same man—he still experiences life through his senses, and, yet, he still cannot speak his thoughts and feelings. But his POV shows that the events of the story, both the terrorist attacks and his ex-wife's forgiveness, have changed him and have taught him the value of experiencing the eternity of a moment, not just its fleeting quality. Notice the connections and differences set up between the two passages, one early and one late. Both have to do with his broken wrist, but in the first, he is a passive patient inside a metal MRI tube, getting his damage diagnosed. In the second, however, he is doing the exercises that are healing him. In the first, he can only "hear," but in the later passage, he is acting and feeling.

Look for similar parallel scenes in the books you read, and then try to create your own scenes that are connected in some way—one early in your story and one late—and use the difference in POV to show the journey the character has made. The reader will make a subconscious link between the two scenes and sense the change.

It's paradoxical: Deeply emotional issues like 9/11 or the loss of a loved one are best handled elliptically. If DeLillo had attempted a straight-on narration of the events of that day, his readers might have, like Keith, shut down in emotional overload. But using the metaphor of a broken bone and the motif of sound, the author gets around our instinctive resistance to the pain of memory. That's how our minds work; we come at these things sideways, thinking of tragedy in metaphors and motifs. Character POV in deeply emotional moments like this should reflect that human need to symbolize in order to find meaning.

EXERCISE

THE POV JOURNEY

1. Think about the POV character you described in the exercise on pages 216–217. Read over those hallmarks of POV, and jot down notes about the character's temperament, values, perceptive strengths and weaknesses—anything that might affect narration.

2. Choose one point early in your story where this character has to experience an event or take an action—important or trivial. Write two or three paragraphs deep in his viewpoint, trying to show the

uniqueness of this person's perspective. Keep it simple. You don't need to overdo it, but make it distinctly this character.

3. Then write a paragraph or two of analysis of this: How did it feel to write that way? Reading it over, do you feel that it captured or revealed this character? If you were going to take this passage and put it into your story, what would you change or keep? What about his POV will you use in other scenes?

4. Consider the events you'll be taking this character through. How will his POV change in response? Think of an event that happens late in the story, something connected to that earlier event, and put yourself in his mind and body to experience that. Quickly freewrite a POV passage. How does he perceive and respond differently now?

10

LEVELS OF POV

Even after you've chosen your POV approach and gotten to know your characters, there's still one more element to consider as you craft a scene. That's the level of POV you'll be in at any given moment, from a surface perspective to a deep emotional level, no matter whether you're using single POV or multiple. In fact, in any scene, perhaps even within a paragraph, the POV can shift from surface level (camera-eye) to the deepest level (deep immersion/voice). So even if you're in the POV of someone primarily in the perception mode, you can and probably will still narrate his actions, though not in great detail as you might if you were primarily in action mode.

But don't worry. You probably already instinctively vary how deeply you delve into the POV depending on what's happening in the scene—at least to some degree. In this chapter, you'll learn to become more conscious about the choices you make and use them to enhance the reader's experience.

LEVELS OF POV (IN DESCENDING ORDER OF DEPTH)

- Camera-eye/Objective
- Action
- Perception
- Thought
- Emotion
- Deep immersion/Voice

LEVEL ONE: CAMERA-EYE OR OBJECTIVE

Camera-eye level is observation, not participation, similar to the objective type of POV described in chapter six. While this is a good way to start scenes, very few writers stay in camera-eye level for very long because it's so distancing for readers. However, it's effective for showing an event happening from a perspective outside the POV of any character. Here's an example from *Prince of Fire* by Daniel Silva:

> Most heard the truck before they saw it. The convulsive roar of its diesel engine was a violent intrusion on the otherwise still morning. It was impossible to ignore. The Italian security men paused in mid-conversation and looked up, as did the group of fourteen strangers gathered outside the entrance of the embassy. The tubby Jesuit, who was waiting for a bus at the opposite end of the street, lifted his round head from his copy of L'Osservatore Romano and searched for the source of the commotion.

Because the "camera" does not stay with any one character in this scene, the reader is allowed to take in the larger picture and orient herself in the story before diving in to one POV.

LEVEL TWO: ACTION

The next level down is much more interesting because it's more personal: action. This allows a bit of participation in that the reader gets to experience the character's physical actions and reactions. This works really well in combat or danger scenes, when you have to narrate what's going on and don't want to wreck the pacing by getting into a character's thoughts.

Consider the POV of a character who is far too busy surviving to have time to think. He's being shot at or chased by a tiger, and his instincts are guiding his actions. This POV character might still have an individual perception of events (the soldier down in the foxhole is going to have a different view of the action than the fighter pilot above the battle looking for his target), but there won't be much thought or feeling expressed.

On the action level, it's important to make the narration interesting and exciting. The reader should participate in the adventure through the unique perceptions of the character, but without getting bogged down by feelings. Richard Stark does a good job at describing action and setting pace in this excerpt from *Breakout*:

> As Parker ran down the long aisle, Armiston a dozen paces behind, Bruhl appeared, coming fast out of the first side aisle down there. Walheim tried to clutch at him, but Bruhl hit him with a backhand that knocked the thinner man down.
>
> Parker yelled, "Bruhl! Stop!" but Bruhl kept going. He jumped to the ground outside the loading dock, next to the truck, then ran toward the front of it. He was going to take it, leave the rest of them here on foot.

Just as I described above, this scene gives no thought, no real feeling, just the minimum of perception and action. You'll always have access to the action level of POV, and there are several intriguing opportunities to use it. Of course, the most obvious one is when a protagonist is in danger or intent upon a task so very little other "stimuli" are coming into his perspective.

Since an action-focused passage is often stripped of most of its emotion and color, you need to compensate with strong verbs and active sentence construction. See how inventive you can get with what action you have—for example, a woman who is facing a carjacking could grab a tire iron, but she can also do something more interesting, like break off the leg of the department-store male mannequin she keeps on her passenger seat to ward off rapists.

The action level can also be used to block thought. Again, you'll want to establish whatever the unthinkable thought is before turning up the action to block it. For example, consider a pacifist loading his gun to go out and avenge his family's slaughter. It can be very effective to set up all the conflict of pacifism versus revenge, and then show his decision playing out in action only, as if he cannot bear to think it through—he just has to act.

The action level can also be used to emphasize the character's need to block other stimuli, like physical pain (perception) or fear (emotion).

What you want to do here is establish the unwanted stimuli and then show the character blocking it with action, as Alafair Burke does here in *Missing Justice*:

> The walls of the stairway pass as a man follows me upstairs. I force myself to focus on my own movements, trying to block out thoughts of the other man downstairs, armed and determined to kill me when I return.
>
> Time slows as I duck beside my bed, reach for the pistol hidden inside my nightstand, and rise up to surprise him. The .25 caliber automatic breaks the silence; more shots follow downstairs. Glass shatters. Heavy footsteps thunder through the house .... I see bullets rip through flesh and muscle, the scene tinted red like blood smeared across my retinas.

This passage is effective because it replicates the inner state of someone intent upon blocking his thoughts of the danger downstairs so he can react to the danger right behind him. The narrator is focused, and so the narrative is focused as well.

Highly emotional moments are often paradoxically more effective from a more surface-level POV. Once again, you have to set up the situation earlier so the reader can know what the character is feeling here. For example, say Alice comes home after ten years of working in the city, eager to see her mother because she has saved some money and is going to tell her mom, "I'm taking you to Paris, just like we always dreamed!" I'd show her thinking about it in the cab from the airport, show her great anticipation, and then, when she gets to her old house and sees the ambulance out in front, I'd move to action level. Alice withdraws from her own emotions so that she can get through the next few minutes; show her walking up to the back door of the ambulance, twisting the knob, opening it, looking in. This is much more powerful than letting her emote; the reader will experience the dread *for* her. The more emblematic the actions, the stronger the experience will be. Maybe she climbs into the ambulance, sits down, and takes her mother's limp hand, and with her other hand, she reaches into her pocket and crumples up the tickets to Paris. Use the actions to show what she would be feeling if she could let herself feel. Letting the body express the emotion in action will, oddly enough, give the reader space to feel the blocked emotion. In other words, the reader can cry because the character won't.

You won't be parked in this action level, though, because no one can block perception, thought, and emotion for long. As Alice emerges from the ambulance, she's going to feel the hot asphalt under her feet and the summer breeze tease her face, and hear her own breathing and the ambulance's siren. So very likely, you'll start descending into the level of perception.

LEVEL THREE: PERCEPTION—THE SENSORY LEVEL

The perception level lets the reader experience not just action but also the perceptions of the POV character. We are in her body. We see what she sees, we hear what she hears, we feel what she feels.

A POV character will be primarily in the perception level when she enters a new setting, especially one that's unfamiliar. This is where you might want to spend a paragraph or so describing a room before the character starts engaging in action. But keep the description unique to this character. What would she notice when she enters this room? Look back at what you identified as the perceptual hallmarks of her POV and make use of them.

At the same time, however, remember that this story moment is unique, too. This isn't just one of a number of room entrances. There's something special about this one, and she'll notice whatever seems most relevant in this situation. This is the sheriff's office, and her gaze goes immediately to the rack of guns on the wall. This is the church, and she's feeling guilty, so she glances at the confessional and looks away. This is her mother's hospital room, and she goes right to the foot of the bed and picks up the chart and looks at the nurse's notations.

Here is a passage from *Endymion Spring* by Matthew Skelton, in which a student waits in a familiar place, the library, but it's different today:

> All around him the library was sleeping in the hot, still afternoon. Shafts of sunlight hung in the air like dusty curtains and a clock ticked somewhere in the distance, a ponderous sound that seemed to slow down time. Small footsteps crept along the floorboards

above. That was probably his sister, Duck, investigating upstairs. But no one else was around.

Only Mephistopheles, the college cat, a sinewy black shadow with claws as sharp as pins, was sunbathing on a strip of carpet near the window and he only cared about one thing: himself.

As far as Blake could tell, he was entirely alone. Apart, that is, from whatever was lurking on the shelf.

Keep these sensory openings interesting by making sure he has unique perceptions. Who is this guy, and how does he perceive the world? How does he get the information he needs about his environment? That's where you get the interesting perceptions. For example, if he's a sailor, he'll perceive the weather very differently than a land-lubber will. He'll feel the coming of a storm in his bones or on the wind on his face. He'll smell it in the air. He won't just turn on the Weather Channel.

In this example from *H.M.S. Surprise* by Patrick O'Brian, the sailor-protagonist is used to interpreting the sea, so readying his ship for a battle calms him:

> "Mr. Church," [Jack] said, "be so good as to fetch me a mango."
>
> The minutes passed; the juice ran down his chin. The French frigates stood on to the north-northwest, growing smaller. First the *Semi-llante* and then the *Belle Poule* crossed the wake of the *Surprise*, gaining the weather-gauge; there was no changing his mind now. The *Marengo*, her two tiers of guns clearly to be seen, lay on the starboard beam, sailing a parallel course. There was no sound but the high steady note of the wind in the rigging and the beat of the sea on the frigate's larboard bow. The far-spaced ships scarcely seemed to move in relation to one another from one minute to another—there seemed to be all the peaceful room in the world.

The perception level, like the action level, can be used to show the blocking of thought or emotion, as in the above example, where the captain is embarking on a dangerous mission and can't think about the hazards ahead. But very soon the situation will likely demand thought, and the POV will descend to that level.

LEVEL FOUR: THOUGHT—THE POV PARKING PLACE

The thought level is actually where most scenes spend the most time. As the POV character is acting and reacting to the environment, he's also generally thinking. He might be planning his next move, deciding between two options, remembering the last time he was in this room, realizing that he's lost or talking to himself, or mentally interpreting what's going on around him.

In the thought level, the reader is very close to the POV character, not just in his body but in his mind. Here's an example from *The Blessing Way* by Tony Hillerman:

> Leaphorn went through his solution again, looking for a hole. The Big Navaho must have found the Army's missing rocket on the Mesa. Why, Leaphorn asked himself angrily, had he been so quick to reject this solution when he learned the reward was cancelled? A Navaho would not kill for money, but he would kill in anger.

In this case, the detective, Leaphorn, figures out the solution to the mystery, and this takes place on the thought level. There is also emotion (he gets angry at himself), but it's tied to what he figured out.

If you have a character think through a problem, consider having the catalyst for his thought be something concrete in the real world. For Leaphorn, it's the discovery of truck tracks in the desert that gives him the final clue he needs to puzzle out the mystery. Be wary, however, of too much "introspection" unlinked to what's going on around him. An editor once remarked that I had two scenes of the hero walking around analyzing a problem before finally coming up with a solution. She said, "While he's thinking, nothing's happening!" His thought processes weren't all that exciting as he methodically sorted through his options, choosing the most sensible one. In the editor's estimation (and mine, too, eventually), the scenes were bogged down for lack of action.

Even when the character is deep in thought, give him something to *do*, or at least the prospect of an event to bring him back to reality. Leaphorn, for example, is driving onto the mesa and, in a nice touch, his speed is in inverse proportion to his thought—the closer he gets to his solution, the slower he drives. This sort of dynamic between action and contemplation keeps the thought level from getting too inert.

LEVEL FIVE: EMOTION

The next level deeper into character is emotion. This is very intimate, just once removed from the character's soul. In some books, we don't ever need to get this deep. Just as in some fictional relationships, we might never need to know how some protagonists feel. Think of Miss Jane Marple in Agatha Christie books. We didn't need to know that she misses her nephew. We are content to spend most of our time in her fertile mind, sharing her clever thoughts.

But for the characters the reader needs to know well, you'll want to occasionally descend to the emotional level, not just to describe the POV character's feelings but to present the emotional experience. In this passage from Laura Kinsale's *Flowers from the Storm*, Jervaulx, a wealthy, handsome rake, embarks on a sort of cruel flirtation, one meant to disquiet and disorient the shy, inexperienced POV character, Maddy. He tells her blind father, a Quaker, that he will describe Maddy's face. Jervaulx uses inappropriately sexualized terms, and concludes with the following:

> "This serious mouth might have been insipid, but instead it goes with the wonderful long lashes that haven't got that silly debutante curl. They ... shadow her eyes and turn the hazel so gold, and she seems as if she's looking through them at me. ..."
>
> In his house, at his table, she felt she could not say precisely what she thought .... Besides that, her father appeared enraptured. "Maddy," he whispered. "Thou hast your mother's look."
>
> "Of course, Papa," she said helplessly. "Has no one ever told thee?"
>
> "No. No one ever did."
>
> He said it without any particular emotion. But by the candlelight, she could see that his eyes had tears in them. "Papa," she said, reaching for his hand ... he lifted his fingers, touching her face. He explored her slowly, intently, over her cheeks, and across her eyelashes. She held her hands locked tight, embarrassed and suddenly close to foolish tears herself.

"I thank thee, Friend," her father said, turning his face toward Jervaulx. "I thank thee. For one of the finest days of my life."

Jervaulx didn't answer. He didn't even seem to have heard, but sat gazing into the shadowed folds of the tablecloth, his dark blue eyes meditative and his pirate mouth turned grim.

In Maddy's POV, we not only "hear" about her emotion, but experience its development, from her annoyance at Jervaulx's insulting behavior, to her new understanding of her father's love. Using Maddy's POV this way is considerably more powerful than a mere description of her emotion would be, as it invites the reader to participate in the emotion.

A long sojourn in this emotion is usually reserved for major characters. Astute readers expect that if we're let in on the emotional life of a character, he will end up being important, and the emotion described will somehow affect the plot. There's no problem being in the POV of a butler as he enters an empty room and discovers a dead body on the floor. But maybe you should dip only to the perception or thought level; otherwise, you'll risk giving him too much emotional importance in the plot. Then again, you would want to go into the emotion level if the body is that of his son or the boss he hated.

Certainly don't waste the impact of sharing emotions on someone who will never appear again in the story, unless you have a very good reason. Sharing emotions is like sharing a bed: if you're promiscuous about it, it lessens the importance of any one emotional experience. That's why you might want to be wary of using the emotional level of viewpoint with minor characters. And you might even consider how often you want to use it with the major characters.

Adding a Little Distance

I know this sounds contradictory, but sometimes, a little narrative distance can make characters and their emotions even more appealing. (As I mentioned earlier when talking about action, if the POV character can't or won't have a good cry, the reader feels compelled to do the crying for him.) Let the *scene* provide the emotion, not the POV. This can be accomplished by a deliberate shifting of levels: At the most emotional moment, retreat to the level of thought, or even higher.

In this example from Patrick O'Brian's *The Reverse of the Medal*, the proud Captain Jack Aubrey is caught up in a swindle and must suffer the stocks as punishment. The worst punishment will be, he imagines, the shame of being pelted with stones from bystanders. He cannot deal with the humiliation, so his POV ascends to the perception level, where he can observe as if from above. However, what he sees is intensely emotional and draws him back. Hearing of his plight, every sailor in several counties has come to London to stand with him:

> Jack was led out of the dark room into the strong light, and as they guided him up the steps he could see nothing but the glare. "Your head here, sir, if you please," said the sheriff's man in a low, nervous, conciliating voice, "and your hands here."
>
> The man was slowly fumbling with the bolt, hinge and staple, and as Jack stood there with his hands in the lower half-rounds, his sight cleared; he saw that the broad street was filled with silent, attentive men, some in long togs, some in shore-going rigs, some in plain frocks, but all perfectly recognizable as seamen. And officers, by the dozen, by the score: midshipmen and officers. Babbington was there, immediately in front of the pillory, facing him with his hat off, and Pullings, Stephen of course, Mowett, Dundas .... He nodded to them, with almost no change in his iron expression, and his eye moved on: Parker, Rowan, Williamson, Hervey ... and men from long, long ago, men he could scarcely name, lieutenants and commanders putting their promotions at risk, midshipmen and master's mates their commissions, warrant-officers their advancements.
>
> "The head a trifle forward, if you please, sir," murmured the sheriff's man, and the upper half of the wooded frame came down, imprisoning his defenseless face. He heard the click of the bolt and then in the dead silence a strong voice cry, "Off hats." With one movement, hundreds of broad-brimmed tarpaulin-covered hats flew off, and the cheering began, the fierce full-throated cheering he had heard so often in battle.

This narration doesn't use emotional words but, instead, sets up the event to provide the emotional experience for the reader. And when emotion returns to Jack, it is an experience of love that he characteristically associates with the solidarity of men in battle. It is his deliberate use of perception to distance himself from emotion that creates for the reader the space needed to fully feel the emotion.

Author Laura Kinsale even suggests that if there is another character in the scene, you let that character be the POV character to observe and narrate the highly charged moment. The example above from her book *Flowers from the Storm* demonstrates this. Maddy, the POV character, definitely experiences emotion, but it's not a new emotion—she loves her father and knows her father loves her, even if they are too reserved to show it often. But notice that it's the non-POV character, Jervaulx, who perhaps experiences the most profound emotional shift:

> "I thank thee, Friend," her father said, turning his face toward Jervaulx. "I thank thee. For one of the finest days of my life."
>
> Jervaulx didn't answer. He didn't even seem to have heard, but sat gazing into the shadowed folds of the tablecloth, his dark blue eyes meditative and his pirate mouth turned grim.

Jervaulx starts the scene just wanting to exert his powerful sexual magnetism over the plain Maddy, who dislikes and distrusts him. But he doesn't count on the moral clarity of these two Quakers, who care nothing for wealth and power and have something he has always lacked: a certainty of family love. In fact, his teasing brings them together, and puts him on the outside, looking in. What he sees is something pure and true—and perhaps for the first time, he realizes how empty his "superiority" is.

Generally, you want to be in the POV that matters most at that time. But sometimes a more distant POV allows the reader to *participate* more by filling in the blanks ("He must be so worried! But he's so brave ..."), and that participation is the ultimate triumph of story writing. I tried this once in a scene where the heroine had been ostracized. I put it in the hero's POV. She was clearly hurt, but he saw her with respect as well as pity, so she came across as heroic, not just as a victim. This distance transformed the scene from maudlin to intensely controlled.

When you do a distant or lighter viewpoint, remember to compensate with increased perception or action. Make the actions resonant with meaning. (*He crumbles up a note. He goes to the window, opens it,*

leans out, and breathes deeply the night air, which tastes clean and pure.)
Make the action show the emotion. Men often express emotion through
action, so take advantage of this.

Another emotional situation that might benefit from a higher level
is the "revelation" scene in a romance, when characters realize and
confess their love. As a romance writer, I battle my tendency to explain too much in the revelation scene in every book. It always helps
to consider who these characters are and how they would realize
their love in actions and speech, not just inner monologue. I like
to go straight to dialogue to let their exchange of love carry all the
weight. You don't need internalization when you have them talking
to each other! Surely, at the moment of confession, they are speaking
their hearts in whatever language fits their passion.

For example, in my novel *Poetic Justice*, I considered that John
and Jessica's relationship was based on their competitiveness and
their equal appreciation for puzzles. When he solves the mystery
Jessica sets up for him, their mutual declaration is characteristically
contentious (you can see in brackets the "explainer" material I must
always cut out):

> "I was worried that you were so stupid you couldn't figure out where
> I'd gone." [She hoped that he'd understand how frightened she'd
> been and wouldn't take offense.]
>
> [He replied with mock disgruntlement,] "It isn't as if you made
> it easy for me. Why didn't you tell me you were planning on scarper-
> ing, and why?"
>
> "That would have been too easy. I had to know—" [she paused
> and thought, now I do know.]
>
> "What?" That was only a whisper. [John could hardly wait for
> her answer.]
>
> "That you cared enough to find me." [It was hard to say it, but
> she did, and it didn't hurt as much as she'd worried.]
>
> [His anger left him and he knew finally he could confess the
> truth.] "Well, now you know. I care more than enough. And—and
> I know you. I knew right away why you ran off. To test me. To
> challenge me."

Spelling out the emotional internalization through inner monologue is fine when there isn't a way to *show* it through action and dialogue. But don't let it substitute, for example, for them talking to each other. Our heroine doesn't have the reader's ability to "read" the hero's emotions—he has to speak them to her. So make him do the work. (I advise that in relationships, too—let the guy do the work!)

As I said, you are likely to be sliding up and down the POV slope in every scene, sometimes within a paragraph. But if you can put yourself inside the POV character, you can manipulate these levels to create an intense reader identification.

LEVEL SIX: DEEP IMMERSION/VOICE

In truly intense moments, when action, perception, thought, and emotion are all engaged, the narrative can reach the deepest level of intimacy with the character—what I call "deep immersion," where the narrative itself takes on the nature of the character's voice.

In deep immersion, the narrative actually descends into the character. You don't just present his thoughts and feelings; you write as transparently as possible, putting as little filter as you can between the character's experience and the reader's experience. Within reasonable limits, the terminology used, the phrasing, the thoughts expressed, the perspective, even the grammar of the narration should be that of the POV character. For example, here is another passage from *Flowers from the Storm* by Laura Kinsale; the narration is done by a man who lost much of his speech ability after a stroke:

> Any changes in the room made him angry. He was afraid only a crazy person cared so much about such things, and tried not to care, and still did. He looked down at his feet in topboots. A madman. Crazy, mute, imprisoned animal. He caught the bars on the door and shook them against the steel frame, filling the room and hall with clanging metal.
>
> *Know, Maddygirl? Hear this? Understand feel no self, no pride, sick shame dress coat boots spurs can't go? Understand?*

This is the most intense and intimate POV level, more intimate, in fact, than first-person narration. Why? Because an effective first-person narrator can and probably will lie. In deep-immersion third person, the reader can assume that what's reported is the deepest of personal truth, at least as far as the character knows.

This is also the ultimate in "show, don't tell" because the character's perspective is all the reader gets. This means if the POV character wouldn't think it or notice it, it doesn't get said. While you can use this level in multiple-POV scenes, the longer you can stay in one POV, the more effective this is. Moving from one narrative voice to another every couple pages can be jarring to the reader.

Here's an example from Alice Munro's *Hateship, Friendship, Court-ship, Loveship, Marriage.* Notice how deep immersion limits the narrative (within reason—it's in *language,* so there's a certain layer of externality—most of us don't think entirely in language) to the perceptions of the viewpoint character. Head words (like *he thought*) are used as seldom as possible because we're already inside his head:

> She spoke to him in a loud voice as if he was deaf or stupid, and there was something wrong with the way she pronounced her words. An accent. He thought of Dutch—the Dutch were moving in around here—but she didn't have the heft of the Dutch women or the nice pink skin or the fair hair. She might have been under forty, but what did it matter? No beauty queen, ever.
>
> The station agent would have said, without thinking about it, that he knew everybody in town. Which meant that he knew about half of them. And most of those he knew were the core people, the ones who really were "in town" in the sense that they had not arrived yesterday and had no plans to move on. He did not know the woman who was going to Saskatchewan because she did not go to his church or teach his children in school or work in any store or restaurant or office that he went into. Nor was she married to any of the men he knew in the Elks or the Oddfellows or the Lions Club or the Legion. A look at her left hand while she was getting the money out had told him—and he was not surprised—that she was not married to anybody. With those shoes, and ankle socks instead of stockings, and no hat or gloves in the afternoon, she might have been a farm woman. But she didn't have the hesitation

they generally had, the embarrassment. She didn't have country manners—in fact, she had no manners at all. She had treated him as if he was an information machine.

You'll notice first that this POV passage is long. Showing usually takes longer than telling because we perceive in elaboration, not summary ("... shoes, and ankle socks instead of stockings, and no hat and gloves ..."). We see what we see, register it, and only then try to categorize it. Deep immersion will often narrate that whole process, especially when what's being perceived (like her style of dress) is unfamiliar to the viewpoint character. So the stationmaster has to *see* her clothing, register its faculties (dowdy), and put it into a category in his knowledge base, which includes respectable town women, beauty queens, and farm wives. This is effective in conveying what this man knows and how he thinks. We are clearly deep in his head, seeing not just from his eyes, but from his mind, too.

Note, also, that as much as possible, Munro used the stationmaster's own terminology and syntax. The sentences are long and stringy when they're not fragments. If you do this, you might have to bend grammar rules (using sentence fragments, for one thing) to more closely mimic his narrative voice. This works best if you're in the character's voice for long stretches so the editor and the reader realize it's the character with lousy grammar, and not you.

You have to walk a fine line here between annoying fidelity and author intrusion. It's hard. But before you use a ten-dollar word with a two-bit POV character, ask yourself, "Would he think this?" That doesn't mean you can't be creative and exciting in your prose—even illiterate people can speak and think poetically, as the narrator does here in *Walkin' the Dog* by Walter Mosley:

> At first he thought the trill and bleating note was part of a dream. A sweet note so high it had to be the angel that Aunt Belladra said the blue god sent, "to save the black mens from falling out the world complete."

But this does mean that, to some extent, you give over control of the narrative to the voice of the POV character. Your extensive vocabulary and lush descriptions aren't going to fit if you decide to write in deep-third. This is why Elmore Leonard once said, "If I come across anything in my work that smacks of 'good writing,' I immediately strike it out." Leonard is famous for subsuming his own author voice into the voice of his usually criminal characters, as in this excerpt from *Rum Punch*:

> "This way," Ordell said, and they started up South County ahead of the parade, couple of old buddies: Ordell Robbie and Louis Gara, a light-skinned black guy and a dark-skinned white guy, both from Detroit originally where they met in a bar, started talking, and found out they'd both been to Southern Ohio Correctional and had some attitudes in common. Not long after that Louis went to Texas, where he took another fall. Came home and Ordell had a proposition for him: a million-dollar idea to kidnap the wife of a guy making money illegally and hiding it in the Bahamas. Louis said okay. The scheme blew up in their face and Louis said never again. Thirteen years ago ...
>
> And now Ordell had another scheme. Louis could feel it. The reason they were here watching skinheads and coneheads marching up the street.

You don't have to completely dedicate yourself to deep immersion, as it can be claustrophobic for the reader if it goes on too long or if the "voice" is annoying. (Try narrating an entire book in the voice of a six-year-old. Groan!) Even Elmore Leonard usually starts scenes in his own voice before descending into the voice of his POV character. But in some scenes, such as action scenes or deeply emotional scenes, it can be effective to help the reader "channel" the character.

EXERCISE

POV LEVELS

Now it's time to try and put it all together—to plan out an intense scene and craft the narrative to reflect the potential of POV.

You can either perform this exercise with a scene from your own story, or start with a sample scene where a hero finally tracks down his runaway wife. He thought she was dead, but now she's left clues so that he can find her; he thinks she's playing some cat-and-mouse game.

1. Do you want one perspective or multiple perspectives on this scene? If multiple, when and how will you shift?

2. Of the possible major POV characters, what are the intriguing "slants" of their perspectives? That is, what gives each a particularly interesting viewpoint on the event? How might that perspective play out?

3. What are the hallmarks of the POV(s) you've chosen? What distinguishes the perspective, the perception, the approach, the internal thoughts of the character(s) in this situation?

4. Now take your character through the various levels of POV, from action down to voice, and for each, jot down one or two ideas about how to power it up. (For example, for "action," think about what the POV character is going to be doing physically in the scene, and what you can do to make that more interesting.)

THE POWER OF POINT OF VIEW

11

CREATING ALTERNATIVE AND UNUSUAL VOICES

In today's new interactive age, a generic voice isn't likely to attract much interest. More and more, readers are looking for unique perspectives and voices—and that means unique POVs. So knowing your characters inside and out becomes even more important. You might go back and read the "Voice" section on page 75. That will translate pretty easily into third-person deep immersion, too. Following are a few other considerations when you are trying to create your character's voice in the narrative.

WRITING THE HISTORICAL CHARACTER: CONSIDERING TIME PERIOD

In a historical novel, a nineteenth-century character shouldn't sound like a twenty-first-century character. You can read fiction and diaries from that time to get a sense of the voice, but be careful. If it's entirely authentic, a modern reader might find the narrative difficult to understand. What is enjoyable in short bursts of dialogue becomes difficult in long stretches of narrative. So aim for a plausible cadence and use period-authentic wording, but keep the voice lively enough for modern readers. Here's an example from Elizabeth Peters's Victorian mystery, *The Deed of the Disturber*:

> Thoughtless persons have sometimes accused me of holding an unjust prejudice against the male sex. Even Emerson has hinted at it—and Emerson, of all people, should know better. When I assert that most of the aggravation I have endured has been caused by members of that sex, it is not prejudice, but a simple statement of fact. Beginning with my estimable but maddeningly absent-minded father and five despicable brothers, continuing through assorted murderers, burglars, and villains, the list even includes my own son.

> In fact, if I kept a ledger, Walter Peabody Emerson, known to friends and foes alike as Ramses, would win the prize for the constancy and the degree of aggravation caused me.

In this case, the long and complex sentence structure gives a Victorian flavor, but the vocabulary is accessible and the wry tone appealing. Peters makes this voice sound authentic by replacing common words with synonyms that have a slightly archaic sound but are still in use today (no dictionary needed!): *aggravation* rather than *hassle*, *estimable* rather than *excellent*, *maddeningly* rather than *irritatingly*, *despicable* rather than *disgusting*.

When you are writing a historical story, remember this: The character isn't historical in her own estimation. Her vocabulary might be a bit formal to our ear, but to hers, it's the way she expresses herself. So before you start to write, descend into the character and learn who she is, what she values, and how she sees herself. Then let her speak for herself. If you need to, later revise in older words and sentence constructions to create that historical feel. But the way to avoid the dreaded "stiltedness" is to let the character be herself, a product of her past background and her present personality, and not just a mouthpiece for an era.

Peters keeps the voice of her heroine from becoming stilted by making her individual. This is not just a period voice; this is the voice of the proto-feminist Amelia who wears a Gibson Girl outfit while shaking her dainty little fist. That is, she's a character first, and a Victorian afterward. Her self-image is not of a stiff matron in an old daguerreotype, but a modern woman in a world that doesn't appreciate women.

Remember, you must aim for verisimilitude rather than authenticity in your character's POV; your goal is to offer the appearance of a period voice rather than its reality. If you too faithfully replicate the vocabulary and sentence constructions of an earlier time, your readers may be turned off by the stiffness. This becomes a greater problem the earlier the period. Try and get the rhythm of the period voice, some of the easily guessed words and phrases, and avoid words that are clearly modern (no "laser-like gaze" from your medieval warrior!).

If you've set your historical novel in a non-English culture, you actually have more flexibility. After all, you're already "translating" their thoughts and speech from whatever language they're using. Modern historical writers like Dorothy Dunnett tend to go with a lush style for the deep POV passages but without self-conscious attempts to sound "period." Most important is staying true to your characters' POVs, couching their thoughts and narration in terms they would use if they could tell the story.

CREATING DISTINCT VOICES: USING DIALECT

Everyone has a dialect, which is simply a nuanced version of the native tongue. This is as true of Queen Elizabeth as it is of a Jamaican reggae singer. Done well, dialect can give a great flavor to a character's manner of speaking. For some reason, however, less experienced writers often rely on dialect to note some contrast between characters' socio-economic positions, races, or regional backgrounds. Done poorly (especially with alternate spellings), dialect becomes patronizing and discriminatory.

"Listen" to your character's dialect, which includes accent, pronunciation, word choice, and sometimes sentence structure. Don't assume that the British aristocrat has no dialect while his Irish maid does. Here, Evelyn Waugh mimics the "posh dialect complete with italics" in *Brideshead Revisited*:

> Sebastian's life was governed by a code of such imperatives: "I *must* have pillar-box red pyjamas," "I *have* to stay in bed until the sun works round to the windows," "I've absolutely *got* to drink champagne to-night!"

You can probably hear the fluting upper-class tones in that speech, and the excessive language (*pillar-box red, absolutely*) of the affected young aristocrat. Notice how much you can accomplish with word choice and emphasis.

No one does the "young aristocrat" dialect quite as effectively as P.G. Wodehouse. His narrator Bertie's dialect consists of half-remembered phrases from his reading, trendy slang (that is, trendy for the 1920s), and the fairly sophisticated sentence structure of one educated at an exclusive school. Here's a passage from *Right Ho, Jeeves*:

Too often, when a chap of your acquaintance is planning to marry a girl you know, you find yourself knitting the brow a bit and chewing the lower lip dubiously, feeling that he or she, or both, should be warned while there is yet time. But I have never felt anything of this nature about Tuppy and Angela. Tuppy, when not making an ass of himself, is a soundish sort of egg. So is Angela a soundish sort of egg. And, as far as being in love was concerned, it had always seemed to me that you wouldn't have been far out in describing them as two hearts that beat as one.

Notice the careful "he or she, or both," and the sophisticated use of "yet" (instead of "still") in "while there is yet time." These signal words and phrases identify Bertie as educated. But the "soundish sort of egg" shows that he is young and speaking the language of the youth of his time. So we can deduce that Bertie is young, but he does not wish to *sound* young. Consider not only your character's age but also the way he wishes to be perceived.

The conflicts inherent in an ethnic group or socioeconomic class's situation will also affect characters' POV passages. For example, in *Walkin' the Dog* by Walter Mosley, an African American man is trying his best to succeed in a world where lives are still subject to the whims of the majority culture. In this passage, a young man reacts to his boss putting a warning hand on him:

"I say, keep your hands to yourself if you wanna keep 'em at all." All the reserve he had built up, all the times he told himself that men like Jason Fullbright were just fools and not to be listened to—all of that was gone. Just a few hours of missing sleep and a strong dream—a fool playing his trumpet in the middle of the night—that's all it took, one bad morning, and Socrates was ready to throw everything away.

It's best to avoid phonetic spelling, as it's hard to read and is usually just annoying. I still remember reading *Gone with the Wind* and puzzling over the word "gwine," which the slaves were always using. It took me a long time, and a lot of irritation, to figure out it was the author's attempt to put "going" into dialect. Well, I grew up in the South and was familiar with both black and white Southern dialects, and if I couldn't figure that out, I couldn't imagine what a Yankee made of it.

Most of us aren't really familiar with any dialect but our own (and we don't necessarily realize we even have a dialect). So unless your narrator shares your dialect, you will need to do some research. It's not enough to read books, however. You'll get a better sense of the rhythm of a dialect through audiobooks, such as the recording of *Angela's Ashes*, read by author Frank McCourt in an authentic (and irresistible!) Irish accent. Consider the following passage:

> [Dad's] in great form altogether and he thinks he'll play awhile with little Patrick, one year old. Lovely little fella. Loves his Daddy. Laughs when Daddy throws him up in the air. Upsy-daisy, little Paddy, upsy daisy in the air in the dark, so dark, oh, Jasus, you miss the child on the way down and poor Patrick lands on his head, gurgles a bit, whimpers, goes quiet. ... Little Pat, my uncle, was never the same after that. He grew up soft in the head with a left leg that went one way, his body the other. He never learned to read or write but God blessed him in another way. When he started to sell papers at age eight, he could count money better than the Chancellor of the Exchequer himself.

This passage shows that it's the rhythm of the sentences, not the spelling of the words, that usually distinguishes the dialect. Write dialect passages so that your reader can "hear" the Irish or the Scottish or the Appalachian voice come through the arrangement of words.

You might check at your local library for "acting tapes"—the audiobooks that train actors how to do different accents. Or, rent videos of movies that feature actors playing roles within their own ethnic group, where they're not just making up a dialect or accent. For example, Nicholas Cage (whose true surname is Coppola) is Italian, and his rough-poetic "voice" in *Moonstruck* gives you a good sense of a working-class Italian-American dialect.

As you're listening to dialect samples, pay attention not only to what's said and how it's said, but also to the rhythm of the speech and the characteristics of phrasing. For example, McCourt above refers to "little Paddy," while a Yorkshireman might refer to "our Pat" and a Scotsman to "wee Pat." Watch for distinctions like exaggeration—"better than the Chancellor of the Exchequer himself." Cultures with a strong oral tradition like the Irish will use more mimicking (*Upsy-daisy, little Paddy, upsy daisy in the air in the dark, so dark*).

If you are writing a character of a different ethnic group, look for models in books written by members of that group. For example, if you want some tough Chicago talk, go with Nelson Algren, but if you're going for the educated Jewish Chicago sound, try absorbing the prose of Saul Bellow. No one writes better black dialect than Walter Mosley. But gender might play a role, too, so check out Alice Walker, Maya Angelou, or Terry McMillan for models for black women characters. Of course, your character won't sound exactly like the model, but you can get a sense of the rhythm of the dialect from reading the prose of someone who grew up speaking it.

It all comes back, however, to respecting your characters and getting inside them enough to know how they'd narrate a story—not just word choice and accent, but what they'd emphasize and what they'd leave out; how they'd tell a joke; and how they'd talk when they're trying not to cry. POV voice is more than just an expression of their background; it's a manifestation of all that they are.

FROM THE MOUTHS OF BABES: WRITING THE CHILD

You can represent a child's POV without sounding childish. The trick is using a child's sensibilities and concerns without resorting to using childlike speech patterns and vocabulary. This is appropriate for long sections narrated by a child, where authentic kid-speak (which might work in small doses) could get seriously annoying.

Dean Koontz creates convincing children's POVs by getting a real sense of his child character as a *person*, not just as a child—by treating her with as much respect as he would an adult character, allowing her values and vanities, and considering how she perceives the world. Her unique perception is only partly due to her youth; the rest comes from who she is and what she finds interesting. Kids are people first, after all, and when it comes to viewpoint characters, there's no such thing as "an average ten-year-old." Here's the voice of ten-year-old Charlotte from Koontz's *Mr. Murder*:

> [At the restaurant] sandwiches and fries were served in baskets, and the ambiance was Caribbean. *Ambiance* was a new word for Charlotte, and she liked the sound of it so much she used it every chance she got, though Emily, hopeless child, was confused and kept asking, "Ambulance? I don't see an ambulance."
>
> Charlotte was ten, or would be in seven weeks, and Emily had just turned seven in October. Em was a good sister, but of course, seven-year-olds were so ... so ... sevenish. ... Sometimes she pretended to be smashed after two glasses of root beer, which was stupid and embarrassing ... Everyone was understanding—from a seven-year-old, what else could be expected? But it was embarrassing nonetheless.

The sentence structure and vocabulary are a bit advanced, even for a smart kid like Charlotte ("nonetheless"), but even taken out of context, it's clear that it's a kid narrating this scene. Notice the sibling rivalry, the fixation with age, the chronic embarrassment, the mix of sophistication and naiveté. And it's not hard to imagine what sort of kid Charlotte is—thoughtful, curious, a little obsessive about words, and easily embarrassed but not easily discomfited. The deeper Koontz descends into her POV, the more childlike the diction gets ("so sevenish"), but that gradual descent keeps it from being too annoying.

Listen to children who are the same age as your POV character, and note their diction, tone, and word choice. When you sit down to write, don't condescend to your fictional children by making them sound like idiots. I've seen manuscripts in which a writer has given a child the line "Me want a cookie," which grated on me as a reader and ruined the scene. In reality, children absorb most of the rules of their native language by the time they're five. The mistakes they do make are logical, often more logical than the language. (For example, my kids say that something happened "on accident" [rather than "by accident"], which is wrong but logical—after all, things happen "on purpose.")

If you can, draft a friend with a child about the age of your character to read over the passages of child POV and make suggestions. A grade-school teacher is likely to be "bilingual," moving from kid-speak to adult-speak without a jolt, and she'd be another good resource. A children's librarian can direct you to the books that are currently entrancing children. The voices in those books are "kid-approved" and are worth absorbing, even if you're writing an adult novel with only a few scenes with a child's POV.

The brains of children are designed for language acquisition, and from year to year, even month to month, a child's vocabulary and ability to describe the world will expand. Children and teenagers are the ones who use slang and catchphrases, but these change annually, too: *Cool* becomes *awesome* becomes *tight* becomes *sweet* becomes whatever it is now. TV, like slang, is ephemeral, so Nickelodeon, the Disney Channel, and MTV are going to be more up-to-date than published novels, which might be a year out of date. Another resource for a youth's POV is teen magazines like *Teen People* and *Seventeen*. The articles, and particularly the letters, will sound like kids today. Make use of the Internet, too—the kids certainly do. Check out blogs concerned with video games, popular music, and other kid-oriented interests, and try to see beyond their text-message butchery of English spelling.

Again, the key is respecting the character. She's a child, but that's only one important aspect of her POV. In this excerpt from *The Lovely Bones* by Alice Sebold, the character isn't just a child, but a still-angry victim:

> My name was Salmon, like the fish; first name, Susie. I was fourteen when I was murdered on December 6, 1973. In newspaper photos of missing girls from the seventies, most looked like me: white girls with mousy brown hair. This was before kids of all races and genders started appearing on milk cartons or in the daily mail. It was still back when people believed things like that didn't happen.

There's the diction of a kid there, but also kid concerns—she has to mention her funny name and her "mousy" appearance. Kids are not just little adults in croptops and crew socks. They think differently and value different things. Their fears and their passions are exaggerated, and this will be reflected in their POVs. They will not have had time to build that protective armor most of us adults have. They probably aren't discreet, but they can be shy. Don't infantilize them in a misguided attempt to make them "sound" young. Rather, give them the benefit of real thought, and imagine how this person of this age, this class, and this region, and, most important, with this personality, would narrate a story.

THE DARK SIDE: A VILLAIN'S POV

Villains are tricky. They are evil, for one thing, and we might not want to reside in their minds for long. But they are often important drivers of plot, and occasionally their POV is elucidating or entertaining. So when you're considering slipping into your villain's POV, the first question to ask yourself is: Why do I need this passage in *this* POV?

It's important to consider why you want to get into the villain's head. Is it to tantalize the reader with clues to the identity, to increase the horrific factor of the narrative, or to provide a glimpse into the damaged psyche of a psychopath? Once you identify your major purpose, think about how that can be accomplished, and at what cost.

The most important consideration is whether you want to reveal the villain's identity. If not, beware that you might end up writing yourself into a corner. It's especially hard if you also want to conceal the gender, because then you are barred from the ever-helpful *he* or *she* pronoun. So you get things like "the person who killed Jonah sat at the window, warming hands over tea." The prose gets awkward and seldom matches the more intimate and smooth passages with the main character. Here's a passage from *The Night Watcher* by John Lutz that successfully gives the villain's motivation but not his (or her) identity by using a pseud-onym instead of a name or personal pronoun:

> Death itself wasn't the object, the Torcher thought. Fire and change and balance and justice, those were the objects of the purity of flame. The man and his child weren't supposed to die. The Torcher felt sympathy for the woman who was left; how deep must be her loss. But in a way, it was fate.

If you decide to conceal the villain's identity, understand you're going to have to do it very well. A half-hearted effort might let slip details like "a Princeton alumna" or "his long, tapered fingers" that could accidentally give more information than you want the reader to have. Once you've written a passage in your villain's POV, go back and look for clues that might tip off the savvy reader. Gender is a big one in some equal-opportunity books, when there are suspects of both sexes.

Another method for avoiding villain identification is using first person for the villain's POV. Here's an example from *The Bride* by Julie Garwood:

> God, it was a satisfying moment. The fear of being found out made my hands sweat, yet the thrill of it sent a burst of strength down my spine at the same time.
>
> I got away with murder! Oh, how I wish I could boast of my cunning.
>
> I cannot say a word, of course, and I dare not let my joy show in my gaze.
>
> I turn my attention to Alec Kincaid now. Helena's husband stands by the gaping hole in the ground. His hands are fisted at his sides and his head is bowed. I wonder if he's angry or saddened by his bride's sinful death. It's difficult to know what's going on inside his mind, for he always keeps his emotions carefully masked.
>
> It doesn't matter to me what Kincaid is feeling now. He'll get over her death, given the passage of time. And time is what I need, too, before I challenge him for my rightful place.

This passage drops the clue (intentionally) that the villain is probably someone in the family. But the first-person POV clearly separates these passages from the more standard third-person narration of the main story. I don't generally recommend mixing first person and third person in a novel, just because it can violate the narrative logic. But readers are remarkably flexible, and as long as the passages are short and taking place in the villain's mind, I think this can work. I've also seen villain POV done in second person (Dennis Schofield's *Slackwire*), and that raises all sorts of intriguing questions (like, "Are *you* evil?").

If revealing gender is not an issue, you've got more options. I'd suggest getting analytical here. Identify what information you want to convey—say, that he's a man, that he's connected to the bank somehow, that he salts his beer, and that he has an intense hatred of the CIA. Then list what you don't want to reveal, like his name, the fact he once worked for the CIA, his occupation, and how he knows the protagonist. Once you've identified what you can write about and what's off-limits, you might find it easier to craft the scene.

Another option is to go into camera-eye or objective POV. This will allow you to "film" the scene without giving the internal information that might give away too much information. The problem with this, of course, is that you're not actually getting into the villain's head, so I'd suggest this method if you just want to show the action of the scene (such as the villain setting fire to the warehouse or conspiring with the bank manager).

Using the camera-eye perspective eliminates one danger in using villain POV: The perspective might be so repellent (the villain describing the crime) or so trite (a villain whining about his bad childhood) that the reader will be turned off. If you're unsure about whether to go into the villain's head or just report the scene, look at what other writers have done in similar books, and consider why they made the choices they did.

Standard mysteries seldom use the villain's POV because the stories are not as much about the crime as the investigation. The reader's experience is meant to be one of following the detective through the crime scene and investigation, and coming up with her own conclusion. This experience will likely be diminished if the reader has access to the villain's thoughts and therefore knows more than the detective, because there will be a separating of perspectives, a distancing between the POV character and the reader (the opposite of what you want to achieve in a mystery).

Thrillers, however, are much more likely to feature villain POV. The intended reader experience in a thriller is more expansive—a vicarious sharing not just of the investigator's perspective but also that of the victim (and the villain). Thrillers aren't usually as tightly focused as mysteries, and they tend to be more emotional than intellectual in expression; they inspire fear, horror, and dread rather than curiosity. For this reason, thriller readers might enjoy (if that's the word!) the experience of sharing a mind, for just a short time, with a villain.

Even if villain POV is unexceptional in your chosen genre, it's still not always advisable. The same rule of thumb applies to this as to every other scene in your book: Does it advance the plot? If not, if all it does is reveal that the villain is ruthless or nasty or psychopathic, consider whether you need this passage, because presumably the villain's acts will brand him ruthless and nasty and psychopathic already. What else do you want this passage to accomplish?

For example, suppose the murderer isn't the only villain; there's someone behind him, pulling the strings. You might use the murderer's POV to hint at that secret master villain. Here's another passage from Koontz's novel *Mr. Murder* that not only gives a glimpse into the terrifying sadness of evil but also indicates the villain's not the only, or even the most, evil one in the book:

> Curiously, he has no recollection of having seen, let alone studied, a map, and he can't imagine where this detailed information was acquired. He doesn't like to consider the holes in his memory because thinking about them opens the door to a black abyss that terrifies him. So he just drives. ... At times like this, he desperately needs a mirror. His reflection is one of the few things that can confirm his existence. ...
>
> He doesn't know his name, only the names he will use while in Kansas City. He wants so much to have a name of his own that is not as counterfeit as the credit cards on which it appears. ... In a profound way, he does not know who he is. He has no memory of a time when his profession was other than murder.

There is a real *person* in there—not just a generic serial murderer. Notice the present tense (the rest of the book is in past tense), which focuses our attention on his inability to remember the past or predict the future. There is only this moment for this man, and that is part of the horror of who he is.

Keep in mind that the villain's POV has to be interesting both on the character level and the plot level. This is not a place to get lazy with characterization and figure all serial murderers are the human equivalents of the shark in *Jaws*: just another killing machine. Do some real examination of who this person is and why he commits the crimes he does.

With that in mind, you'll need to consider creating some sympathy for this villain. Going into his POV will almost automatically do that, just because it's hard for the reader to be inside someone without coming to identify with him. Just be wary of setting the villain and protagonist in a rivalry for the reader's affections. Your protagonist should probably be the most interesting or identifiable character, not the bad guy! You also don't want to weaken the villain by making him too emotionally vulnerable. He should still seem like a major threat. One way to balance these two elements of your villain is to let his actions speak for him in the first part of the story, and then only late in the story, show his motivation, guilt, regret, or other "soft" emotions that might get in the way of his evildoing.

If you want the villain to be judged just on his actions, also consider using the levels of POV. Try staying in the upper levels of POV in the first part of the story—let him narrate his action, his perceptions of what's going on, and his thoughts (especially if the thoughts are about his nefarious plans). Later in the book, go into his emotion level only judiciously, considering what effect you mean to have.

Shakespeare often plays with villain POV by giving the bad guys extended monologues, thus shamelessly manipulating our responses. For example, in his eponymous play, Richard III is shown to be a villain in his actions (he does kill the little princes), but in his own eyes, he's entirely justified. In fact, the very first lines of the play are Richard's justification: he deserves a bit of good fortune, considering that he's been deformed since birth and is now "rudely stamped." If Shakespeare had stopped him right at that point, we might feel a little sorry for him, and more likely to forgive at least some of his actions. But this master of characterization lets Richard go on and on about the evil done to him by fate, and by the end of the first monologue, we're tired of his self-pity and ready to think the worst of him.

For contrast, look at the portrayal of Caliban's POV in *The Tempest*. He, too, whines more than a little bit about the unfairness of his fate. But that doesn't win us over; rather, it is his song of love for his stolen home ("Be not afeard; the isle is full of noises, Sounds and sweet airs, that give delight and hurt not") that makes him sympathetic and makes it understandable, if not justifiable, when he then plots to kill the invader, Prospero.

It's when Caliban's emotion is directed away from himself and to the island that we respond sympathetically. That's something to remember:

a character whose love is reserved mostly for himself isn't going to win much love from us. You can manipulate this as Shakespeare did. If you want the reader to dislike the villain, make his POV introspection all about himself. But if you are looking to create sympathy and fellow feeling, have him contemplate something else, something that matters outside himself.

Remember that the villain is a character, not just a plot device. You should still ask the usual POV questions: What do you want to reveal about him? What do you want to conceal? What do you want to show about how this person perceives reality? How do you want the reader to experience this perspective—deeply or distantly? How long should we stay with this character? When in doubt, a short passage in villain POV would probably be more effective and less risky than a long one.

IT'S A JUNGLE IN HERE:
THE ANIMAL'S PERSPECTIVE

Writers sometimes joke about their early works, "I went into every POV in the room, including the dog's!" But there's actually a bit of a tradition of "animal viewpoint," and it's fascinating to see how imaginatively some authors portray the way a non-human thinks.

Choosing an animal as your POV character isn't actually something I'd advise unless you're either writing comedy or writing a book primarily about animals. There are books with animal protagonists, like Jack London's masterwork *Call of the Wild*, and part of the pleasure readers get in these books is the exploration of the animal's thought process. Any pet owner knows that animals can think, but he also knows that they think rather differently than humans. So these books are shaped by the eternal desire to know what the alien but beloved creature is thinking behind those big brown eyes.

How do authors portray the thoughts of other species? One hallmark of animal viewpoint is a heavy emphasis on sensory perception and physical action and feeling. What the animal sees and experiences is reported faithfully, often with an interpretation that is reflective of whether it thinks as a predator or as a prey. The animal's thoughts are generally portrayed as fairly simple and linear, possessing a flat common sense.

THE POWER OF POINT OF VIEW

Of course, animals probably don't think in words at all, but rather, in images, associations, and emotions. But you still have to convey their perspectives using language, so consider using diction that would reflect their levels of intellect relative to your human characters. You can also show the animal's personality through the narrative.

Here's a thoroughbred racehorse's impression of his human trainer from *Horse Heaven* by Jane Smiley:

> The thing the Iron Plum found most intriguing about the Round Pebble was her fragrance. He often put his nose up to her face and snuffled her in .... She let him. Her hand never came up to touch or pet him, she never looked at him or spoke to him, but she was available for investigation, and the Iron Plum investigated. ... The Iron Plum recognized that the Round Pebble was absolute stillness ... so he snuffled and nosed and probed and pushed her gently with his head, and dropped his manure in one spot in the corner of the pen, where it was easy for her to pick it up.

Notice that Smiley has made up the term "snuffle in," which exactly describes what a horse does to a favorite groom. The concreteness of physical detail demonstrates the deeply sensual (especially olfactory) nature of the horse's perception. But this isn't any ordinary horse. This is a contemplative, quiet horse, sensitive to too much chaos and longing for stillness, which is the dominant emotion Smiley uses in this passage. Additionally, she uses the horse's action (the orderly manure-dropping) to indicate his rudimentary cause-and-effect reasoning. ("I like her. She is stillness and order. I will make life easier for her by being orderly.")

Animal POV is likely to remain exotica, and that's just as well. It's hard enough imagining how other people perceive and think. But certainly this POV is an option if you're writing a book where animals play a large role (as in *Horse Heaven*), or when you want to add a bit of comedy by showing how a non-human would regard this situation. (Dave Barry does this well with a silly dog and his conflict with a huge, wily frog in his novel *Big Trouble*.) If you're going to try this, seek out models. There are lots of good books and movies that are told from an animal's perspective, such as E.B. White's *Charlotte's Web*. You could also spend some time observing a model animal's behavioral patterns and imagining what's going on in its head (if it's my cat, all thoughts have to do with food and how and when I will bring it) and how that might be conveyed in narrative. We anthropomorphize our pets enough as it is; be sure and give your POV animal a unique way of presenting thoughts.

THE DANGEROUS MAGIC OF POV

POV isn't only about a character's viewpoint. It's where character meets language, the actual essence of fiction in print. We novelists don't have the tone of voice of singers, or the physical presence of actors, or the visual display of filmmakers. We have to tell the whole story, create the character, craft the mood—all through mere words.

Of course, we aren't using mere words. We can also use three thousand years of storytelling tradition, uniting our own story with the wisdom of our human culture. We can use a common language to connect with the reader's own understanding of how human beings think, perceive, and behave. And we can use our own perceptions to explore our similarities and our differences, and to invite the reader to become, if only momentarily, someone else. All of this is accomplished through POV.

There's something breathtakingly dangerous about that, and it's only by trusting ourselves and our readers that we can create characters so compelling and worlds so comprehensive that for a little while, fiction becomes as true as reality itself.

Best of luck in your quest to provide readers with the magic of a good story!

READING RECOMMENDATIONS

- *Fight Club* by Chuck Palahniuk. This book, later made into a film, manipulates the reader's understanding through a careful first-person POV. It's a good example of how to embed a trick secret in a tight POV.

- The Jessica Darling series by Megan McCafferty. This series of books, popular with teen girls, follows a smart but unmotivated student through her high school and college life. The narration is told almost exclusively through diary entries and letters.

- The Animorphs series by K.A. Applegate. This series, aimed at middle-grade students, features the first-person POV of five children who have the ability to transform into animals. Each child's POV is distinct and sharp, and changes appropriately to reflect what animal the child has morphed into.

- *Foucault's Pendulum* by Umberto Eco. A renowned semiotician explores his subject of "signs" through the paranoia of a conspiracy theorist. It is also a good example of how to show a story within a story.

- The Rabbit series by John Updike. This modern master of the literary novel and short story uses this series to follow a man from youth to old age. This series demonstrates what fundamentals of a person's POV remain constant, and which reflect the influence of age and culture.

- *Tinker, Tailor, Soldier, Spy* by John le Carré. This spy novel, set in the years of the Cold War, gets its moody tone mostly from the POV of a discarded agent trying to accept betrayal as a fact of life.

- *White Teeth* by Zadie Smith. This uproarious debut novel uses occasional omniscience to control its large cast, whose lives interweave in late twentieth-century Britain.

INDEX

THE POWER OF POINT OF VIEW

ABOUT THE AUTHOR

Alicia Rasley is a RITA Award-winning novelist and a nationally known writing workshop leader. She teaches writing at a state university and conducts online writing classes for writers' groups. Her Web site, www.rasley.com, features her many writing articles. Writing workshop information for groups is available by e-mailing her at rasley@juno.com.